ARCHITECTURAL DESIGN

Integration of Structural and Environmental Systems

Carl Bovill

School of Architecture and Environmental Design
California Polytechnic State University, San Luis Obispo

VNR VAN NOSTRAND REINHOLD
New York

The information in this book is intended for approximate sizing in the concept-formation stage of architectural design. It is not to be used for design development or final design of any building or construction.

Professional judgment and traditional engineering procedures, in concert with the advice of professional consultants, should be used in design development and final design.

The author and publisher have attempted to make this book as accurate as possible, but do not warrant its suitability for any specific purpose other than as an introduction to concept formation and assume no liability for its accuracy or completeness.

Copyright © 1991 by Van Nostrand Reinhold

Library of Congress Catalog Card Number 90-47862
ISBN 0–442–00440–0

Printed in the United States of America.

Van Nostrand Reinhold
115 Fifth Avenue
New York, New York 10003

Nelson Canada
1120 Birchmount Road
Scarborough, Ontario MIK 5G4, Canada

Chapman and Hall
2–6 Boundary Row
London, Se1 8HN, England

Thomas Nelson Australia
102 Dodds Street
South Melbourne 3205, Victoria, Australia

16 15 14 13 12 11 10 9 8 7 6 5 4 3 2 1

Library of Congress Cataloging-in-Publication Data

Bovill, Carl.
Architectural design : integration of structural and
environmental systems / Carl Bovill.
p.   cm.
Includes index.
ISBN 0-442-00440-0
1. Buildings—Environmental engineering.   2. Building fittings.
I. Title.
TH6021.B64   1991
696—dc20   90-47862
                                                   CIP

To Anna, Mia, and Jean

Contents

Preface

This book addresses broadbased technical system inclusion in architectural design. The intent is to provide the information and procedures necessary to incorporate building code constraints, structure, HVAC, lighting, acoustics, plumbing, and electricity into the concept sketch level of architectural design formation. It is intended to be used as a studio reference, but its top-down approach should make it useful as a text for an introduction to architectural technology class. The information provided is geared for concept formation purposes only. (For design development and contract documents the designer must use traditional engineering procedures.)

The first part of the book contains information that the designer can use to help develop the requirements that surround an architectural program. The information developed by the suggested procedures in this part of the book does not involve the form of the building. The intent is for the designer to collect constraint information concerning technical system integration in order to be prepared for the ensuing design process.

The second part of the book is a description of the major components of the technical systems that are necessary for an architectural design to be built, accompanied by rule-of-thumb sizing and layout information and procedures. Architectural design is a puzzle that first needs to be conceived and then put together properly. Used loosely in a sketch fashion, the information in this book can help with both the conceiving and putting together of the puzzle.

The integration of the many components that are required to design a constructible building is a complex problem that has no direct algorithmic solution. The problem is beyond logic. A tool that can take the designer beyond logic is play. Technical integration can be conceived as a cooperative game played between the technical systems, interlinked with a cooperative game played between the designer's logical and intuitive minds. It is the combination of rule systems explored through logic, and chance provided by the creative leaps of the intuitive mind, that creates harmonious form.

This book grew out of the need for a reference book for the fourth-year architecture students in the required Structural and Mechanical Integration Design Studio at the University of Tennessee. A small art museum design project is used periodically throughout the book as an example of how to incorporate technical information into design. Appendix A is a set of drawings produced by Greg Blaylock in the technical integration studio using the information in this book; the examples in the body of the book are the author's restating of technical integration design procedure steps based on Greg Blaylock's design solution.

I would like to thank the students and faculty of the School of Architecture at the University of Tennessee for their comments and criticism. I would like to especially thank Greg Blaylock and Professors Richard Kelso, William Martella, Robert Holsaple, and Gerald Anderson.

PART I

Predesign Information Ordering

The first part of this book focuses on the constraints that are generated by the technical systems that surround the architectural design problem. The purpose of this approach is to clarify the initial stage of the design process and offer a method of narrowing down the range of design possibilities. The early stage of design involves a sketching out of the architectural program. Implied as well as explicitly stated constraints on the design problem are examined and documented. This process enables the designer to avoid wasting time on solutions that are not buildable. ■

1

Architectural Information

The architect is faced with a completely new problem every time he or she designs a building. The elements of the "puzzle" (Fig. 1.1) must be defined before it can be solved (Archea 1987). At its core, the architectural design process is more like Newton inventing statics than an engineer using statics: The design idea that relates the pieces to the whole has to be reinvented on each new job. There is no preexisting body of knowledge like statics that the architect can use in an analytic fashion to produce the design idea or central concept holding an architectural design together. In its place is a combination of modified precedents and metaphors.

Each new program and site present a different set of desires and constraints that must be ordered into a coherent system. Highly subjective features, such as the context of the neighborhood or the symbolic intent of the building, should be stated as clearly as possible, but are not within the scope of this book. There are other criteria, however, that can be derived in a more defined fashion from the architectural program, the site and its zoning, and the technical requirements of the building process. This book is concerned with these more definable constraints. Before considering these constraints in detail, the architect needs information on the more general parameters of the project, its scope, site, and zoning.

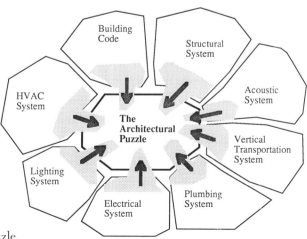

Figure 1.1 The architectural puzzle.

GROSS BUILDING AREA VERSUS NET BUILDING AREA

Many architectural programs list only the net building area that the owner desires, failing to include the areas necessary for circulation, mechanical and electrical equipment, and the walls of the building. Table 1.1 provides a list of types of building occupancies with a multiplier that will provide a good first estimate of the gross building area based on a given net building area. Table 1.2 provides an estimate of the gross building area as a function of the type of occupant unit. Table 1.3 provides preliminary information on construction costs.

TABLE 1.1. Multipliers to calculate gross building area from net building area[a]

Building Occupancy	Gross Area/Net Area
Apartment	1.56
Auditorium	1.42
Bank	1.40
Church	1.42
Community center	1.72
Courthouse	1.62
Department store	1.23
Garage	1.18
Gymnasium	1.42
Hospital	1.83
Hotel or dormitory	1.58
Laboratory	1.71
Library	1.32
Museum	1.25
Office	1.35
Restaurant	1.41
Warehouse	1.08

Source: Adapted with permission from: *Means Assemblies Cost Data* 1989.
[a]The gross area includes the circulation areas, the mechanical/electrical equipment areas, and the area taken up by the construction materials. The mechanical/electrical equipment areas take from 6 to 10% of the net area.

TABLE 1.2. Space planning information as a function of occupant unit

Building Type	Unit	Gross Area (sq ft)
Apartment	Unit	860
Auditorium	Seat	25
Bowling alley	Lane	940
Church	Seat	28
Dormitory	Bed	200
Parking garage	Car	355
Hospital	Bed	600
Hotel	Room	600
Elderly housing	Unit	635
Public housing	Unit	875
Ice skating rinks	Total	27,000
Motel	Room	465
Nursing home	Bed	290
Restaurant	Seat	29
Elementary school	Student	77
Junior high school	Student	110
High school	Student	130
Theater	Seat	15

Source: Adapted with permission from *Means Assemblies Cost Data* 1989.

TABLE 1.3.   Square foot cost information

Building Type	Cost (per sq ft)	Typical Gross Size (sq ft)	Building Type	Cost (per sq ft)	Typical Gross Size (sq ft)
Low-rise apartment	42	21,000	Public housing	50	36,000
High-rise apartment	59	310,000	Jail	123	14,000
Auditorium	70	25,000	Library	75	12,000
Bank	97	4,200	Motel	53	27,000
Church	65	9,000	Nursing home	72	23,000
Country club	63	6,500	Low-rise office	57	8,600
College class room	85	50,000	Mid-rise office	62	52,000
College science lab	102	45,000	High-rise office	76	260,000
Student union	92	33,000	Post office	72	12,000
Community center	67	9,400	Restaurant	85	4,400
Court house	89	32,400	Schools	62	50,000
Factory	35	26,000	Sports arena	49	15,000
Parking garage	21	160,000	Theater	58	10,500
Gymnasium	60	20,000	Town hall	69	10,800
Hospital	118	55,000	Warehouse	27	25,000

Source: Adapted with permission from *Means Assemblies Cost Data* 1989.

ZONING CONSTRAINTS AND LEGAL RESTRICTIONS

Because zoning is locally determined, the categories and constraints will vary in different areas of the country and from municipality to municipality. The zoning area, usually a city, is divided into districts such as agricultural, open space, residential, office, commercial, historical, industrial, and floodway. Each district has a specific list of permitted uses allowed within its boundaries. Each of these districts will also have constraints defining where on the site a building can be built and how large and how high a building can become. A clear understanding of these zoning constraints is essential to a successful design.

The following list of important constraints on the design solution can be used as a guide to the type of information needed.

· Front yard setback
· Side yard setback
· Rear yard setback
· Maximum lot coverage
· Floor area ratio
· Height regulations
· Landscape regulations
· Off-street parking requirements

Legal restrictions must also be taken into account. An *easement* is a legal restriction on building within a

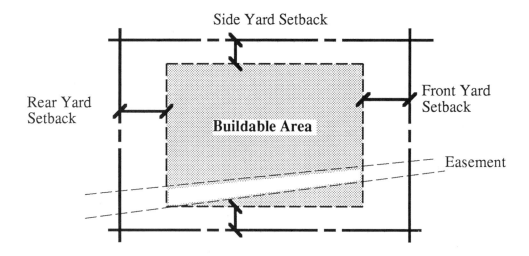

Figure 1.2 Determining the buildable area from zoning constraints.

defined area. There may be easements through a site protecting utility lines or providing access to adjacent sites.

Figure 1.2 shows a sample site with front, side, and rear yard setbacks as well as an easement through the remaining buildable area.

ACCESS ONTO THE SITE

The local planning commission will have a say in where a driveway can be located for vehicle access onto a site because the commission needs to control the effects driveways will have on traffic patterns. It is also important to determine how people will arrive at the site: Will they walk, drive, or take public transportation? This will have an effect on where the entrance to the building should be located.

LOCAL CLIMATE: WIND AND SUN

Access to or exclusion of wind and sun are the main climate features that can influence the building design. Local wind patterns are usually not accurately recorded except at the nearest airport. It is useful to determine

wind direction and intensities by season, especially in areas where wind is a major climatic factor. Most of the time wind information is at best qualitative. If a wind diagram can be constructed (even a qualitative one), it should be placed on the site plan.

The location of the sun relative to the earth at different points of time and place is well documented (see Appendix B.). A sun path diagram that is closest to the latitude of the site should be chosen to determine the desirable levels of access to (or exclusion of) sunlight for the building. The sun path diagram (see Fig. 1.3) is an equidistant plan projection of the sky dome showing azimuth as radial lines and altitude as concentric circles. The sun's position is then plotted on the sky dome projection as a function of month of the year and time of day. The appropriate sun path diagram should be placed on a site plan with north located at the top of the page. The sun path diagram provides sun angles throughout the year, from which shading strategies can be formed.

Using a sundial is another method of exploring solar access and exclusion (Fig. 1.4). The sundial can be mounted on a model of the site or building and used to study shadow patterns at any time of the year. When the shadows cast by the sundial are aligned to the month and time of interest, the shadows cast on the model will be equivalent to that month and time. The position of the shadows should be sketched on a site plan for future reference. The sundial can also be used to map solar obstructions in winter (Fig. 1.5).

Information on wind and solar patterns is then integrated into the site plan (Fig. 1.6).

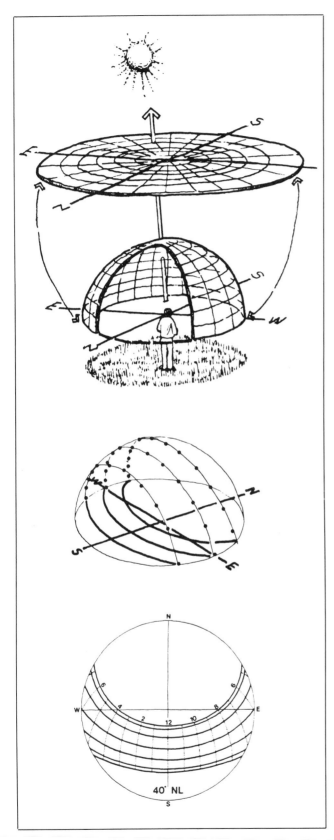

Figure 1.3 The sun path diagram. Adapted by permission from Moore (1985).

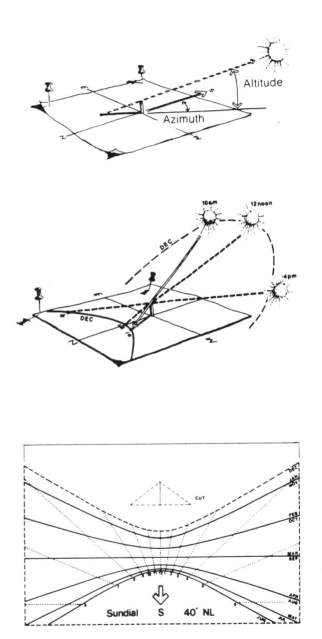

Figure 1.4 A sundial is constructed by plotting the path of a shadow cast by a stick as a function of month of the year and time of day. Adapted by permission from Moore (1985).

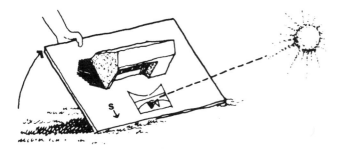

Figure 1.5 Using the sundial to map solar obstructions in winter. Attach the sundial to the site model and take it outside. Tilting the model so the shadow cast on the sundial points to a particular month of the year and time of day will produce accurate shadows on the site model for that month and time. Adapted by permission from Moore (1985).

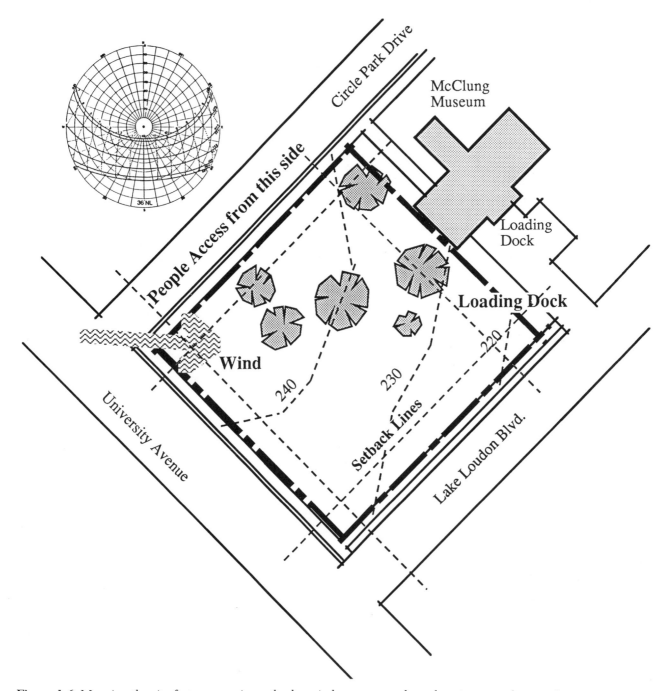

Figure 1.6 Mapping the site features, zoning setbacks, wind patterns, and sun location onto the site plan.

2

Building Code Information

THE *UNIFORM BUILDING CODE*

Building code constraints, which determine the features of building configuration and construction that ensure occupant safety, are a major concern for architects. Configuring a building that meets the building code's fire safety constraints, for example, is one of the architect's primary responsibilities. The building code constrains architectural design into a firesafe configuration by relating the materials that a building is constructed with to the allowable floor area, and to the number of stories that can be built for a given occupancy.

The *Uniform Building Code*, published by the International Conference of Building Officials (1988), will be used in this book as an annotated example of a building code. The major constraint features described in the code relating to construction type, occupancy, allowable floor area, number of stories, and egress system will be discussed. For a complete understanding of all constraints and exceptions as they apply to specific locations and buildings, a copy of the actual building code must be consulted.

CONSTRUCTION TYPES AND FIRE RATING OF BUILDING MATERIALS

The building code construction types are based on whether or not the building construction material is combustible, and on the hours that a wall, column, beam, floor, or other structural element can resist fire. Steel and concrete are examples of noncombustible building materials. Steel, however, will lose structural strength as it begins to soften in the heat of a fire. Wood is an example of a building material that is combustible.

There are two ways that a construction can be resistant to fire. First, it can be *fire-resistive*—built of a monolithic noncombustible material like concrete. Second, it can be *protected*—encased in a noncombustible material such as steel columns or wood studs covered with gypsum plaster. Local building codes may include differences in allowable construction types. The following are the allowable building construction types as defined in the *Uniform Building Code*.

Type I and *Type II fire-resistive* construction are noncombustible construction. They are built from concrete, masonry, and/or steel, and require substantial fire-resistance ratings.

Type II 1-hour and unprotected construction is also built from concrete, masonry, and/or steel, but the fire resistance ratings are substantially less. Light steel framing would fit in this category.

Type III 1-hour and unprotected construction has noncombustible exterior walls of masonry or concrete and interior construction of any material allowed by the code, including wood.

Type IV construction is combustible heavy timber framing. It achieves its fire rating from the large size of the timber framing used to construct it. The outer surface of the wood chars in a fire creating a fire-resistant layer protecting the remaining wood. Exterior walls have to be built from noncombustible materials.

Type V 1-hour and unprotected construction is light wood framing.

The required fire resistance ratings for these construction types are listed in Table 17-A of the *Uniform Building Code* (Fig. 2.1).

The amount of concrete or plaster cover needed over steel or wood members to achieve the listed fire ratings of 4, 3, 2, and 1 hour is included in Chapter 43 (Fire Resistive Standards) of the *Uniform Building Code*. The information is sometimes supplied by the manufacturers of the building component. We can leave the detail of how much encasing material is necessary until later in design development. The designer should be aware, however, of where 4-, 3-, 2-, and 1-hour fire protection is required by the building code.

OCCUPANCY

The building code classifies buildings by occupancy in order to group similar life safety problems together. For example, a theater with its dense population of people will require more attention to fire safety than a low-rise office building. Table 5-A of the *Uniform Building Code* (Fig. 2.2) provides a concise definition of all the occupancy classifications. It also provides exterior wall criteria for Type II 1-hour, Type II unprotected, and Type V construction. Refer to the code itself for more detail on each of the occupancies. Table 33-A of the

---

TABLE NO. 17-A—TYPES OF CONSTRUCTION—FIRE-RESISTIVE REQUIREMENTS
(In Hours)
For details see chapters under Occupancy and Types of Construction and for exceptions see Section 1705.

BUILDING ELEMENT	TYPE I Fire-resistive	TYPE II (NONCOMBUSTIBLE) Fire-resistive	TYPE II 1-Hr.	TYPE II N	TYPE III (COMBUSTIBLE) 1-Hr.	TYPE III N	TYPE IV H.T.	TYPE V 1-Hr.	TYPE V N
Exterior Bearing Walls	4 Sec. 1803 (a)	4 1903 (a)	1	N	4 2003 (a)	4 2003 (a)	4 2103 (a)	1	N
Interior Bearing Walls	3	2	1	N	1	N	1	1	N
Exterior Nonbearing Walls	4 Sec. 1803 (a)	4 1903 (a)	1 1903 (a)	N	4 2003 (a)	4 2003 (a)	4 2103 (a)	1	N
Structural Frame[1]	3	2	1	N	1	N	1 or H.T.	1	N
Partitions—Permanent	1[2]	1[2]	1[2]	N	1	N	1 or H.T.	1	N
Shaft Enclosures	2	2	1	1	1	1	1	1 1706	1 1706
Floors-Ceilings/Floors	2	2	1	N	1	N	H.T.	1	N
Roofs-Ceilings/Roofs	2 Sec. 1806	1 1906	1 1906	N	1	N	H.T.	1	N
Exterior Doors and Windows	Sec. 1803 (b)	1903 (b)	1903 (b)	1903 (b)	2003 (b)	2003 (b)	2103 (b)	2203	2203

N—No general requirements for fire resistance.   H.T.—Heavy Timber.

[1]Structural frame elements in the exterior wall shall be protected against external fire exposure as required for exterior bearing walls or the structural frame, whichever is greater.
[2]Fire-retardant treated wood (see Section 407) may be used in the assembly, provided fire-resistance requirements are maintained. See Sections 1801 and 1901, respectively.

Figure 2.1 Table 17-A, Types of Construction—Fire-Resistive Requirements. Reproduced by permission from *Uniform Building Code*. Copyright © 1988, the International Conference of Building Officials.

TABLE NO. 5-A—WALL AND OPENING PROTECTION OF OCCUPANCIES BASED ON LOCATION ON PROPERTY

TYPES II ONE-HOUR, II-N AND V CONSTRUCTION: For exterior wall and opening protection of Types II One-hour, II-N and V buildings, see table below and Sections 504, 709, 1903 and 2203.

This table does not apply to Types I, II-F.R., III and IV construction, see Sections 1803, 1903, 2003 and 2103.

GROUP	DESCRIPTION OF OCCUPANCY	FIRE RESISTANCE OF EXTERIOR WALLS	OPENINGS IN EXTERIOR WALLS
A See also Section 602	1—Any assembly building or portion of a building with a legitimate stage and an occupant load of 1000 or more.	Not applicable (See Sections 602 and 603)	
	2—Any building or portion of a building having an assembly room with an occupant load of less than 1000 and a legitimate stage 2.1—Any building or portion of a building having an assembly room with an occupant load of 300 or more without a legitimate stage, including such buildings used for educational purposes and not classed as a Group E or Group B, Division 2 Occupancy	2 hours less than 10 feet, 1 hour less than 40 feet	Not permitted less than 5 feet Protected less than 10 feet
	3—Any building or portion of a building having an assembly room with an occupant load of less than 300 without a legitimate stage, including such buildings used for educational purposes and not classed as a Group E or Group B, Division 2 Occupancy	2 hours less than 5 feet, 1 hour less than 40 feet	Not permitted less than 5 feet Protected less than 10 feet
	4—Stadiums, reviewing stands and amusement park structures not included within other Group A Occupancies	1 hour less than 10 feet	Protected less than 10 feet
B See also Section 702	1—Gasoline service stations, garages where no repair work is done except exchange of parts and maintenance requiring no open flame, welding, or use of Class I, II or III-A liquids 2—Drinking and dining establishments having an occupant load of less than 50, wholesale and retail stores, office buildings, printing plants, municipal police and fire stations, factories and workshops using material not highly flammable or combustible, storage and sales rooms for combustible goods, paint stores without bulk handling Buildings or portions of buildings having rooms used for educational purposes, beyond the 12th grade, with less than 50 occupants in any room	1 hour less than 20 feet	Not permitted less than 5 feet Protected less than 10 feet

GROUP	DESCRIPTION OF OCCUPANCY	FIRE RESISTANCE OF EXTERIOR WALLS	OPENINGS IN EXTERIOR WALLS
B (Cont.)	3—Aircraft hangars where no repair work is done except exchange of parts and maintenance requiring no open flame, welding, or the use of Class I or II liquids Open parking garages (For requirements, See Section 709.) Helistops	1 hour less than 20 feet	Not permitted less than 5 feet Protected less than 20 feet
	4—Ice plants, power plants, pumping plants, cold storage and creameries Factories and workshops using noncombustible and nonexplosive materials Storage and sales rooms of noncombustible and nonexplosive materials that are not packaged or crated in or supported by combustible material	1 hour less than 5 feet	Not permitted less than 5 feet
E See also Section 802	1—Any building used for educational purposes through the 12th grade by 50 or more persons for more than 12 hours per week or four hours in any one day 2—Any building used for educational purposes through the 12th grade by less than 50 persons for more than 12 hours per week or four hours in any one day 3—Any building used for day-care purposes for more than six children	2 hours less than 5 feet, 1 hour less than 10 feet[1]	Not permitted less than 5 feet Protected less than 10 feet[1]
H	See Chapter 9		

[1]Group E, Divisions 2 and 3 Occupancies having an occupant load of not more than 20 may have exterior wall and opening protection as required for Group R, Division 3 Occupancies.

GROUP	DESCRIPTION OF OCCUPANCY	FIRE RESISTANCE OF EXTERIOR WALLS	OPENINGS IN EXTERIOR WALLS
I See also Section 1002	1—Nurseries for the full-time care of children under the age of six (each accommodating more than five persons) Hospitals, sanitariums, nursing homes with nonambulatory patients and similar buildings (each accommodating more than five persons)	2 hours less than 5 feet, 1 hour elsewhere	Not permitted less than 5 feet Protected less than 10 feet
	2—Nursing homes for ambulatory patients, homes for children six years of age or over (each accommodating more than five persons)	1 hour	
	3—Mental hospitals, mental sanitariums, jails, prisons, reformatories and buildings where personal liberties of inmates are similarly restrained	2 hours less than 5 feet, 1 hour elsewhere	Not permitted less than 5 feet, protected less than 10 feet
M[2]	1—Private garages, carports, sheds and agricultural buildings (See also Section 1101, Division 1.)	1 hour less than 3 feet (or may be protected on the exterior with materials approved for 1-hour fire-resistive construction)	Not permitted less than 3 feet
	2—Fences over 6 feet high, tanks and towers	Not regulated for fire resistance	
R See also Section 1202	1—Hotels and apartment houses Convents and monasteries (each accommodating more than 10 persons)	1 hour less than 5 feet	Not permitted less than 5 feet
	3—Dwellings and lodging houses	1 hour less than 3 feet	Not permitted less than 3 feet

[2]For agricultural buildings, see Appendix Chapter 11.

NOTES: (1) See Section 504 for types of walls affected and requirements covering percentage of openings permitted in exterior walls.
(2) For additional restrictions, see chapters under Occupancy and Types of Construction.
(3) For walls facing yards and public ways, see Part IV.
(4) Openings shall be protected by a fire assembly having a three-fourths-hour fire-protection rating.

Figure 2.2 Table 5-A, Wall and Opening Protection of Occupancies Based on Location on Property, Types II One-hour, II-N, and V Construction. Reproduced by permission from *Uniform Building Code*. Copyright © 1988, the International Conference of Building Officials.

Uniform Building Code (Fig. 2.3) is included here because an occupant count is necessary to distinguish between a large (1000 or more people), medium (300 or more people), or small (less than 300 people) assembly occupancy.

The occupancy of the building as defined by the code can be determined from the architectural program information. A listing of architectural program areas by name along with their floor area, occupant classification, and occupant load should be compiled. This information will be necessary to choose the correct occupancy classification for the building. This building-code-defined population of the building will also be necessary for the design of the exiting system as the building form is being conceived. The following art museum example will be used periodically throughout this book to illustrate the development of various types of technical information.

Example: Tabulation of occupancy and occupant load for a small art museum on a college campus.

Program Area	Area (sq. ft.)	Occupancy Type	Square feet/ Person	Occupant Load
Main gallery	6000	Assembly	15 net	400
Gallery	4000	Assembly	15 net	267
Gallery	4000	Assembly	15 net	267
Administration	1500	Business	100 gross	15
Preparation	2000	Business	100 gross	20
Art storage	6000	Storage	500 gross	12

Circulation for the administration and preparation areas at 15% gives 525 sq. ft., at 100 sq. ft./person		5
Total population of the building		986

TABLE NO. 33-A—MINIMUM EGRESS AND ACCESS REQUIREMENTS

USE[1]	MINIMUM OF TWO EXITS OTHER THAN ELEVATORS ARE REQUIRED WHERE NUMBER OF OCCUPANTS IS AT LEAST	OCCUPANT LOAD FACTOR[2] (Sq. Ft.)	ACCESS BY MEANS OF A RAMP OR AN ELEVATOR MUST BE PROVIDED FOR THE PHYSICALLY HANDICAPPED AS INDICATED[3]
1. Aircraft Hangars (no repair)	10	500	Yes
2. Auction Rooms	30	7	Yes
3. Assembly Areas, Concentrated Use (without fixed seats) Auditoriums Churches and Chapels Dance Floors Lobby Accessory to Assembly Occupancy Lodge Rooms Reviewing Stands Stadiums	50	7	Yes[4][5]
Waiting Area	50	3	Yes[4][5]
4. Assembly Areas, Less-concentrated Use Conference Rooms Dining Rooms Drinking Establishments Exhibit Rooms Gymnasiums Lounges Stages	50	15	Yes[4][5][6]
5. Bowling Alley (assume no occupant load for bowling lanes)	50	12	Yes
6. Children's Homes and Homes for the Aged	6	80	Yes[7]
7. Classrooms	50	20	Yes[8]
8. Courtrooms	50	40	Yes
9. Dormitories	10	50	Yes[7]
10. Dwellings	10	300	No

USE[1]	MINIMUM OF TWO EXITS OTHER THAN ELEVATORS ARE REQUIRED WHERE NUMBER OF OCCUPANTS IS AT LEAST	OCCUPANT LOAD FACTOR[2] (Sq. Ft.)	ACCESS BY MEANS OF A RAMP OR AN ELEVATOR MUST BE PROVIDED FOR THE PHYSICALLY HANDICAPPED AS INDICATED[3]
11. Exercising Rooms	50	50	Yes
12. Garage. Parking	30	200	Yes[9]
13. Hospitals and Sanitariums— Nursing Homes	6	80	Yes
14. Hotels and Apartments	10	200	Yes[10]
15. Kitchen—Commercial	30	200	No
16. Library Reading Room	50	50	Yes[4]
17. Locker Rooms	30	50	Yes
18. Malls (see Chapter 56)	—	—	—
19. Manufacturing Areas	30	200	Yes[7]
20. Mechanical Equipment Room	30	300	No
21. Nurseries for Children (Day care)	7	35	Yes
22. Offices	30	100	Yes[7]
23. School Shops and Vocational Rooms	50	50	Yes
24. Skating Rinks	50	50 on the skating area; 15 on the deck	Yes[4]
25. Storage and Stock Rooms	30	300	No
26. Stores—Retail Sales Rooms Basement Ground Floor Upper Floors	11 / 50 / 10	30 / 30 / 60	Yes / Yes / Yes
27. Swimming Pools	50	50 for the pool area; 15 on the deck	Yes[4]
28. Warehouses	30	500	No
29. All others	50	100	

Figure 2.3 Table 33-A, Minimum Egress and Access Requirements. Reproduced by permission from *Uniform Building Code*. Copyright © 1988, the International Conference of Building Officials.

Since the population is greater than 300 and less than 1000 people, and there is no working stage, this building will be classified as an A-2.1 assembly occupancy by the *Uniform Building Code*. The business occupancies are such a small portion of the total that it is easier to call the whole building a small assembly building and not have to worry about creating separation walls between occupancies. The whole building will therefore have to meet the requirements of a small assembly occupancy.

Most buildings will have some mix of occupancies. As demonstrated in the small art museum example, however, if one of the occupancies is a minor area and subservient to the major occupancy, the whole building can often be classified as the major occupancy. It will then have to meet the requirements of the more restrictive occupancy, but no special separation walls will be necessary.

Some buildings will contain different occupancies, none of which is the dominant one. Figure 2.4 shows the required separation in buildings of mixed occupancy (Table 5-B of the *Uniform Building Code*), spe-cifying the fire resistance of the walls and/or floors that separate the occupancies. Openings through occupancy separation walls must meet the following criteria: For 4-hour walls, no opening is allowed; for 3-hour walls, openings must be less than 25% of the length of the wall and no one opening can be larger than 120 square feet; for 2-hour walls, protection of the opening is the only criteria; and for 1-hour walls, protection of the opening is the only criteria.

ALLOWABLE FLOOR AREA

The allowable floor area table in the building code coordinates the level of hazard (occupancy classification) to the required fire resistance (allowable construction type) through a table that defines the allowable floor area for one-story buildings (Fig. 2.5) and another table that specifies the maximum number of stories that can be built for a given occupancy in a particular construction type (Fig. 2.6). High-hazard occupancies like large assemblies can only be built out of the most

TABLE NO. 5-B—REQUIRED SEPARATION IN BUILDINGS OF MIXED OCCUPANCY
(In Hours)

	A-1	A-2	A-2.1	A-3	A-4	B-1	B-2	B-3	B-4	E	H-1	H-2	H-3	H-4-5	H-6-7[1]	I	M[2]	R-1	R-3
A-1		N	N	N	N	4	3	3	3	N		4	4	4	4	3	1	1	1
A-2	N		N	N	N	3	1	1	1	N		4	4	4	4	3	1	1	1
A-2.1	N	N		N	N	3	1	1	1	N		4	4	4	4	3	1	1	1
A-3	N	N	N		N	3	N	1	N	N		4	4	4	3	3	1	1	1
A-4	N	N	N	N		3	1	1	1	N		4	4	4	4	3	1	1	1
B-1	4	3	3	3	3		1	1	1	3		2	1	1	1	4	1	3³	1
B-2	3	1	1	N	1	1		1	1	1		2	1	1	1	2	1	1	1
B-3	3	1	1	1	1	1	1		1	1		2	1	1	1	4	1	1	1
B-4	3	1	1	N	1	1	1	1		1		2	1	1	1	4	N	1	1
E	N	N	N	N	N	3	1	1	1			4	4	4	3	1	1	1	1
H-1	Not Permitted in Mixed Occupancies. See Chapter 9.																		
H-2	4	4	4	4	4	2	2	2	2	4			1	1	2	4	1	4	4
H-3	4	4	4	4	4	1	1	1	1	4		1		1	1	4	1	3	3
H-4-5	4	4	4	4	4	1	1	1	1	4		1	1		1	4	1	3	3
H-6-7[1]	4	4	4	3	4	1	1	1	1	3		2	1	1		4	3	4	4
I	3	3	3	3	3	4	2	4	4	1		4	4	4	4		1	1	1
M[2]	1	1	1	1	1	1	1	1	N	1		1	1	1	3	1		1	1
R-1	1	1	1	1	1	3³	1	1	1	1		4	3	3	4	1	1		N
R-3	1	1	1	1	1	1	1	1	1	1		4	3	3	4	1	1	N	

(H-1 column: Not Permitted in Mixed Occupancies. See Chapter 9.)

Note: For detailed requirements and exceptions, see Section 503.
[1] For special provisions on highly toxic materials, see Fire Code.
[2] For agricultural buildings, see also Appendix Chapter 11.
[3] For reduction in fire-resistive rating, see Section 503 (d).

Figure 2.4 Table 5-B, Required Separation in Buildings of Mixed Occupancy. Reproduced by permission from *Uniform Building Code*. Copyright © 1988, the International Conference of Building Officials.

fire-resistant construction types. A lower-hazard occupancy like a small business office or a residence can be built using any of the construction types.

The allowable construction types are listed in Figure 2.5 from left to right in approximate decreasing order of fire safety, and decreasing order of construction cost. Thus, choosing a construction type as far to the right on the allowable floor area table as possible will provide the least expensive construction type for the occupancy in question.

Allowable area and height of open parking garages, together with specifications for exterior walls, are shown in Figure 2.7 (Tables 7-A and 7-B of the *Uniform Building Code*).

Figures 2.5 and 2.6 (Tables 5-C and 5-D of the *Uniform Building Code*), together with the major modifications listed below, will define the range of classifications of construction types.

Multistory Buildings. The total floor area of a multi-story building can be twice the area of a single-story building. No single story can have more area than is shown in Figure 2-5.

Mezzanines. Mezzanine area is included in the floor area of the floor the mezzanine serves.

Separation on Two Sides. Where public ways or yards exceed 20 feet in width on two sides, the floor area can be increased by 1.25% for each foot of excess yard width. The increase cannot exceed 50%.

Separation on Three Sides. Where public ways or yards exceed 20 feet in width on three sides, the floor area can be increased by 2.5% for each foot of excess yard width. The increase cannot exceed 100%.

Separation on All Sides. Where public ways or yards exceed 20 feet in width on all sides, the floor area can be increased by 5% for each foot of excess yard width. The increase cannot exceed 100%.

Sprinkled Buildings, Floor Area Increases. The allowable floor area for a 1-story building can be tripled.

TABLE NO. 5-C—BASIC ALLOWABLE FLOOR AREA FOR BUILDINGS ONE STORY IN HEIGHT[1]
(In Square Feet)

| OCCUPANCY | I | II | | | III | | IV | V | |
	F.R.	F.R.	ONE-HOUR	N	ONE-HOUR	N	H.T.	ONE-HOUR	N
A-1	Unlimited	29,900	Not Permitted						
A) 2-2.1	Unlimited	29,900	13,500	Not Permitted	13,500	Not Permitted	13,500	10,500	Not Permitted
A) 3-4[2]	Unlimited	29,900	13,500	9,100	13,500	9,100	13,500	10,500	6,000
B) 1-2-3[3]	Unlimited	39,900	18,000	12,000	18,000	12,000	18,000	14,000	8,000
B-4	Unlimited	59,900	27,000	18,000	27,000	18,000	27,000	21,000	12,000
E	Unlimited	45,200	20,200	13,500	20,200	13,500	20,200	15,700	9,100
H-1	15,000	12,400	5,600	3,700	Not Permitted				
H-2[4]	15,000	12,400	5,600	3,700	5,600	3,700	5,600	4,400	2,500
H-3-4-5[4]	Unlimited	24,800	11,200	7,500	11,200	7,500	11,200	8,800	5,100
H-6-7	Unlimited	39,900	18,000	12,000	18,000	12,000	18,000	14,000	8,000
I) 1-2	Unlimited	15,100	6,800	Not Permitted[8]	6,800	Not Permitted	6,800	5,200	Not Permitted
I-3	Unlimited	15,100	Not Permitted[5]						
M[6]	See Chapter 11								
R-1	Unlimited	29,900	13,500	9,100[7]	13,500	9,100[7]	13,500	10,500	6,000[7]
R-3	Unlimited								

[1]For multistory buildings, see Section 505 (b).
[2]For limitations and exceptions, see Section 602 (a).
[3]For open parking garages, see Section 709.
[4]See Section 903.
[5]See Section 1002 (b).
[6]For agricultural buildings, see also Appendix Chapter 11.
[7]For limitations and exceptions, see Section 1202 (b).
[8]In hospitals and nursing homes, see Section 1002 (a) for exception.

N—No requirements for fire resistance
F.R.—Fire Resistive
H.T.—Heavy Timber

Figure 2.5 Table 5-C, Basic Allowable Floor Area for Buildings One Story in Height. Reproduced by permission from *Uniform Building Code*. Copyright © 1988, the International Conference of Building Officials.

TABLE NO. 5-D—MAXIMUM HEIGHT OF BUILDINGS

OCCUPANCY	TYPES OF CONSTRUCTION								
	I	II			III		IV	V	
	F.R.	F.R.	ONE-HOUR	N	ONE-HOUR	N	H.T.	ONE-HOUR	N
	MAXIMUM HEIGHT IN FEET								
	Unlimited	160	65	55	65	55	65	50	40
	MAXIMUM HEIGHT IN STORIES								
A-1	Unlimited	4	Not Permitted						
A) 2-2.1	Unlimited	4	2	Not Permitted	2	Not Permitted	2	2	Not Permitted
A) 3-4[1]	Unlimited	12	2	1	2	1	2	2	1
B) 1-2-3[2]	Unlimited	12	4	2	4	2	4	3	2
B-4	Unlimited	12	4	2	4	2	4	3	2
E[3]	Unlimited	4	2	1	2	1	2	2	1
H-1[4]	1	1	1	1	Not Permitted				
H-2[4]	Unlimited	2	1	1	1	1	1	1	1
H-3-4-5[4]	Unlimited	5	2	1	2	1	2	2	1
H-6-7	3	3	3	2	3	2	3	3	1
I-1[5]	Unlimited	3	1	Not Permitted	1	Not Permitted	1	1	Not Permitted
I-2	Unlimited	3	2	Not Permitted	2	Not Permitted	2	2	Not Permitted
I-3	Unlimited	2	Not Permitted[6]						
M[7]	See Chapter 11								
R-1	Unlimited	12	4	2[8]	4	2[8]	4	3	2[8]
R-3	Unlimited	3	3	3	3	3	3	3	3

Figure 2.6 Table 5-D, Maximum Height of Buildings. Superscript numbers refer to occupancy types. Reproduced by permission from *Uniform Building Code*. Copyright © 1988, the International Conference of Building Officials.

The allowable floor area for a multistory building can be doubled. These area modifications can be compounded on top of the area increases for separation on two, three, and all sides of the building. The floor area increase can be taken even if the code requires sprinklers for the occupancy. The floor area increase cannot be used for Group H, Division 1, 2, or 3 occupancies or for atria.

Sprinkled Buildings, Height Increases. A building that is not otherwise required to be sprinkled can have one additional story if it is sprinkled. You cannot take both a height increase and an area increase because of the sprinklers. You have to choose one or the other.

Sprinkled Buildings, 1-Hour Fire Protection Substitution. A sprinkler system can be used to substitute for 1-hour fire protection if it is not required by the code for some other reason and is not used for area or height increases. Exit access corridors, exit stairs, shafts, area separation walls, and similar structures must still maintain their required fire protection.

TABLE NO. 7-A—OPEN PARKING GARAGES AREA AND HEIGHT

TYPE OF CONSTRUCTION	AREA PER TIER (Square Feet)	HEIGHT		
		RAMP-ACCESS	MECHANICAL-ACCESS	
			Automatic Fire-extinguishing System	
			No	Yes
I	Unlimited	Unlimited	Unlimited	Unlimited
II-F.R.	125,000	12 Tiers	12 Tiers	18 Tiers
II-1-hour	50,000	10 Tiers	10 Tiers	15 Tiers
II-N	30,000	8 tiers	8 Tiers	12 Tiers

TABLE NO. 7-B—OPEN PARKING GARAGES—EXTERIOR WALLS[1]

FIRE RESISTANCE OF EXTERIOR WALLS	OPENINGS IN EXTERIOR WALLS
One hour less than 10 feet	Not permitted less than 5 feet. protected less than 10 feet

[1]See Section 709 (f).

Figure 2.7 Table 7-A, Open Parking Garages Area and Height; and Table 7-B, Open Parking Garages—Exterior Walls. Reproduced by permission from *Uniform Building Code*. Copyright © 1988, the International Conference of Building Officials.

SPRINKLER SYSTEM REQUIREMENTS

A sprinkler system is the most effective way to provide for fire safety in a building. A correctly operating sprinkler system will extinguish a fire before it can spread out of control. The *Uniform Building Code* requires sprinkler systems in the following situations.

· Group A occupancy drinking establishments with floor areas greater than 5000 square feet.
· Group A occupancy basements with floor areas greater than 1500 square feet.
· Group A occupancy exhibition and display rooms with floor areas greater than 12,000 square feet.
· Group A occupancies in stage and backstage areas.
· Group B, Division 2 office buildings and Group R, Division 1 occupancies with floors located 75 feet above the lowest level of fire truck access.
· Group B, Division 2 occupancy retail sales areas where the floor area is greater than 12,000 square feet on one floor, or greater than 24,000 square feet on all floors, or the building is more than three stories in height.
· Group E occupancy basements with floor areas larger than 1500 square feet.
· Group H, Division 1, 2, 3, 6, and 7 occupancies.
· Group H, Division 4 occupancies with floor areas greater than 4000 square feet.
· Group I occupancies.
· Group R, Division 1 occupancy apartment houses three or more stories in height, or with more than 15 dwelling units.
· Group R, Division 1 occupancy hotels 3 or more stories in height, or with more than 20 guest rooms.
· All occupancies (except Group R, Division 1 and Group M) where there is not sufficient fire department access through the outside walls. Sufficient access is 20 square feet of openings with a minimum dimension of 30 inches per 50 linear feet of wall. If these openings are on only one side, the floor dimension cannot exceed 75 feet from the openings.

AREA SEPARATION WALLS

One building can be divided into what the building code considers separate buildings through the use of area separation walls. The allowable floor area criteria of the code is then applied individually to each of the separated areas. The following criteria apply to area separation walls:

· *Type I* and *Type II fire-resistive* require a 4-hour fire wall.
· *Type II 1-hour and unprotected* requires a 2-hour fire wall.
· *Type III 1-hour and unprotected* requires a 4-hour fire wall.
· *Type IV heavy timber* requires a 4-hour fire wall.
· *Type V 1-hour and unprotected* requires a 2-hour fire wall.
· The total width of openings in area separation walls cannot be more than 25% of the length of the wall and must be protected by a fire assembly with a 3-hour rating for a 4-hour separation wall or a 1½-hour rating for a 2-hour separation wall.
· Area separation walls must extend from the foundation to a point 30 inches above the roof unless the roof has a 2-hour fire rating.

Figure 2.8 is an example of a *protected opening*. The door is constructed to withstand fire for a specified period of time, and is equipped with an automatic release so it will close in case of fire.

ATRIA

Atria have special restrictions since they provide an easy path for smoke and fire to spread up through a building.

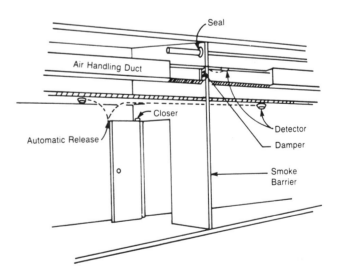

Figure 2.8 Some form of automatic closure of the opening when a fire is detected is termed a protected opening. Reproduced by permission from *Life Safety Code Handbook*. Copyright © 1988, National Fire Protection Association.

TABLE NO. 17-B—ATRIUM OPENING AND AREA		
HEIGHT IN STORIES	MINIMUM CLEAR OPENING[1] (Ft.)	MINIMUM AREA (Sq. Ft.)
3-4	20	400
5-7	30	900
8 or more	40	1600

[1]The specified dimensions are the diameters of inscribed circles whose centers fall on a common axis for the full height of the atrium.

Figure 2.9 Table 17-B, Atrium Opening and Area. Reproduced by permission from *Uniform Building Code*. Copyright © 1988, the International Conference of Building Officials.

Minimum opening sizes are defined in Figure 2.9 (Table 17-8 of the *Uniform Building Code*). A sprinkler system is required together with a smoke control system that supplies air at the base and exhausts air at the top. Adjacent spaces must be separated from the atrium by 1-hour construction or protected openings or by sprinkler-protected fixed glass (if the spaces are not dwelling units the separation requirement may be omitted at three floor levels). Travel distance through the atrium to an exit must be no more than 100 feet.

DOCUMENTING BUILDING CODE CONSTRAINTS

The constraints discussed above give an indication of the main thrust of the *Uniform Building Code*. The designer needs to read through the code carefully looking for and documenting the passages that relate to the design problem in question. Particular attention should be given to the introduction to the occupancy chapter, the sections covering the specific occupancies of the design, the introduction to the construction types chapter, and the section that defines the construction type of the design.

For example, consider the following excerpt from Chapter 18, "Type I Fire-Resistive Buildings," of the *Uniform Building Code*. Section 1806 discusses roofs. One paragraph states:

> Where every part of the structural framework of the roof of a group A or E occupancy or of an atrium is not less than 25 feet above any floor, balcony or gallery, fire protection of all members of the roof construction including those of the structural frame may be omitted. Heavy-Timber members in accordance with Section 2106 may be used for such unprotected members in one story buildings.

DETERMINING THE APPROPRIATE CONSTRUCTION TYPE

The following is an example of an analysis of basic *Uniform Building Code* provisions applied to a specific architectural project.

Example: Determination of the possible construction types for the small art museum project.

Museum Area	Square Feet
Galleries	14,000
Administration	1,500
Preparation	2,000
Art storage	6,000
Total net area	23,500
Plus 25 percent	5,800
Total gross area	29,300

The building is an A-2.1 assemble occupancy without a working stage. Scanning across Figure 2.5, Basic Allowable Floor Areas for Buildings One Story in Height, and Figure 2.6, Maximum Height of Buildings, from the *Uniform Building Code*, one can determine the types of construction the building code will allow.

1. *Type I fire resistant* construction has no floor area limits and no height limits for an A-2.1 occupancy. It will be an acceptable construction type.
2. *Type II fire-resistant* construction has a single-story limit of 29,900 square feet and a 4-story height limit with a total floor area limit of 59,800 square feet for the 4-story building. No single story can exceed 29,900 square feet. Since the small museum will easily fit inside these constraints, this is an acceptable construction type.
3. *Type II 1-hour* construction only allows 13,500 square feet on a single floor and only 2 stories with a total floor area of 27,000 square feet for a multistory building. The museum will exceed the size specified for this construction type. The code, however, allows the following modifications to increase the allowable floor area of this construction type.
   a) *Type II 1-hour* construction with *area separation on three sides* will probably be an acceptable option on the site being used. The building is about 30,000 square feet. A 10% safety margin would bring the area up to 33,000 square feet. This is 6000 square feet above the allowable multistory floor area limit. For separation

beyond 20 feet on 3 sides, the code allows 2.5% additional area per foot of extra separation.

$$0.025 \times 27,000 \text{ sq. ft.} = 675 \text{ sq. ft.}$$
$$6000 \text{ sq. ft.}/675 \text{ sq. ft.} = 8.89 \text{ ft.}$$

Therefore, we would need to locate the building to allow approximately 9 to 10 extra feet of separation on three sides for this type of construction.

b) *Type II 1-hour sprinkled* construction allows $3 \times 13,500$ sq. ft. $= 40,500$ sq. ft. on one floor, or $2 \times 13,500$ sq. ft. $\times 2$ stories $= 54,000$ sq. ft. for two stories.

Therefore, this construction type will be acceptable.

4. *Type II unprotected* construction is not allowed by the *Uniform Building Code* for an A-2.1 assembly occupancy.

5. *Type III 1-hour* construction and *Type IV heavy timber* construction have the same constraints as *Type II 1-hour* construction. Thus both these construction types will have to have enough separation on two or more sides, or they will have to be sprinkled to gain the extra allowable floor area needed for acceptable construction.

6. *Type V 1-hour* construction allows only 10,500 square feet on a single floor, or 21,000 square feet on 2 floors. This is not enough area to build the museum as it is being designed.

a) *Type V 1-hour* construction with *area separation on three sides* might be an option.

$$0.025 \times 10,500 = 262.5 \text{ sq ft.}$$
$$33,000/262.5 = 125.7 \text{ ft.}$$

This is clearly too large an extra separation for area separation to be a viable method of extending the floor area.

b) *Type V 1-hour sprinkled* construction would allow: $3 \times 10,500$ sq. ft. $= 31,500$ sq. ft. on 1 floor, or $2 \times 10,500$ sq. ft. $\times 2$ stories $= 42,000$ sq. ft. for 2 stories.

Therefore, this construction type will be acceptable.

7. *Type V unprotected* construction is not allowed by the *Uniform Building Code* for an A-2.1 assembly occupancy.

3

The Structural System

Deciding which structural system to use is one of the most prominent choices the architect will make. Much of a building's appearance will be affected by the structural system choice. The constraints governing this choice make a decision easier to achieve. The most important element is the construction type or types the building code allows for the occupancy and size of building being designed. Other constraints involve long versus short span, low-rise versus high-rise, construction costs, and ease of long-term maintenance.

CHOICE OF STRUCTURAL MATERIAL FROM AMONG CODE OPTIONS

The allowable heights and floor area tables in the building code determine what construction types are acceptable. The following sections link building code construction types to structural systems and their typical spans.

Type I and Type II Fire-Resistive Construction
Type I and Type II fire-resistive constructions require noncombustible materials (concrete, masonry, and steel) and substantial fire-resistance ratings (2-, 3-, and 4-hour fire resistance). Both these construction types can be used to build large, tall buildings. The difference is that Type I construction has no height or area limits for most occupancies. Type I construction requires 3- and 4-hour fire resistance for structural members. Type II construction has a maximum height limit of 160 feet as well as floor area and maximum story limitations as a function of occupancy. Type II construction requires 3- and 2-hour fire-resistance ratings and will thus be less expensive than Type I construction. Structural systems used for these types of construction are listed in Table 3.1.

Type II 1-Hour and Unprotected Construction
Type II 1-hour and unprotected construction uses structural members of noncombustible construction materials for exterior walls, interior bearing walls, columns, floors and roofs. Construction is steel framing combined with concrete or masonry walls. Structural systems for Type II 1-hour and unprotected construction are listed in Table 3.2.

TABLE 3.1. Structural systems for Type I and Type II fire-resistant construction

Structural System	Typical Span (feet)
Concrete solid slabs	10–25
Concrete slabs with drop panels	20–35
Concrete 2-way slab on beam	20–35
Conctete waffle slabs	30–40
Concrete joists	25–45
Concrete beams	15–40
Concrete girders	20–60
Concrete arches	60–150
Concrete thin shell roofs	50–70
Steel decking	5–30
Steel beams	15–60
Steel girders	40–100

Source: Adapted with permission from Lin and Stotesbury 1988. Note: The steel must be encased in fireproof material of sufficient thickness to provide the 4-, 3-, or 2-hour fire resistance required by the code.

TABLE 3.2. Structural systems for Type II 1-hour and unprotected construction

Structural System	Typical Span (feet)
Steel decking	5–30
Steel beams	15–60
Steel joists	15–60
Steel girders	40–100
Steel trusses	40–80

Source: Adapted with permission from Lin and Stotesbury 1988.

Type III 1-Hour and Unprotected Construction
Type III 1-hour and unprotected construction has exterior walls of noncombustible construction material, usually masonry or concrete; interior columns, beams, floors, and roofs can be constructed of any material, including wood. Table 3.3 lists structural systems used for Type III 1-hour and unprotected construction.

Type IV Heavy Timber Construction Type IV heavy timber construction achieves its fire resistance from the large size of the timber members used to frame it. (It is often referred to simply as heavy timber construction.) Exterior walls must be noncombustible. Structural systems for Type IV are listed in Table 3.4.

Type V 1-Hour and Unprotected Construction
Type V 1-hour and unprotected construction is essentially light wood framing (see Table 3.5).

TABLE 3.3. Structural systems for Type III 1-hour and unprotected construction

Structural System	Typical Span (feet)
Steel decking	5–30
Steel beams	15–60
Steel joists	15–60
Steel girders	40–100
Steel trusses	40–80
Plywood	3–5
Wood planks	2–6
Wood joists	10–25
Wood beams	15–30
Wood girders	20–35
Glue laminated beams	15–120
Wood trusses	30–100

Source: Adapted with permission from Lin and Stotesbury 1988.

TABLE 3.4. Structural systems for Type IV heavy timber construction

Structural System	Typical Span (feet)
Wood planks: minimum tongue and grooved 3 in. nominal thickness	2–6
Wood beams: minimum size 6 by 10 in. nominal	15–30
Wood girders: minimum size 6 by 10 in.	20–35
Wood trusses: supporting floors 8 in. minimum dimension; supporting roofs 6 by 8 in.	30–100
Wood arches: supporting floors 8 in. minimum dimension; supporting roofs 6 by 8 in.	30–120
Wood glue laminated beams	15–120

Source: Adapted with permission from Lin and Stotesbury 1988.

TABLE 3.5. Structural systems for Type V 1-hour and unprotected construction

Structural System	Typical Span (feet)
Plywood	3–5
Wood planks	2–6
Wood joists	10–25
Wood beams	15–30
Wood girders	20–35
Glue-laminated beams	15–150
Wood trusses	30–100

Source: Adapted with permission from Lin and Stotesbury 1988.

Usually there are a number of construction types that are acceptable. Some factors to consider when choosing among allowable construction types are the permanence of the structure, the context of the site, the expense of the construction, and client motivation. For example, in a corporate or institutional setting, where life-cycle costs, including maintenance and fire insurance, are considered, Type II fire-resistive concrete construction becomes very attractive.

Example: Choosing the structural system for the art museum (see example in Chapter 2).

For the example in Chapter 2 we listed the construction types that the *Uniform Building Code* will allow for a small assembly without a stage. Construction types are discussed below in relation to the specific project. The client is a large university.

1. *Type I fire resistive.* There is no point in building the museum to these specifications since Type II fire-resistive construction is acceptable; since it is less restrictive it will also be less expensive.
2. *Type II fire resistive.* The university has a long-term approach to its facilities. The life-cycle costs of maintenance and fire insurance play an important role in decision making. The university likes to use *Type II fire-resistive* concrete construction to minimize life-cycle costs. A further advantage of this type of construction is its high degree of fire resistance. Traveling art exhibits may have restrictions on what type of building the art can be displayed in to insure the fire safety of the art.
3. *Type II 1-hour sprinkled* construction (light steel framing), *Type III 1-hour sprinkled* construction, *Type IV sprinkled* construction (heavy timber), or *Type V 1-hour sprinkled* construction (wood framing) would all be cheaper construction types than *Type II fire-resistive* construction.
4. *Type II fire-resistive* concrete construction will be considered because the institutional client desires life-cycle value.
5. *Type II 1-hour, sprinkled,* light steel construction will also be considered because of its lower construction cost but still relatively high fire safety.

LONG VERSUS SHORT SPANS

The architectural program lists the required spaces that the building should accommodate. Spaces should be classified according to the following question: Does this area require a long span enclosure system or will shorter, more economical spans serve this function just as well?

Short spans (10, 20, or 30 feet) suggest beams, girders, and slabs in bending. This method encloses the space economically with a minimum structural depth.

Long spans (50 to 100 feet and beyond) suggest the use of shape to aid the structural material. Arches, shells, domes, space frames, trusses, and similar structures use their shape to help the structural material span the long distance (see Fig. 3.1).

Extra long spans (such as stadiums) involve roofs spanning great distances. The economics suggest tension and inflatable membrane structures (Fig. 3.2).

Construction cost is always a concern. Figure 3.3 lists the cost per square foot for a range of structural systems. Note how the relative cost of different structural systems changes as a function of span and superimposed load.

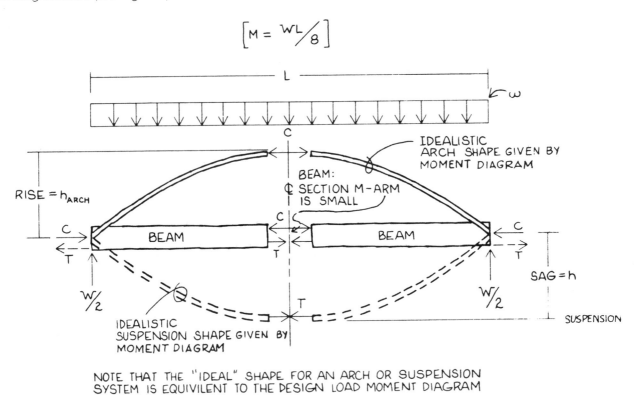

Figure 3.1 An arch or suspension system. The additional overall depth of an arch or truss shape reduces stresses in the material so that longer spans can be achieved. Reproduced by permission from Lin and Stotesbury, (1988).

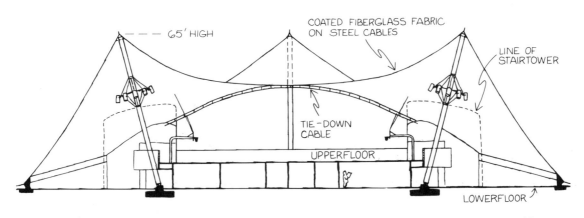

Figure 3.2 For very long spans, tension and inflated structures use shape to produce a roof structure supported by tension only. Reproduced by permission from Lin and Stotesbury, (1988).

BAY SIZE	Cast In Place Concrete						Precast Concrete			Structural Steel					Wood	
	1 WAY BM & SLAB (3.5-120)	2 WAY BM & SLAB (3.5-130)	FLAT SLAB (3.5-140)	FLAT PLATE (3.5-150)	JOIST SLAB (3.5-160)	WAFFLE SLAB (3.5-170)	BEAMS & HOLLOW CORE SLABS (3.5-242)	BEAMS & HOLLOW CORE SLABS TOPPED (3.5-244)	BEAMS & DOUBLE TEES TOPPED (3.5-254)	BAR JOISTS on COLS. & BRG. WALLS (3.5-440)	BAR JOISTS BEAMS on COLS (3.5-460)	COMPOSITE BEAMS & C.I.P. SLAB (3.5-520)	WIDE FLANGE BEAMS COMPOSITE (3.5-530)	COMPOSITE BEAM & DK., LT. WT. SLAB (3.5-540)	WOOD BEAMS & JOISTS (3.5-720)	LAMINATED WOOD BEAMS & JOISTS (3.5-730)
Superimposed Load = 40 PSF																
15x15	7.85	7.39	6.71	6.32	7.73	—	—	—	—	—	—	—	—	—	4.74	5.84
15x20	7.83	7.72	6.97	6.70	7.77	—	—	—	—	4.67	5.45	—	8.32	—	5.25	5.93
20x20	7.94	8.08	7.17	6.69	7.74	8.53	9.21	10.74	—	4.77	5.83	—	8.90	—	5.32	6.13
20x25	8.06	8.55	7.71	7.38	7.84	8.62	8.78	10.28	—	5.25	6.44	9.13	8.98	7.78	—	—
25x25	8.10	8.79	7.92	7.52	7.72	8.84	9.28	11.11	—	5.56	6.86	9.40	9.87	7.67	—	—
25x30	8.27	9.13	8.37	—	8.10	8.94	8.93	10.36	12.43	5.66	7.08	10.14	9.92	7.75	—	—
30x30	9.15	9.87	8.82	—	8.34	9.36	9.28	11.11	13.16	5.62	7.10	10.11	10.75	7.77	—	—
30x35	9.55	10.58	9.38	—	8.69	9.51	9.45	11.05	—	6.22	7.91	10.45	11.53	8.04	—	—
35x35	10.17	11.08	9.55	—	8.77	9.96	10.05	11.35	—	6.38	8.06	10.85	11.77	8.50	—	—
35x40	10.42	11.70	—	—	9.05	10.21	10.16	12.07	11.95	—	—	11.75	12.21	9.29	—	—
40x40	—	—	—	—	9.36	10.50	10.71	12.52	12.61	—	—	—	—	—	—	—
40x45	—	—	—	—	9.74	10.85	—	—	—	—	—	—	—	—	—	—
40x50	—	—	—	—	—	—	—	—	—	—	—	—	—	—	—	—
Superimposed Load = 75 PSF																
15x15	7.91	7.57	6.81	6.32	7.74	—	—	—	—	—	—	—	—	—	5.74	7.31
15x20	8.12	8.34	7.17	6.99	7.96	—	—	—	—	5.06	6.16	—	9.01	—	6.46	7.80
20x20	8.58	8.78	7.46	7.01	8.21	8.67	9.76	11.24	—	5.39	6.66	—	9.78	—	6.36	7.60
20x25	8.86	9.55	8.13	7.53	8.25	8.83	8.78	10.65	—	5.94	7.01	10.15	10.75	7.98	—	—
25x25	8.79	9.46	8.25	7.84	8.21	9.09	9.68	11.11	—	6.13	7.65	10.75	11.08	8.27	—	—
25x30	8.84	9.93	8.81	—	8.43	9.18	9.23	11.16	12.43	5.95	7.53	11.35	11.58	8.14	—	—
30x30	9.84	10.68	9.28	—	8.67	9.58	9.68	11.81	13.16	6.39	8.11	11.20	12.25	8.32	—	—
30x35	9.99	11.13	9.89	—	8.78	9.51	10.05	11.27	—	7.25	9.07	11.95	13.07	8.63	—	—
35x35	11.07	11.55	10.12	—	9.20	10.19	10.55	12.48	—	7.75	9.71	12.35	13.34	9.52	—	—
35x40	11.23	12.10	—	—	9.43	10.50	—	—	11.82	—	—	13.05	13.90	9.90	—	—
40x40	—	—	—	—	9.65	10.90	—	—	13.05	—	—	—	—	—	—	—
40x45	—	—	—	—	9.83	11.15	—	—	—	—	—	—	—	—	—	—
40x50	—	—	—	—	—	—	—	—	—	—	—	—	—	—	—	—
Superimposed Load = 125 PSF																
15x15	8.01	7.86	7.00	6.47	7.87	—	—	—	—	—	—	—	—	—	7.62	10.60
15x20	8.44	9.04	7.45	7.40	8.38	—	—	—	—	5.68	7.04	—	10.12	—	8.80	11.59
20x20	9.01	9.09	7.98	7.40	8.35	8.82	—	—	—	6.39	7.58	—	10.86	—	11.01	11.25
20x25	9.39	9.77	8.61	7.95	8.73	8.98	—	—	—	6.64	8.19	11.35	12.35	9.69	—	—
25x25	10.17	10.31	8.69	8.17	9.10	9.28	—	—	—	7.14	8.89	12.20	13.02	8.76	—	—
25x30	10.24	10.75	9.11	—	9.07	9.41	—	—	—	7.20	8.99	13.25	12.94	9.35	—	—
30x30	10.51	11.28	9.58	—	9.15	9.72	—	—	—	7.95	10.06	13.10	14.15	9.80	—	—
30x35	11.17	12.20	10.18	—	9.24	9.98	—	—	—	8.15	10.27	14.50	15.00	10.07	—	—
35x35	11.79	12.65	10.35	—	9.23	10.36	—	—	—	9.06	10.75	14.15	15.65	11.03	—	—
35x40	11.91	12.75	—	—	9.44	10.90	—	—	—	—	—	15.20	16.10	11.25	—	—
40x40	—	—	—	—	10.06	11.10	—	—	—	—	—	—	—	—	—	—
40x45	—	—	—	—	10.22	11.40	—	—	—	—	—	—	—	—	—	—
40x50	—	—	—	—	—	—	—	—	—	—	—	—	—	—	—	—
Superimposed Load = 200 PSF																
15x15	8.38	8.44	7.25	—	8.19	—	—	—	—	—	—	—	12.05	—	13.07	16.35
15x20	9.15	9.70	7.60	—	8.60	—	—	—	—	—	—	—	12.68	—	11.86	14.78
20x20	9.81	9.58	8.10	—	8.73	9.23	—	—	—	—	—	—	—	—	—	15.54
20x25	10.09	10.64	8.87	—	9.18	9.36	—	—	—	—	—	13.80	13.65	10.73	—	—
25x25	11.03	11.61	9.00	—	9.51	9.53	—	—	—	—	—	14.30	14.70	11.18	—	—
25x30	10.99	11.69	9.57	—	9.63	10.12	—	—	—	—	—	15.15	15.60	11.25	—	—
30x30	11.66	12.10	10.11	—	9.67	10.50	—	—	—	—	—	15.85	18.45	11.60	—	—
30x35	11.79	12.80	—	—	9.97	10.90	—	—	—	—	—	17.15	17.90	11.57	—	—
35x35	12.75	13.25	—	—	9.97	11.10	—	—	—	—	—	17.45	19.45	12.54	—	—
35x40	12.85	13.65	—	—	10.19	11.85	—	—	—	—	—	18.80	19.95	13.36	—	—
40x40	—	—	—	—	—	—	—	—	—	—	—	—	—	—	—	—
40x45	—	—	—	—	—	—	—	—	—	—	—	—	—	—	—	—
40x50	—	—	—	—	—	—	—	—	—	—	—	—	—	—	—	—

Figure 3.3 Comparative cost of floor-framing systems in dollars per square foot as a function of structural system type, bay size, and superimposed load. Reproduced by permission from R. S. Means Co. (1989).

LOW-RISE VERSUS HIGH-RISE DESIGN

Low-rise structural design is dominated by the collection of dead and live loads through slabs, beams, and girders onto the walls and columns where the load is taken down to the foundation and onto the earth below.

High-rise design is dominated by the need to with-stand the lateral loading of wind and earthquake on the building. This domination of lateral loading forces a building to become more symmetrical as it gets taller. There is substantial additional cost involved in a high-rise solution because of this increased need to resist lateral loads from wind and earthquake (see Fig. 3.4).

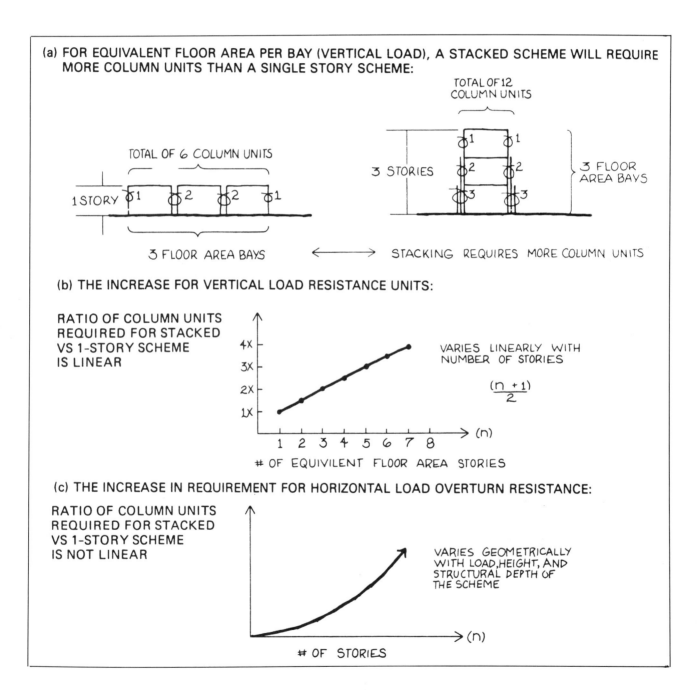

Figure 3.4 A comparison of the added cost in materials for gravity and horizontal load resistance in a high-rise structure relative to a low-rise design for vertical load only. Reproduced by permission from Lin and Stotesbury, (1988).

4

The HVAC System

In architectural design it is very easy for engineering features to be partitioned in a coincidental manner. For example, the heating, ventilating, and air conditioning (HVAC) system is often divided into air-handling units on each floor because it is physically easy to do so. The designer should be thinking about functional associations. In the HVAC system design, an example of functional association would be building areas having similar air quality requirements or similar schedules. Considering and listing HVAC functional associations in predesign will provide the information necessary for the design to respond in sympathetic fashion to the HVAC requirements it is creating. Physical space for equipment can then be considered as the design is forming.

DIVISION INTO HVAC USE GROUPS

The partitioning of the HVAC design problem should relate to the functional characteristics of the architectural program, and the ability of the HVAC system to respond. A functional partitioning of the building into major zones will be achieved by grouping architectural program areas into sets with similar schedules, similar temperature set points, similar ventilation and air quality, similar internal heat generation, and similar need for heating, cooling, and/or ventilation.

Start at the top of the list: Divide the architectural program areas into groupings with similar schedules.

Then, continue down through the list adding new groupings as necessary to meet the other four criteria. The result will be a partitioning of the areas listed in the architectural program as a function of HVAC requirements into HVAC use groups. These groups will become a guidance overlay for the concept formation of the architecture.

Each of the HVAC use groups will become a major zone served by some form of HVAC delivery system. For the HVAC delivery system to serve the group easily, the architectural program areas listed in an HVAC use group need to be located physically next to or near each other. This is not always possible, but an attempt should be made to achieve proximity.

This method of zoning a building creates a HVAC system that can respond to functional requirements for thermal and air quality comfort. It also creates a HVAC system that has a maximum capacity to save energy since it can be set back or shut down or can control the amount of outside air in close relationship to the building's functional requirements. An arbitrary HVAC subdivision by physical expediency would not be as well matched to the functional nature of the HVAC design problem.

SAMPLE ANALYSIS FOR AN HVAC SYSTEM

The following example continues the analysis of the architectural program begun in Chapter 2.

Example: Partitioning the architectural program for the art museum example according to the needs of the HVAC system.

1. Group the spaces by similar operational schedule.
    a) The galleries, art storage, and exhibit preparation areas will need 24-hour HVAC operation to maintain the thermal environment for the art work.
    b) The administrative areas operate for about 10 hours per day. They could be shut down or set back during off hours.
2. Note any change in groupings because of similar temperature set point. In this example all the areas will have similar temperature set points during operating hours. Thus no new groups are generated by this criterion.
3. Note changes in groupings because of similar ventilation and air quality needs.
    a) The galleries need conditioning for art and for people.
    b) The art storage will need less ventilation than the galleries because there will be very few people in the storage areas. For periods of time there will be no people.
    c) The exhibit preparation area will require high ventilation rates at times when fumes from painting and other preparation activities become high. The HVAC system should not spread these fumes to other areas of the building.
    d) The administrative areas need conditioning for people.
4. Note changes in grouping because of similar internal heat generation. The storage area might have somewhat less internal heat generation but it is already a separate group. All the other areas have similar internal heat generation. This criterion does not change the groupings.
5. Note changes arising from similar needs for heating, cooling, and/or ventilation. This whole building needs heating, cooling, and ventilation. There is no covered parking that needs only ventilation or bulk storage that might only need heating and ventilation.
6. The partition of the HVAC system will reflect the following separate groupings: the galleries, art storage, exhibit preparation, and administrative areas. When the design concept forms, additional partitions might appear because of the differences between internal and external loading.

5

The Lighting System

Building form is displayed to us through light. The amount and quality of natural and artificial lighting should reinforce the building design concept.

DAYLIGHTING

Daylight is an important connection with the outside world. Even if daylight is not to be used as a primary lighting source, in most buildings there should be some penetration of daylight. The architectural program can be partitioned into spaces where daylighting can or should be used and spaces where daylight will not be a major factor. The best opportunities for daylight use are in areas where task lighting is not the primary consideration. As the task lighting needs to be more controlled, daylighting becomes more problematic as a lighting solution.

Good daylighting opportunity happens where task lighting needs are not too critical, as in corridors, waiting rooms, lobbies, and residences. A more difficult daylighting problem is produced where task light is more important, as in classrooms, offices, and museums.

Daylighting is probably not a good idea where task light constraints are very restrictive, as in lecture rooms and hospital operating rooms.

ARTIFICIAL LIGHTING

If the client's lighting needs and motivations have not been explicitly stated in the architectural program, they need to be determined and recorded for each area of the program. It is important that the descriptive words used by the client and the designer are interpreted to mean the same thing by both people. Words are of limited use, however. The best way to get a client to understand and commit to a lighting concept is to show him or her similarly lit environments on a field tour of buildings.

Where task lighting needs to be more controlled, as in classrooms, offices, operating rooms, and museum galleries, freedom of expression in lighting design must give way to functional illumination criteria. Freedom of expression in lighting design is less constrained where task lighting needs are not as critical, as in corridors, waiting rooms, and lobbies.

SAMPLE CRITERIA FOR LIGHTING DESIGN

Example: Lighting criteria for the art museum project.

1. Daylighting
   a) Daylighting is desirable in areas of public circulation, the main gallery and the secondary gallery (in a controlled fashion), and in the administration areas.
   b) Daylight is *not* necessary in the preparation area or areas of private circulation.
2. Electrical lighting
   a) The galleries will require incandescent spot lighting that can be flexibly focused onto changing displays.
   b) The administration and preparation areas will need fluorescent light for task illumination with a mix of incandescent spots for the art that will be displayed.
   c) The art storage area will need fluorescent illumination for the task of placing and finding things.
   d) Public circulation areas are probably best illuminated with incandescent spots or wall sconces to blend with the galleries.
   e) Private circulation areas could be illuminated with fluorescent light for efficiency.

6

The Plumbing System

The plumbing system must enter and leave the building and thread itself through the structure, usually in a hidden manner. The plumbing code specifies the minimum plumbing fixtures (toilets, lavatories, drinking fountains, and so on) that are necessary as a function of the occupancy type and the number of people served. It is therefore helpful to determine plumbing requirements in the predesign stage so they can be considered during design formation. (For design development and contract documents, the designer must consult the actual plumbing code directly and use traditional engineering procedures.)

LOCATING UTILITY LINES ON THE SITE PLAN

The location of the water main, sanitary sewer, and storm drain needs to be recorded on the site plan (see Fig. 6.1 for these locations on a sample plan).

The water supply is under pressure so there is flexibility in connecting the water main to the building. The connection to the sanitary sewer and storm drainage system, however, is most appropriately located downhill from the building because these systems are gravity flow systems. The sanitary sewer receives the effluent from the building plumbing system (toilets, lavatories, sinks, showers, and drinking fountains). This

fluid needs to be treated in a sewage treatment plant before being discharged to nature.

The storm drainage system receives the rain water runoff from the roof and grounds of the building. Rain water runoff does not have to be treated in a sewage treatment facility. It can be discharged directly into whatever body of water is available.

DETERMINING BATHROOM FIXTURE REQUIREMENTS

The plumbing code lists the number of plumbing fixtures that are necessary as a function of occupancy type and the number of people served. This information can be determined from the architectural program area requirements and from Figure 6.2 (Appendix C of the *Uniform Plumbing Code*), which lists minimum plumbing facilities. From a plumbing standpoint, the population of the building is the same as the population determined by the *Uniform Building Code* for occupancy and egress purposes. This population should be divided into male and female before determining the number of fixtures necessary for each sex. It is important to remember that these are minimum requirements. You might want to exceed the minimum to provide more accessible facilities. In addition, keep in

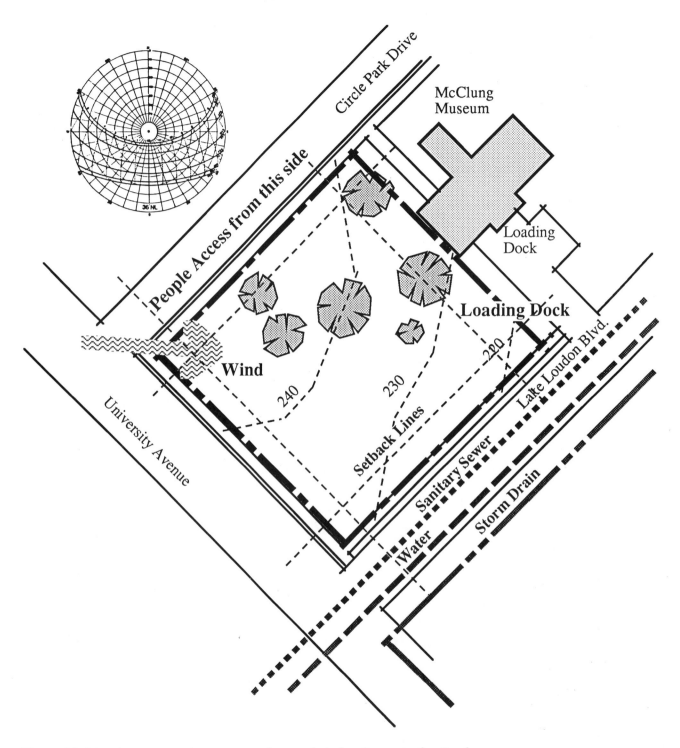

Figure 6.1 Mapping water, sanitary sewer, and storm drain locations onto the site plan.

mind that good practice distributes bathrooms around a building facility for convenient use. Convenient distribution of facilities often requires the installation of more then the minimum numbers listed in the tables.

Example: Determination of the minimum plumbing fixture requirements for the small art museum project.

First, the population of the building as defined in the

Uniform Building Code needs to be determined. The following table shows the occupant load calculation.

Program Area	Area (sq. ft.)	Occupancy Type	Square feet/ Person	Occupant Load
Main Gallery	6000	Assembly	15 net	400
Gallery	4000	Assembly	15 net	267
Gallery	4000	Assembly	15 net	267
Administration	1500	Business	100 gross	15
Preparation	2000	Business	100 gross	20
Art storage	6000	Storage	500 gross	12
Circulation for the administration and preparation areas at 15% gives 525 sq. ft. at 100 sq. ft./person				5
Total population of the building				986

With this information, Figure 6.2 can be used to determine the minimum plumbing fixture requirements.

1. The plumbing fixtures for the assembly areas of the building for public use are determined as follows.

   Total assembly area population = 400 people + 267 people + 267 people = 934 people

   Male population =
   934 people/2 = 467 people

   The required fixtures for the males are 4 water closets, 4 urinals, 3 lavatories, and 6 drinking fountains.
   a) The water closets can be reduced by one because of the urinals.
   b) Where urinals are used, a water closet can be eliminated for each urinal for up to two-thirds of the required water closets.
   c) Note 12 modifies the number of drinking fountains to 1 for the first 75 people, then 1 per each additional 150 people. Even this tends to produce too many drinking fountains. Judgment needs to be used.
   Thus, 3 water closets, 4 urinals, 3 lavatories, and 1 drinking fountain are required for the male population.

   Female population = 934 people/2 = 467 people

   The required fixtures for the females are 9 water closets, 3 lavatories, and 1 drinking fountain.

2. The plumbing fixtures for the office, preparation, and storage areas of the building for employee use are determined as follows.

   Total office, preparation, and storage population = 15 people + 20 people + 12 people = 47 people

   Male population = 47 people/2 = 23.5 people = 24 people

   The required fixtures for the males are 2 water closets, 1 urinal, and 1 lavatory.
   a) The water closets cannot be reduced by one because of the urinal because it would be more than a two-thirds reduction.

   Female population = 47 people/2 = 23.5 people = 24 people

   Required fixtures for the females are 2 water closets and 2 lavatories.

It is important to remember that the number of fixtures calculated above is the minimum required number, not the suggested quantity for good design. Some expansion of the numbers listed above is probably wise.

SPECIAL PLUMBING FIXTURE REQUIREMENTS

The architectural program might require either explicitly or implicitly that other plumbing fixtures be included. It is a good idea to determine which spaces will require plumbing fixtures so that grouping of the plumbing in the building can be a consideration as the design is forming.

WATER SUPPLY PUMPS

The city water pressure will push water up through two or three stories. Buildings taller than this will need a surge tank and water pressure pumps. A hot water heater will also have to be included in the plan.

SPRINKLER SYSTEM

A sprinkler system is the most effective way to provide for fire safety in a building. A correctly operating sprinkler system will extinguish a fire before it can spread out of control. The sprinkler system includes pumps and control valves that need to be planned.

APPENDIX C
MINIMUM PLUMBING FACILITIES[1]

Each building shall be provided with sanitary facilities, including provisions for the physically handicapped as prescribed by the Department having jurisdiction. In the absence of such requirements, this Appendix — which provides a guideline for the minimum facilities for the various types of occupancies (See Section 910, Plumbing Fixtures Required, of the Uniform Plumbing Code) may be used. For handicapped requirements, ANSI A117.1-1961 (R1971). Specifications for Making Buildings and Facilities Accessible to, and Usable by, the Physically Handicapped, may be used.

Type of Building or Occupancy[2]	Water Closets (Fixtures per person)		Urinals[10] (Fixtures per person)	Lavatories (Fixtures per person)		Bathtubs or Showers (Fixtures per person)	Drinking Fountains[3,13] (Fixtures per person)
Assembly Places — Theatres Auditoriums, Convention Halls, etc. — for permanent employee use.	*Male* 1:1-15 2:16-35 3:36-55 Over 55, add 1 fixture for each additional 40 persons	*Female* 1:1-15 2:16-35 3:36-55	1 per 50	*Male* 1 per 40	*Female* 1 per 40	----------------	----------------
Assembly Places — Theatres Auditoriums, Convention Halls, etc. — for public use	*Male* 1:1-100 2:101-200 3:201-400 Over 400 add 1 fixture for each additional 500 males and 2 for each 300 females	*Female* 3:1-100 6:101-200 8:201-400	1:1-100 2:101-200 3:201-400 4:401-600 Over 600 add 1 fixture for each additional 300 males	*Male* 1:1-200 2:201-400 3:401-750 Over 750, add 1 fixture for each additional 500 persons	*Female* 1:1-200 2:201-400 3:401-750	----------------	1 per 75[12]
Dormitories[9] — School or Labor	*Male* 1 per 10 Add 1 fixture for each additional 25 males (over 10) and 1 for each additional 20 females (over 8)	*Female* 1 per 8	1 per 25 Over 150, add 1 fixture for each additional 50 males	*Male* 1 per 12 Over 12, add 1 fixture for each additional 20 males and 1 for each 15 females	*Female* 1 per 12	1 per 8 For female, add 1 bathtub per 30. Over 150, add 1 per 20	1 per 75[12]
Dormitories — for staff use	*Male* 1:1-15 2:16-35 3:36-55 Over 55, add 1 fixture for each additional 40 persons	*Female* 1:1-15 2:16-35 3:36-55	1 per 50	*Male* 1 per 40	*Female* 1 per 40	----------------	-------------
Office or Public Buildings	*Male* 1:1-15 2:16-35 3:36-55 4:56-80 5:81-110 6:111-150 Over 150, add 1 fixture for each additional 40 persons	*Female* 1:1-15 2:16-35 3:36-55 4:56-80 5:81-110 6:111-150		*Male* 1:1-15 2:16-35 3:36-60 4:61-90 5:91-125 Over 125, add 1 fixture for each additional 45 persons	*Female* 1:1-15 2:16-35 3:36-60 4:61-90 5:91-125	----------------	1 per 75[12]
Office or Public Buildings For employee use	*Male* 1:1-15 2:16-35 3:36-55 Over 55, add 1 fixture for each additional 40 persons	*Female* 1:1-15 2:16-35 3:36-55	1 per 50	*Male* 1 per 40	*Female* 1 per 40	----------------	-----------
Penal Institutions— For employee use	*Male* 1:1-15 2:16-35 3:36-55 Over 55, add 1 fixture for each additional 40 persons	*Female* 1:1-15 2:16-35 3:36-55	1 per 50	*Male* 1 per 40	*Female* 1 per 40	---------------- ----------------	1 per 75[12]
Penal Institutions— For prisoner use Cell	1 per cell		-------------	1 per cell		----------------	1 per cell block floor
Exercise Room	1 per exercise room		1 per exercise room	1 per exercise room		----------------	1 per exercise room
Restaurants, Pubs and Lounges[11]	*Male* 1:1-50 2:51-150 3:151-300 Over 300, add 1 fixture for each additional 200 persons	*Female* 1:1-50 2:51-150 4:151-300	1:1-150 Over 150, add 1 fixture for each additional 150 males	*Male* 1:1-150 2:151-200 3:201-400 Over 400, add 1 fixture for each additional 400 persons	*Female* 1:1-150 2:151-200 3:201-400	----------------	-----------
Schools—For staff use All schools	*Male* 1:1-15 2:16-35 3:36-55 Over 55, add 1 fixture for each additional 40 persons	*Female* 1:1-15 2:16-35 3:36-55	1 per 50	*Male* 1 per 40	*Female* 1 per 40	----------------	-----------

Figure 6.2 Appendix C, Minimum Plumbing Facilities. Reproduced by permission from *Uniform Plumbing Code* (International Association of Plumbing and Mechanical Officials 1988).

Type of Building or Occupancy[2]	Water Closets (Fixtures per person)		Urinals[10] (Fixtures per person)	Lavatories (Fixtures per person)		Bathtubs or Showers (Fixtures per person)	Drinking Fountains[3],[13] (Fixtures per person)
Dwellings[4]							
Single Dwelling	1 per dwelling		------------	1 per dwelling		1 per dwelling	----------
Multiple Dwelling or Apartment House	1 per dwelling or apartment unit			1 per dwelling or apartment unit		1 per dwelling or apartment unit	
Hospitals							
Waiting Room	1 per room		------------	1 per room		----------------	1 per 75[12]
For employee use	*Male* 1:1-15 2:16-35 3:36-55 Over 55, add 1 fixture for each additional 40 persons	*Female* 1:1-15 2:16-35 3:36-55	1 per 50	*Male* 1 per 40	*Female* 1 per 40	----------------	
Hospitals							
Individual Room	1 per room		------------	1 per room		1 per room	----------
Ward Room	1 per 8 patients		------------	1 per 10 patients		1 per 20 patients	1 per 75[12]
Industrial[6] Warehouses Workshops, Foundries and similar establishments (for employee use)	*Male* 1:1-10 2:11-25 3:26-50 4:51-75 5:76-100 Over 100, add 1 fixture for each additional 30 persons	*Female* 1:1-10 2:11-25 3:26-50 4:51-75 5:76-100		Up to 100, 1 per 10 persons Over 100, 1 per 15 persons[7],[8]		1 shower for each 15 persons exposed to excessive heat or to skin contamination with poisonous, infectious, or irritating material.	1 per 75[12]
Institutional—other than Hospitals or Penal Institutions (on each occupied floor)	*Male* 1 per 25	*Female* 1 per 20	1 per 50	*Male* 1 per 10	*Female* 1 per 10	1 per 8	1 per 75[12]
Institutional—other than Hospitals or Penal Institutions (on each occupied floor)—for employee use	*Male* 1:1-15 2:16-35 3:36-55 Over 55, add 1 fixture for each additional 40 persons	*Female* 1:1-15 2:16-35 3:36-55	1 per 50	*Male* 1 per 40	*Female* 1 per 40	----------------	----------
Schools—For student use Nursery	*Male* 1:1-20 2:21-50 Over 50, add 1 fixture for each additional 50 persons	*Female* 1:1-20 2:21-50	------------	*Male* 1:1-25 2:26-50 Over 50, add 1 fixture for each additional 50 persons	*Female* 1:1-25 2:26-50	----------------	1 per 75[12]
Elementary	*Male* 1 per 30	*Female* 1 per 25	1 per 75	*Male* 1 per 35	*Female* 1 per 35	----------------	1 per 75[12]
Secondary	*Male* 1 per 40	*Female* 1 per 30	1 per 35	*Male* 1 per 40	*Female* 1 per 40	----------------	1 per 75[12]
Others (Colleges, Universities, Adult Centers, etc.)	*Male* 1 per 40	*Female* 1 per 30	1 per 35	*Male* 1 per 40	*Female* 1 per 40	----------------	1 per 75[12]
Worship Places Educational and Activities Unit	*Male* 1 per 250	*Female* 1 per 125	1 per 250	1 per toilet room		----------------	1 per 75[12]
Worship Places Principal Assembly Place	*Male* 1 per 300	*Female* 1 per 150	1 per 300	1 per toilet room		----------------	1 per 75[12]

Whenever urinals are provided, one (1) water closet less than the number specified may be provided for each urinal installed, except the number of water closets in such cases shall not be reduced to less than two-thirds (⅔) of the minimum specified.

1. The figures shown are based upon one (1) fixture being the minimum required for the number of persons indicated or any fraction thereof.
2. Building categories not shown on this table shall be considered separately by the Administrative Authority.
3. Drinking fountains shall not be installed in toilet rooms.
4. Laundry trays. One (1) laundry tray or one (1) automatic washer standpipe for each dwelling unit or two (2) laundry trays or two (2) automatic washer standpipes, or combination thereof, for each ten (10) apartments. Kitchen sinks. One (1) for each dwelling or apartment unit.
5. Deleted.
6. As required by ANSI Z4.1–1968, Sanitation in Places of Employment.
7. Where there is exposure to skin contamination with poisonous, infectious, or irritating materials, provide one (1) lavatory for each five (5) persons.
8. Twenty-four (24) lineal inches (609.6 mm) of wash sink or eighteen (18) inches (457.2 mm) of a circular basin, when provided with water outlets for such space, shall be considered equivalent to one (1) lavatory.
9. Laundry trays. One (1) for each fifty (50) persons. Slop sinks, one (1) for each hundred (100) persons.
10. General. In applying this schedule of facilities, consideration must be given to the accessibility of the fixtures. Conformity purely on a numerical basis may not result in an installation suited to the need of the individual establishment. For example, schools should be provided with toilet facilities on each floor having classrooms. Temporary workingmen facilities. One (1) water closet and one (1) urinal for each thirty (30) workmen.
    a. Surrounding materials. Wall and floor space to a point two (2) feet (0.6 m) in front of urinal lip and four (4) feet (1.2 m) above the floor, and at least two (2) feet (0.6 m) to each side of the urinal shall be lined with non-absorbent material.
    b. Trough urinals are prohibited.
11. A restaurant is defined as a business which sells food to be consumed on the premises.
    a. The number of occupants for a drive-in restaurant shall be considered as equal to the number of parking stalls.
    b. Employee toilet facilities are not to be included in the above restaurant requirements. Hand washing facilities must be available in the kitchen for employees.
12. Where food is consumed indoors, water stations may be substituted for drinking fountains. Theatres, auditoriums, dormitories, offices, or public buildings for use by more than six (6) persons shall have one (1) drinking fountain for the first seventy-five (75) persons and one (1) additional fountain for each one hundred and fifty (150) persons thereafter.
13. There shall be a minimum of one (1) drinking fountain per occupied floor in schools, theatres, auditoriums, dormitories, offices or public buildings.

Figure 6.2 *(continued)*

STANDPIPES

The *Uniform Building Code* defines three classes of standpipes. Figure 6.3 (Table 38-4-A of the *Uniform Building code*) lists occupancies that require specific types of standpipes.

Class I is a standpipe with 2½-inch outlets. There is a connection point on every landing of every required stairway above or below grade, and on both sides of a horizontal exit door. This type of standpipe is for the fire department to connect their large hoses to.

Class II is a wet standpipe with 1½-inch outlets and a hose. This type is located so that every part of the building is within 30 feet of a nozzle attached to 100 feet of hose. This type of standpipe is for use by building occupants or the fire department. Group A, division 1, 2, and 2.1 occupancies, with an occupant load of more than 1000, need Class II standpipe outlets on either side of the stage, at the rear of the auditorium, and at the rear of the balcony.

Class III is a wet standpipe with 2½-inch outlets and 1½-inch hose connections. These pipes are located according to the rules for both Class I and Class II standpipes.

TABLE NO. 38-A—STANDPIPE REQUIREMENTS

OCCUPANCY	NONSPRINKLERED BUILDING[1]		SPRINKLERED BUILDING[2][3]	
	Standpipe Class	Hose Requirement	Standpipe Class	Hose Requirement
1. Occupancies exceeding 150 ft. in height and more than one story	III	Yes	I	No
2. Occupancies 4 stories or more but less than 150 ft. in height, except Group R, Div. 3	[I and II[4]] (or III)	[5] Yes	I	No
3. Group A Occupancies with occupant load exceeding 1000[6]	II	Yes	No requirement	No
4. Group A, Div. 2.1 Occupancies over 5000 square feet in area used for exhibition	II	Yes	II	Yes
5. Groups I, H, B, Div. 1, 2 or 3 Occupancies less than 4 stories in height but greater than 20,000 square feet per floor	II[4]	Yes	No requirement	No

[1]Except as otherwise specified in Item No. 4 of this table, Class II standpipes need not be provided in basements having an automatic fire-extinguishing system throughout.

[2]Combined systems with their related water supplies may be used in sprinklered buildings.

[3]Portions of otherwise sprinklered buildings which are not protected by automatic sprinklers shall have Class II standpipes installed as required for the unsprinklered portions.

[4]In open structures where Class II standpipes may be damaged by freezing, the building official may authorize the use of Class I standpipes which are located as required for Class II standpipes.

[5]Hose is required for Class II standpipes only.

[6]Class II standpipes need not be provided in assembly areas used solely for worship.

Figure 6.3 Table 38-A, Standpipe Requirements. Reproduced by permission from *Uniform Building Code*. Copyright © 1988, the International Conference of Building Officials.

7

The Electrical and Signal Systems

The electrical and signal systems do not often involve important constraints in the predesign stage since equipment and distribution do not take up much space.

LOCATION OF UTILITY LINES ON THE SITE PLAN

The location of electrical power and telephone lines near the site should be plotted on the site plan. Note whether the power lines are under or above ground. If the utility company has a preference on where connections can be made, these areas should be marked. Figure 7.1 shows the location of electrical and telephone lines on a sample plan.

ELECTRICAL SERVICE VOLTAGE

The utility company transmits electrical power at high voltage to minimize voltage drop and conductor size in its transmission system. For safety reasons, buildings use electrical power at much lower voltages. There are three different electrical system voltages commonly used in buildings.

120/240-Volt Single-Phase Power Residential and residential scale commercial buildings will use 120/240-volt single-phase power. The utility company will provide and maintain the transformer that creates this voltage from its high-voltage distribution lines. The building needs to provide only a residential scale electric meter, main disconnect, and distribution panel board.

120/208-Volt Three-Phase Power Medium-sized commercial buildings will use 120/208-volt 3-phase power to operate efficiently the large motors used for HVAC, elevators, and escalators as well as to provide access to 120 volts for lights and outlets. The building owner can purchase power at high voltage and operate his own transformer. This size building would use a dry type transformer outside the building if the site allows or inside if site space is tight. The inside location, which can be in combination with the main switchboard, is called a unit substation. A wiring diagram for three-phase electrical power is shown in Figure 7.2.

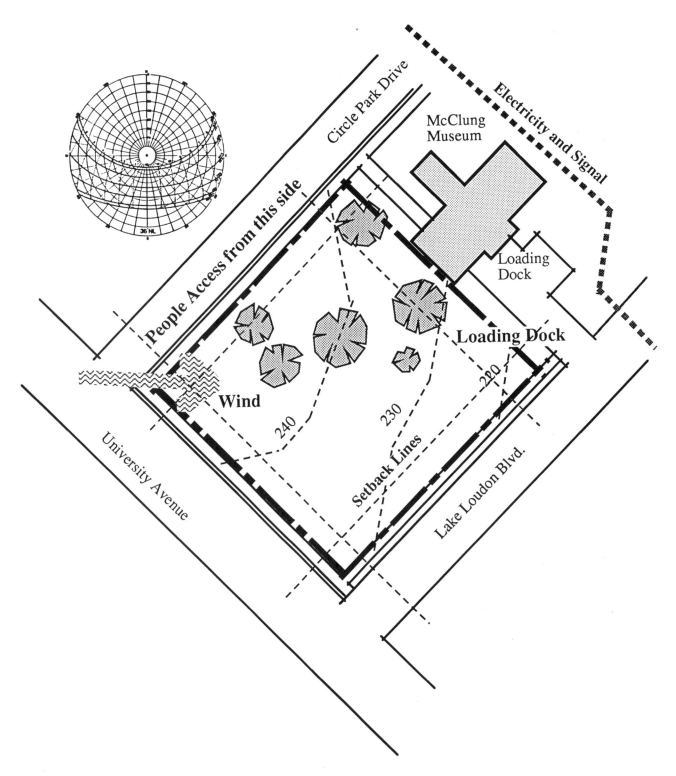

Figure 7.1 Mapping the location of electrical and telephone lines onto the site plan.

277/480-Volt Three-Phase Power Large commercial buildings will purchase their power at high voltage. They will own a large transformer located in a transformer vault (see Fig. 7.3). The transformer will produce 277/480-volt three-phase power for the building. A separate switchboard room will partition the power to the major uses. The large HVAC, elevator, and escalator motors will use the three-phase power. Fluorescent lights will use 277-volt single-phase power.

On each floor of the building, 120-volt single-phase power for electrical outlets will be produced with small dry transformers in electrical closets.

Special Electrical Power and Signal System Requirements Any special requirements for power or signal systems need to be stated up front so they can be considered when the design is forming.

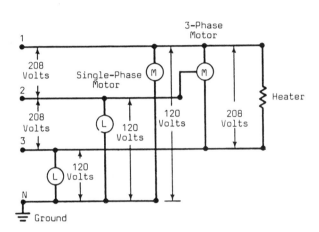

Figure 7.2 Three-phase electrical power wiring diagram. Reproduced by permission from Merritt and Ambrose (1990).

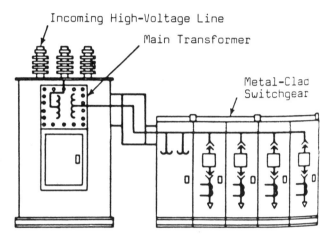

Figure 7.3 Large oil-cooled transformer. Reproduced by permission from Merritt and Ambrose (1990).

PART II

Concept Formation

It is while the building design is first forming out of the architectural program that there is the greatest opportunity to integrate the structural and environmental control systems into the architectural design of the building. These systems need to be considered at the same rough-sketch abstracted level as the architectural design. Detail is inappropriate at this stage. At the concept formation level, the design process should be primarily concerned with the qualitative evaluation of the interacting wholeness of the design. Therefore, the technical information in this book is just quantitative enough so that the qualitative features of technical system interaction in architectural concept formation can be explored.

Technical system knowledge can be used as a constraining aid to architectural concept formation but cannot replace the creative leap at the core of the architectural design problem. Once the creative leap has occurred, however, it is essential that the designer have a method of easily simulating technical constraints so they can be included in design. This section of the book presents the information framework necessary to explore structural and environmental control system inclusion in architectural design. ■

8

The Architectural Concept

Once the architect has a concept, a common method of working out spatial interaction issues is through the use of bubble diagrams. A bubble diagram is what mathematicians call a "planer graph." An understanding of the mathematical implications of planer graphs will improve the usefulness of bubble diagrams.

PLANER GRAPHS

A bubble diagram used as a planer graph can expose hidden conflicts in the interaction requirements of the architectural program and forming concept. Two features that indicate potential conflicts are crossed interaction lines, which are not buildable on a planer surface, and landlocked nodes, which indicate spaces without the possibility of direct connection to outside (Fig. 8.1). It is easier to resolve these problems on a diagram than on a complete floor plan, but the idea that the planer graph is a simulation or abstract model of a floor plan in development should be kept clearly in mind.

A planer graph remains a useful abstraction of the interactions between the spaces of an architectural design only if the graph is not too complicated. Faced with a similar situation, top-down computer programming uses the following heuristic about complexity. When the number of bubbles gets much beyond seven and or the diagram is too big to fit on an 8½-by-11-inch piece of paper, the designer should consider subdividing the diagram in a hierarchical fashion.

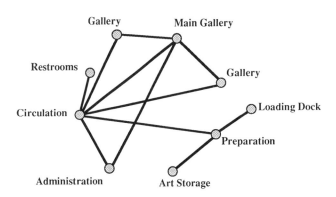

Figure 8.1 Space interaction diagram for a small art museum, laid out in a circle.

A planer graph exploration of a forming architectural design can be produced in the following way (Baglivo and Graver 1983):

1. The nodes representing architectural program areas should be located in a circular form with the desired interactions between areas shown as lines drawn across the center of the circle.
2. Lines that cross each other indicate a physical conflict. The interactions cannot be built on a plane surface as diagrammed. The circular interaction diagram must be resolved into a diagram that has no intersecting lines (Fig. 8.2). This resolution process may require the inclusion of circulation elements like lobbies, halls, and stairs as new nodes.
3. The resolution process may also require reconsideration of some of the interaction requirements of the program. In Figure 8.2 notice how the connection between the administration and the main gallery

creates an enclosure around one of the smaller galleries. This is a buildable condition but not a very likely one. The designer will probably have to pick which connection is more important, administration-circulation or administration-main gallery, in his or her design (see Fig. 8.3).

PLANER GRAPHS WITH FLOOR AREAS

Noting space names and floor areas on the finished planer graph diagram provides a confirmation that the allowable floor area requirements of the building code can be met by the design arrangement being considered (Fig. 8.4). If there is too much area on a floor level, either the design configuration or the building code construction type needs to be reconsidered. It is easier to work out allowable floor area issues at an abstract level on a planer graph rather than on an entire set of floor plans.

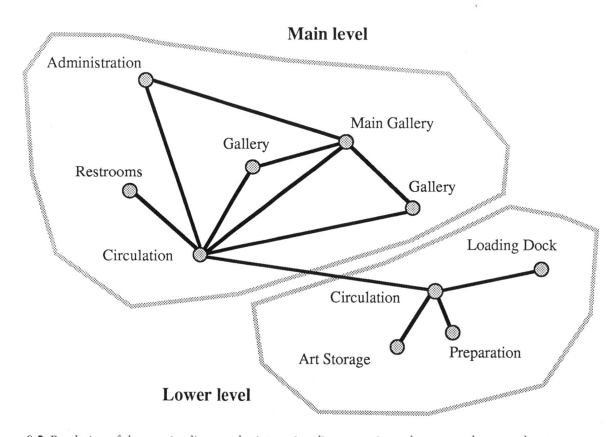

Figure 8.2 Resolution of the crossing lines on the interaction diagram so it can become a planer graph.

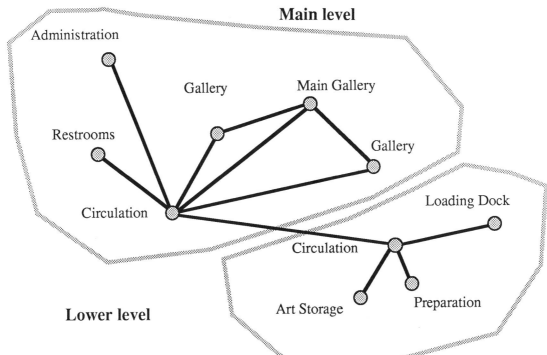

Figure 8.3 Resolution of the landlocked gallery node on the planer graph diagram.

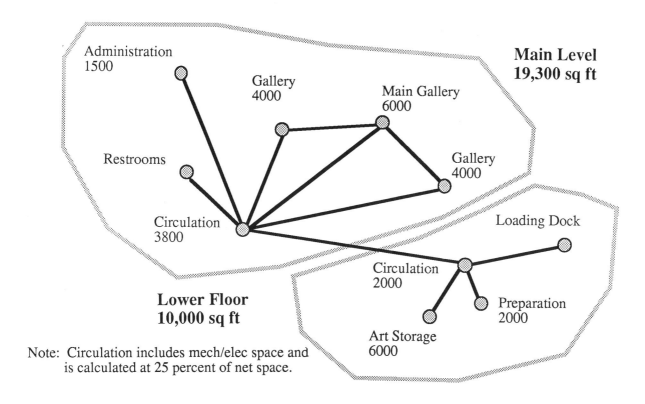

Figure 8.4 Floor areas included on the planer graph layout of the forming architectural concept.

RECTANGULAR AREAS TO SCALE

The architectural programmed areas can now be drawn to scale as rectangular shapes, and arranged as the planer graph diagram suggests (Fig. 8.5). This drawing is an abstract model of an architectural floor plan. This is the point in time and the abstraction level where building code, structural, and environmental control systems need to be considered if they are to be truly integrated into the architectural design concept.

THE ABSTRACT MODEL

As the building begins to form, it is important to work in three dimensions. The designer needs to explore sections and elevations as well as plans at this early sketch level. This is the only way to test the workability of the three-dimensional image that is developing. Keep in mind, however, that you are creating a simplified abstract model of the architectural layout and a simplified abstract model of the structural and environmental control system layouts. To be a useful tool for exploration of the inclusion of technical systems into design formation, the abstract model must remain easy to set up and easy to reconfigure.

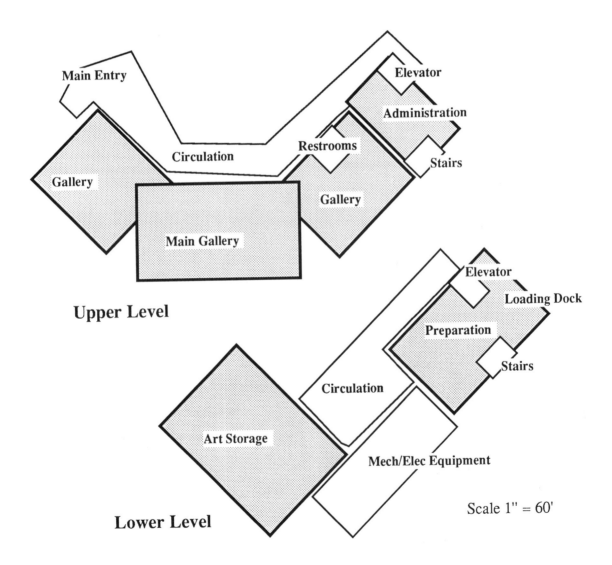

Figure 8.5 Rectangular spaces laid out to scale in the relationship developed with the planer graph.

9

Planning Exits per the Building Code

At the concept formation stage of architectural design, the most important aspect of the building code requirements is the number and distribution of exits. The width of the required exits is also important to ensure that the design concept provides enough room for design development to fill in the details.

MEANS OF EGRESS

A means of egress is a continuous path of travel from any point in a building or structure to the open air outside at ground level. It consists of three separate and distinct parts: the exit access, the exit, and the exit discharge.

The Exit Access   The exit access is that portion of the means of egress that leads to an exit. The exit access usually takes the form of a corridor. A minimum of two exits is almost always required (Fig. 9.1). Other general requirements are the following:

- Corridor width is to be no less than 44 inches for an occupant load of 10 or more people. It can be 36 inches for less than 10 people.
- Dead-end corridors are limited to 20 feet.

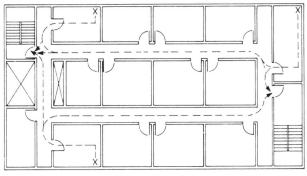

Exit Access On Upper Office Floor – – – ➤

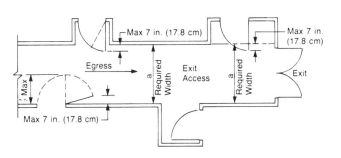

Figure 9.1 Exit access requirements. Reproduced by permission from *Life Safety Code Handbook*. Copyright © 1988, National Fire Protection Association.

- When more than one exit is required the occupant should be able to go toward either exit from any point in the corridor system.
- Corridors used for exit access require 1-hour construction.
- Maximum travel distance from any point to an exit is 150 feet for a nonsprinkled building, or 200 feet if the building is sprinkled. This distance can be increased by 100 feet if the corridor meets all the requirements listed in this section.
- Handrails or fully open doors cannot extend more than 7 inches into the corridor.
- Doors at their worst extension into the corridor cannot obstruct the required width by more than half.

The Number and Size of Exits The exit is that portion of a means of egress that is separated from the area of the building from which escape is to be made, by walls, floors, doors, or other means that provide the protected path necessary for the occupants to proceed with safety to a public space. The most common form the exit takes is an enclosed stairway. In a single story building the exit is the door opening to the outside.

Figure 9.2 (Table 33A of the *Uniform Building Code*) lists occupant loads in square feet of building area per person, as well as the minimum occupant loads for buildings or rooms below which only one exit is required. Per the *Uniform Building Code*:

- Almost all buildings will need at least 2 exits.
- An occupant load of 501 to 1000 people requires three exits.
- An occupant load of 1001 or more people requires four exits.
- In buildings four stories and higher and in Type I and Type II fire-resistive construction, the exit stairs are required to have 2-hour enclosure; otherwise 1-hour construction is acceptable.
- When two exits are required, they have to be separated by a distance equal to half the diagonal dimension of the floor or room the exits are serving. Both distances are measured in a straight line (Fig. 9.3).
- Where more than two exits are required, two of them need to be separated by half the diagonal dimension. The others are spaced to provide good access from any direction.
- The total exit width required is determined by dividing the total occupant load by 50. The answer is in feet of width. This width should be divided equally among the required number of exits.

USE[1]	MINIMUM OF TWO EXITS OTHER THAN ELEVATORS ARE REQUIRED WHERE NUMBER OF OCCUPANTS IS AT LEAST	OCCU-PANT LOAD FACTOR[2] (Sq. Ft.)	ACCESS BY MEANS OF A RAMP OR AN ELEVATOR MUST BE PROVIDED FOR THE PHYSICALLY HANDICAPPED AS INDICATED[3]
1. Aircraft Hangars (no repair)	10	500	Yes
2. Auction Rooms	30	7	Yes
3. Assembly Areas, Concentrated Use (without fixed seats) Auditoriums Churches and Chapels Dance Floors Lobby Accessory to Assembly Occupancy Lodge Rooms Reviewing Stands Stadiums	50	7	Yes[4 5]
Waiting Area	50	3	Yes[4 5]
4. Assembly Areas, Less-concentrated Use Conference Rooms Dining Rooms Drinking Establishments Exhibit Rooms Gymnasiums Lounges Stages	50	15	Yes[4 5 6]
5. Bowling Alley (assume no occupant load for bowling lanes)	50	12	Yes
6. Children's Homes and Homes for the Aged	6	80	Yes[7]
7. Classrooms	50	20	Yes[8]
8. Courtrooms	50	40	Yes
9. Dormitories	10	50	Yes[7]
10. Dwellings	10	300	No

Figure 9.2 Table 33-A, Minimum Egress and Access Requirements. Reproduced by permission from *Uniform Building Code*. Copyright © 1988, the International Conference of Building Officials.

- Total occupant load for calculating exit stair width is defined as the sum of the occupant load on the floor in question, plus 50% of the occupant load of the first adjacent floor, plus 25% of the occupant load of the next adjacent floor. The adjacent floors are usually above the floor in question and exiting is through the floor in question, but they could be below if the exiting was from a basement level. The maximum exit stair width calculated is maintained for the entire exit.
- Minimum exit door width is 36 inches with 32 inches clear opening.
- The width of exit stairs, and the width of landings between flights of stairs, must all be the same and must meet the minimum exit stair width requirements as calculated above or:

USE[1]	MINIMUM OF TWO EXITS OTHER THAN ELEVATORS ARE REQUIRED WHERE NUMBER OF OCCUPANTS IS AT LEAST	OCCU-PANT LOAD FACTOR[2] (Sq. Ft.)	ACCESS BY MEANS OF A RAMP OR AN ELEVATOR MUST BE PROVIDED FOR THE PHYSICALLY HANDICAPPED AS INDICATED[3]
11. Exercising Rooms	50	50	Yes
12. Garage, Parking	30	200	Yes[9]
13. Hospitals and Sanitariums— Nursing Homes	6	80	Yes
14. Hotels and Apartments	10	200	Yes[10]
15. Kitchen—Commercial	30	200	No
16. Library Reading Room	50	50	Yes[4]
17. Locker Rooms	30	50	Yes
18. Malls (see Chapter 56)	—	—	—
19. Manufacturing Areas	30	200	Yes[7]
20. Mechanical Equipment Room	30	300	No
21. Nurseries for Children (Day care)	7	35	Yes
22. Offices	30	100	Yes[7]
23. School Shops and Vocational Rooms	50	50	Yes
24. Skating Rinks	50	50 on the skating area; 15 on the deck	Yes[4]
25. Storage and Stock Rooms	30	300	No
26. Stores—Retail Sales Rooms Basement Ground Floor Upper Floors	11 50 10	30 30 60	Yes Yes Yes
27. Swimming Pools	50	50 for the pool area; 15 on the deck	Yes[4]
28. Warehouses	30	500	No
29. All others	50	100	

Figure 9.2 *(continued)*

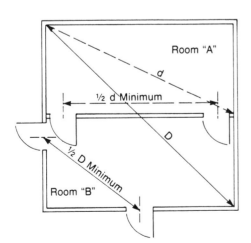

Figure 9.3 Separation of exits. Reproduced by permission from *Life Safety Code Handbook.* Copyright © 1988, National Fire Protection Association.

44-inch minimum width for an occupant load of 50 or more people,

36-inch minimum width for 49 or fewer people, whichever is greater.

Figure 9.4 shows required exit stair dimensions in plan and section.

A *horizontal exit* is a way of passage through a 2-hour fire wall into another area of the same building or into a different building that will provide refuge from smoke and fire. Horizontal exits cannot provide more than half of the required exit capacity, and any such exit must discharge into an area capable of holding the occupant capacity of the exit. The area is calculated at 3 square feet per occupant. In institutional occupancies the area needed is 15 square feet per ambulatory person, and 30 square foot per nonambulatory person.

The Exit Discharge   The exit discharge is that portion of a means of egress between the termination of an exit and a public way. The most common form this takes is the door out of an exit stairway opening onto a public street. Exits can discharge through an enclosed 2-hour passageway that connects the exit with a public way. In Group B, Division 2 occupancy office buildings, 50% of the exits can discharge through a street floor lobby area if the entire street floor is sprinkled, and the path through the lobby is unobstructed and obvious.

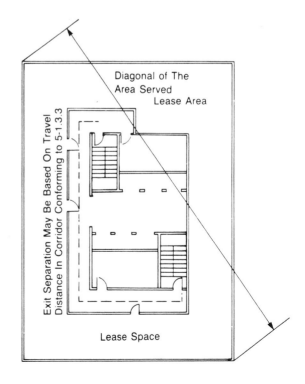

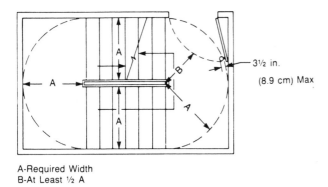

A-Required Width
B-At Least ½ A

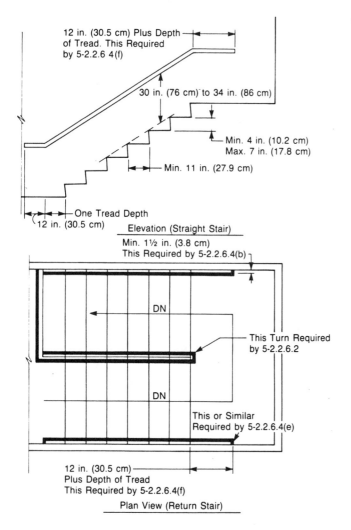

Figure 9.4 Exit stair requirements. Reproduced by permission from *Life Safety Code Handbook*. Copyright © 1988, National Fire Protection Association.

SMOKEPROOF ENCLOSURES

A smokeproof enclosure is an exit stair that is entered through a vestibule that is ventilated by either natural or mechanical means such that products of combustion from a fire will be limited in their penetration of the exit stair enclosure (Fig. 9.5). Smokeproof enclosures are required to be 2-hour construction. They must discharge directly to the outside, or directly through a 2-hour exit passageway to the outside. Smokeproof enclosures for exits are required in any tall building with floors 75 feet above the lowest ground level where fire trucks have access. In a sprinkled building, mechanically pressurized and vented stairways can be substituted for smokeproof enclosures.

EXITS FOR ASSEMBLY OCCUPANCIES

The Main Exit   In an emergency situation people tend to leave a building the way they came in. The code recognizes this fact through special requirements for the main exit from an assembly occupancy. The main exit is required to have a minimum total width large enough to handle one-half of the occupant load, but not less than the total width of all the aisles and stairs that lead to it. The other exits are required to have a minimum total width large enough to handle two-thirds of the total occupant capacity. This size requirement on the main exit from an assembly occupancy makes it difficult to locate large assembly rooms above the level of discharge.

CONVENTIONAL ASSEMBLY SEATING

Conventional seating provides aisles dividing rows and cross aisles that collect people and lead them primarily out the main entrance of the building. The following list can be used for preliminary layout for conventional seating.

1. No seat shall be more than six seats from an aisle. (Space on benches or pews is calculated as 18 inches per person.)
2. A minimum of 12 inches clear space between rows is required.
3. Aisles are to start at 36 inches wide (minimum) for seats on only one side, and at least 42 inches wide for seats on both sides. The aisle width increases from these minimum numbers by 1.5 inches per 5 feet of

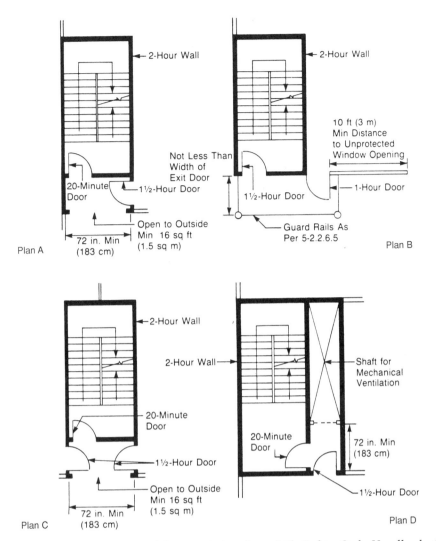

Figure 9.5 Smokeproof enclosures. Reproduced by permission from *Life Safety Code Handbook*. Copyright © 1988, National Fire Protection Association.

aisle length toward the exit, cross aisle, or foyer.

4. Cross aisle width shall be the sum of the width of the widest aisle leading into the cross aisle, and 50% of the width of all the other aisles leading into the cross aisle.

5. Total width of vomitories leading from the cross aisle to the foyer or main exit is determined in the same way as a cross aisle.

6. Dead ends are limited to 20 feet.

7. Maximum travel distance to an exit door is 150 feet unsprinkled and 200 feet sprinkled.

8. Aisle slope shall not be greater than 1 vertical foot per 8 horizontal.

9. Steps in aisles shall always come in groups of two or more risers, and shall not be used if the aisle can be sloped.

CONTINENTAL ASSEMBLY SEATING

Continental seating provides aisles along the side walls with continuous rows of seats between. Exit doors are located along the side walls. The following list can be used for preliminary layout of continental seating.

1. There is no limit on the number of seats in a row as long as all the other exit criteria are met.

2. The clear distance between rows is as follows:
    a) 18 inches between rows for 1 to 18 seats
    b) 20 inches between rows for 19 to 35 seats
    c) 21 inches between rows for 36 to 45 seats
    d) 22 inches between rows for 46 to 59 seats
    e) 24 inches between rows for 60 seats or more

3. The side aisles shall have a minimum width of 44 inches.
4. Exit doors in pairs with 66 inches clear opening are required at a rate of one pair of doors per every 5 rows of seats. The doors lead to the exterior or a foyer, lobby, or exit passageway leading to the exterior.
5. Dead ends are limited to 20 feet.
6. Maximum travel distance to an exit door is 150 feet unsprinkled, and 200 feet sprinkled.
7. Aisle slope shall not be greater than 1 vertical per 8 horizontal.
8. Steps in aisles shall always come in groups of two or more risers, and shall not be used if the aisle can be sloped.

USING AN ABSTRACT MODEL

As in the case of other architectural features, the exit system can be explored using an abstract model of the developing architectural form. This provides the designer with a view of the design problem from the standpoint of the exit system while the design organization is still very flexible. Figure 9.6 shows the exit system for the small museum project outlined in previous chapters.

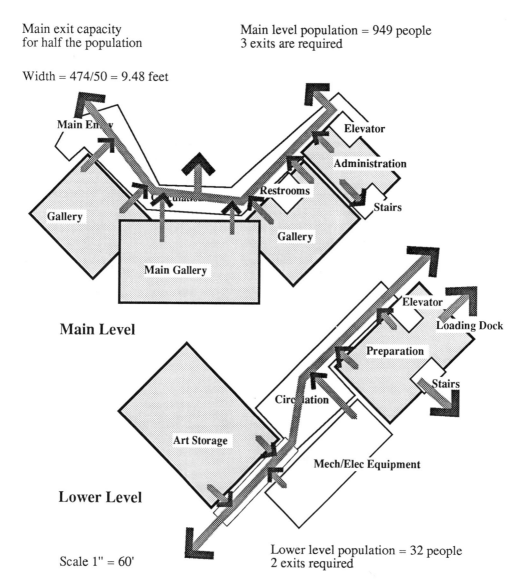

Main exit capacity for half the population

Width = 474/50 = 9.48 feet

Main level population = 949 people
3 exits are required

Main Level

Scale 1" = 60'

Lower Level

Lower level population = 32 people
2 exits required

Figure 9.6 Use of an abstract model of the developing architectural form to explore the exiting system of a small art museum project.

10

The Structural System

The structural system needs to be considered in an abstract fashion early in the design process so that structural concepts can inform and be informed by the architectural design concept. A qualitative explanation of structural concepts is presented in the first section of this chapter. Structure is first visualized as horizontal and vertical planes, and as rigid column beam frames composed into space structures that resist deformation (Lin and Stotesbury 1988). After the concept has been solidified, structural sizing charts are used to explore realistic structural grid spacing in plan, and structural member depth in section.

SHEAR WALLS AND TUBE FORMS

A building has to resist vertical gravity loading through the compressive strength of its walls and columns. It also has to resist the horizontal loads and overturning moments caused by wind and earthquake through the shear and bending strength properties of its overall composition. A useful way of studying this important form-structure interaction is by conceiving the building as being made up of thin vertical and horizontal planes (Lin and Stotesbury 1988).

Consider the building as a rectangular tube standing on the ground (see Fig. 10.1). If the walls are too thin they will buckle and collapse under their own weight.

This represents vertical gravity loading. The building needs to be strong enough to hold up axial loads that are oriented straight down. If there is no horizontal closure at the top, the tube will deform and deflect when a horizontal force (wind or earthquake) is applied to it. A horizontal closure of the top of the tube minimizes deformation of the face of the tube and provides a mechanism for the transfer of the horizontal load to the side walls, which can provide bending and shear resistance. Interacting horizontal and vertical subsystems configured to maintain the shape of the building will provide resistance to the shear and bending forces caused by horizontal loads.

Consider now how these vertical and horizontal planes interact to resist the shear and bending forces caused by horizontal loading (Fig. 10.2). The horizontal diaphragm transfers shear forces to the walls parallel to the horizontal force. Note that the side walls provide some resistance to bending, but not much. The tube action of the overall configuration transfers the major bending resistance to the walls that are perpendicular to the horizontal force. They act in the same way as the flanges of a wide flange beam.

Additional horizontal diaphragms will pick up horizontal loading all the way up the face of the building and distribute it to the shear and moment-resisting vertical planes (Fig. 10.3), thus stiffening the building.

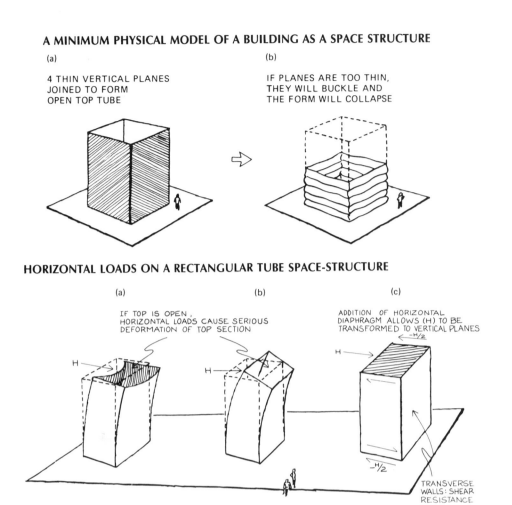

Figure 10.1 Buildings conceived as space forms. Reproduced by permission from Lin and Stotesbury (1988).

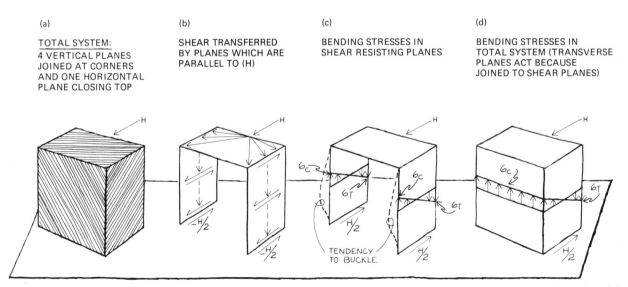

Figure 10.2 Interaction of vertical and horizontal subsystems to provide resistance to shear and bending. Reproduced by permission from Lin and Stotesbury (1988).

ADDITIONAL HORIZONTAL SUBSYSTEMS MUST BE PROVIDED TO PICK UP HORIZONTAL LOADS APPLIED OVER *h*

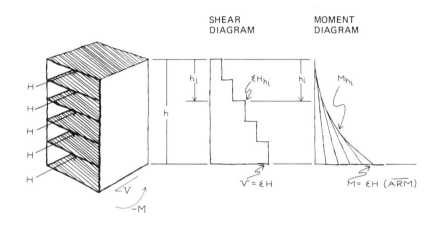

HORIZONTAL SUBSYSTEMS INCREASE THE LOCAL STIFFNESS OF VERTICAL SUBSYSTEMS

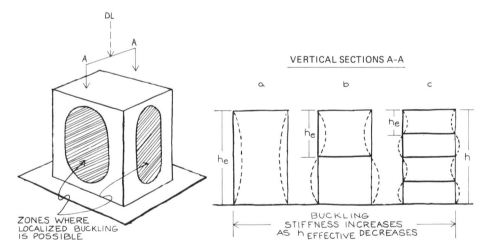

Figure 10.3 Addition of horizontal subsystems to increase the local stiffness of the vertical subsystems. Reproduced by permission from Lin and Stotesbury (1988).

The additional horizontal diaphragms also reduce the effective bending length of the vertical planes, allowing them to carry more vertical load without buckling. Thus, the thickness of the vertical planes is determined by the load they carry and the distance between local horizontal diaphragms rather than by the overall height of the building.

Tube structures that resist the shear and bending caused by the horizontal loading of wind and earthquake can take more complicated shapes than a simple rectangular tube (Fig. 10.4). As the building gets taller it becomes more important that the horizontal force-

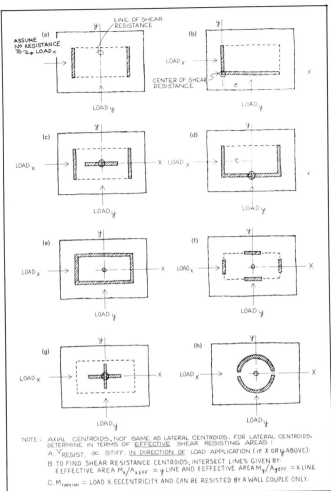

Figure 10.5 Plan views of shear wall layouts. Reproduced by permission from Lin and Stotesbury (1988).

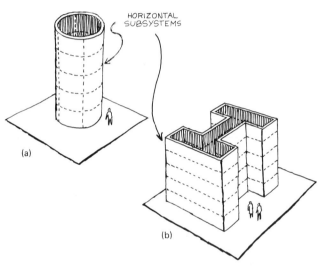

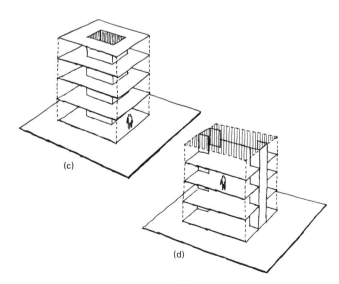

Figure 10.4 Tube action achieved for a variety of sectional shapes and by means of structural core designs. Reproduced by permission from Lin and Stotesbury (1988).

resisting elements are symmetrically arranged or a twisting will be generated in the building by wind and earthquake loads. Figure 10.5 illustrates what can happen if the resultant horizontal load on a building does not pass through the center of shear resistance. In Figure 10.5*b* and *d*, the horizontal load will cause the building to twist. Tube shapes, as in Figure 10.5*e* and *h*, have maximum resistance to twisting that might be induced by uneven loading.

COLUMNS AND BEAMS CONNECTED IN RIGID FRAMES

Columns as vertical load carrying devices provide more internal space planning flexibility than walls. However, columns that have a simple pin type connection to horizontal beams provide very little horizontal stability for the building. If the connection between the columns and the beams is made rigid the horizontal deflection of the frame structure is reduced (see Fig. 10.6). Rigid connections will also minimize the deformation of the building due to vertical loading.

The addition of rigidly connected interior columns and the addition of rigidly connected horizontal members improves the overall stiffness of the frame (Fig. 10.7). The frame stiffness can be increased to the point where a perforated tube structure has a behavior under vertical and horizontal loads very similar to a solid wall tube structure (Fig. 10.8).

INDEPENDENT CANTILEVER ACTION PROVIDES INEFFICIENT RESISTANCE TO HORIZONTAL LOADS

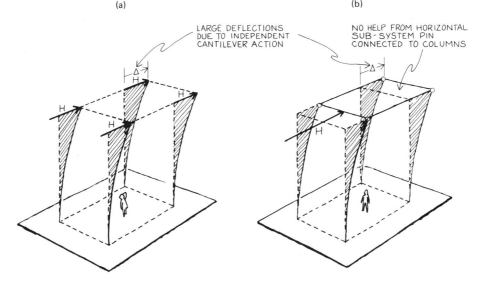

BY FIXING HORIZONTAL SUBSYSTEM TO COLUMNS, ROTATIONAL INTERACTION IMPROVES OVERALL STIFFNESS

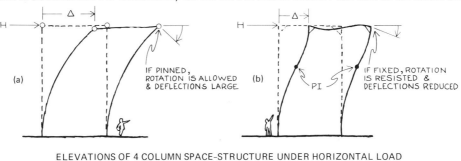

ELEVATIONS OF 4 COLUMN SPACE-STRUCTURE UNDER HORIZONTAL LOAD

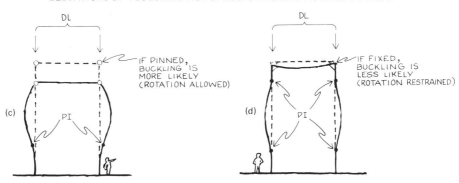

ELEVATIONS OF 4 COLUMN SPACE-STRUCTURE UNDER VERTICAL LOAD

Figure 10.6 Moment-resisting connections between horizontal beams and vertical columns improves overall stiffness. Reproduced by permission from Lin and Stotesbury (1988).

THE OVERALL FRAME ACTION AND STIFFNESS OF A BASIC TWO-COLUMN SUBSYSTEM CAN BE IMPROVED BY THE ADDITION OF INTERIOR COLUMNS

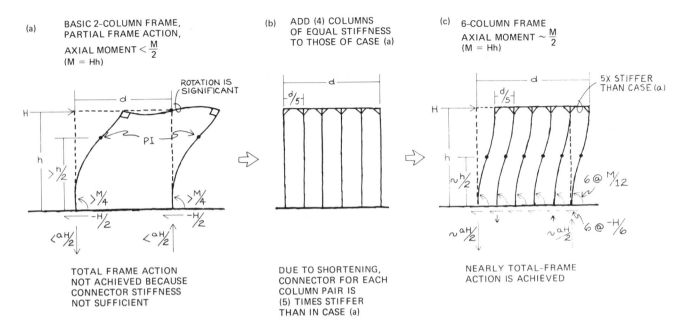

(a) BASIC 2-COLUMN FRAME,
     PARTIAL FRAME ACTION,
     AXIAL MOMENT $< \frac{M}{2}$
     (M = Hh)

TOTAL FRAME ACTION
NOT ACHIEVED BECAUSE
CONNECTOR STIFFNESS
NOT SUFFICIENT

(b) ADD (4) COLUMNS
     OF EQUAL STIFFNESS
     TO THOSE OF CASE (a)

DUE TO SHORTENING,
CONNECTOR FOR EACH
COLUMN PAIR IS
(5) TIMES STIFFER
THAN IN CASE (a)

(c) 6-COLUMN FRAME
     AXIAL MOMENT $\sim \frac{M}{2}$
     (M = Hh)

NEARLY TOTAL-FRAME
ACTION IS ACHIEVED

OVERALL FRAME ACTION STIFFNESS MAY BE INCREASED BY THE USE OF MORE THAN ONE CONNECTOR

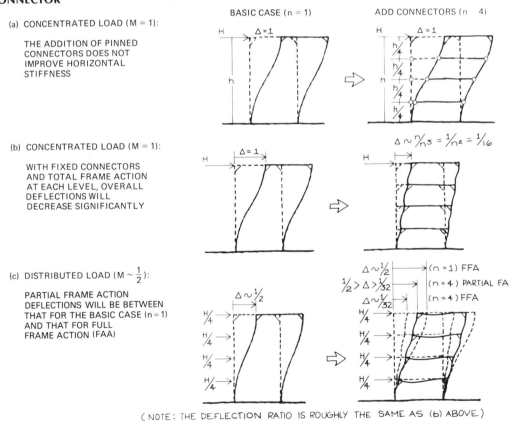

(a) CONCENTRATED LOAD (M = 1):

THE ADDITION OF PINNED
CONNECTORS DOES NOT
IMPROVE HORIZONTAL
STIFFNESS

BASIC CASE (n = 1)   ADD CONNECTORS (n 4)

$\Delta \sim \frac{h}{n^3} = \frac{1}{n^2} = \frac{1}{16}$

(b) CONCENTRATED LOAD (M = 1):

WITH FIXED CONNECTORS
AND TOTAL FRAME ACTION
AT EACH LEVEL, OVERALL
DEFLECTIONS WILL
DECREASE SIGNIFICANTLY

(c) DISTRIBUTED LOAD (M $\sim \frac{1}{2}$):

PARTIAL FRAME ACTION
DEFLECTIONS WILL BE BETWEEN
THAT FOR THE BASIC CASE (n = 1)
AND THAT FOR FULL
FRAME ACTION (FAA)

$\Delta \sim \frac{1}{2}$ →   (n = 1) FFA

$\frac{1}{2} > \Delta > \frac{1}{32}$ →   (n = 4) PARTIAL FA

$\Delta \sim \frac{1}{32}$ →   (n = 4) FFA

(NOTE : THE DEFLECTION RATIO IS ROUGHLY THE SAME AS (b) ABOVE)

Figure 10.7 Increasing overall frame action stiffness by connecting additional vertical and horizontal interior members with moment-resisting connections. Reproduced by permission from Lin and Stotesbury (1988).

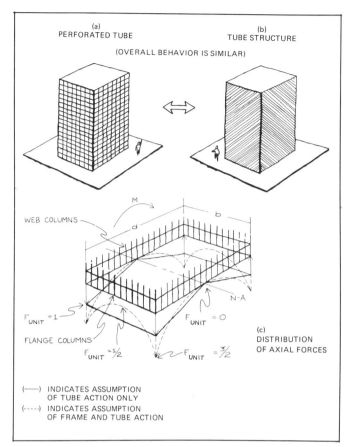

Figure 10.8 A frame design evolving into a perforated tube structure as horizontal and vertical subdivisions increase. Reproduced by permission from Lin and Stotesbury (1988).

STRUCTURAL MATERIAL CONNECTION CHARACTERISTICS

Concrete connections poured in place between columns and beams are inherently rigid. They can be made more rigid as the beam depth increases. Poured-in-place concrete connections between columns and slabs are not as rigid unless there is a drop panel at the connection to provide additional depth at the joint.

Steel connections between columns and girders or beams are normally considered pinned connections but can be made rigid with additional welding or bolting.

Wood connections between columns and beams are pinned connections. Rigid connections are not practical. Horizontal loading must be taken up with shear walls or diagonal bracing.

FOUNDATIONS

The weight of the building comes down through columns and walls to the foundation. The foundation must distribute this load over the ground so that settlement of the building is controlled. Determining the soil's bearing capacity can be a difficult job since the designer cannot see beneath the ground. The services of a soils engineer, who drills test borings into the soil to determine what is beneath the surface, are often used. Table 10.1 lists the average weight-bearing capacities of common types of soils.

TABLE 10.1. Allowable bearing values on soils (tons per square foot)[a]

Soil Type	Tons/Square Foot
Massive crystalline bedrock: granite, gneiss, traprock—in sound condition	100
Foliated rock: schist and slate—in sound condition	40
Sedimentary rock: hard shales, siltstones, sandstones—in sound condition	15
Exceptionally compacted gravels or sands	10
Compact gravel or sand-gravel mixtures	6
Loose gravel; compact coarse sand	4
Loose coarses and or sand-gravel mixtures; compact fine sand, or wet, confined coarse sand	3
Loose fine sand or wet, confined fine sand	2
Stiff clay	4
Medium stiff clay	2
Soft clay	1

Source: Lin and Stotesbury 1988.
Note: Due to variations in the texture of the soil, or the amount of moisture in it, its confinement, and so on, this table is clearly insufficient to yield definite values. The values given here are intended only for schematic considerations at the early stage of the planning of a structure.
[a]Figures drawn from *Code Manual, New York State Building Construction Code.*

Spread Footings Spread footings located under walls and columns are appropriate for low-rise buildings where soil conditions are firm enough to support the weight of the building on the area of the spread footings (Fig. 10.9). These footings can be connected together with grade beams to provide more lateral stability in earthquakes. If the bearing capacity of the soil is four times greater than the overall weight of the building divided by the area of its footprint, spread footings are called for (Lin and Stotesbury 1988). Concrete spread footings are normally about one foot thick.

COLUMN FOOTINGS MUST BE SPREAD OUT TO TRANSFER A CONCENTRATED LOAD TO THE GROUND

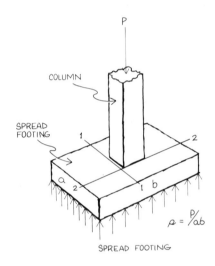

LINE FOOTINGS

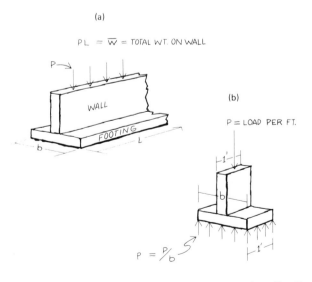

Figure 10.9 Spread footings for columns and walls. Reproduced by permission from Lin and Stotesbury (1988).

COMBINED FOOTINGS

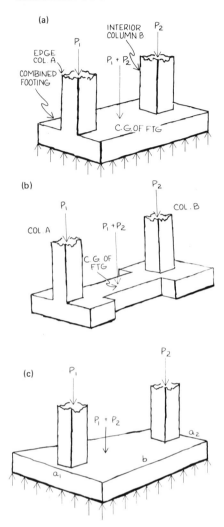

A HEAVY MAT MAY SERVE AS A FOUNDATION FOR THE WHOLE BUILDING

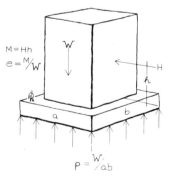

Figure 10.10 Combined footings used to tie a building together. The footing becomes one large mat under the building. Reproduced by permission from Lin and Stotesbury (1988).

Mat Foundations   As the weight of the building increases in relation to the bearing capacity of the soil, the footings need to expand in size. For poor soil conditions, and tall buildings (10 to 20 stories) with their overturning moments, a mat foundation is required (Fig. 10.10). A mat foundation is a large mass of concrete laid under the entire building. Mat foundations range from 4 to 8 feet thick.

Piles and Caissons   If the surface soil cannot support the building because the loads are too big and or the soil is weak, then piles or caissons are used to transfer the load down to a stronger strata under the ground (Fig. 10.11). Piles are long columns that are driven into the ground. Piles transfer the load to a lower, stronger strata or can transfer it to friction along the length of the pile where there is no stronger strata below the building. Piles are usually grouped together under a footing. An individual pile is about 1 foot in diameter and can be wood, precast concrete, or steel. Caissons are large hollow cylindrical enclosures that are driven into the ground and hollowed out. They can be belled out at the bottom to provide more bearing surface. They are then filled with concrete. Caissons range from 3 to 10 feet in diameter.

PILE FOUNDATION

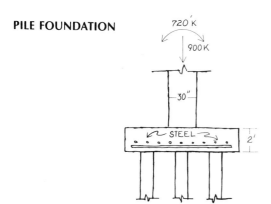

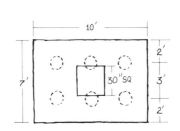

DRILLED-IN CAISSONS: TYPICAL SECTION OF CAISSON FOR A CONCRETE SUPERSTRUCTURE; TYPICAL SECTION OF CAISSON FOR A STEEL SUPERSTRUCTURE; TYPICAL CAISSON CROSS SECTION

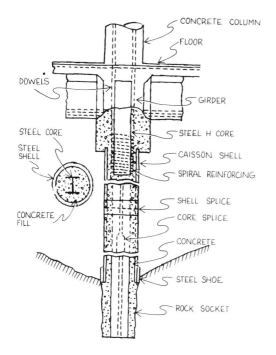

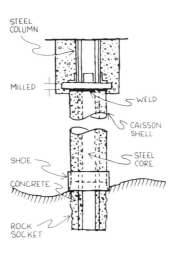

Figure 10.11 Pile and caisson foundations. Reproduced by permission from Lin and Stotesbury (1988).

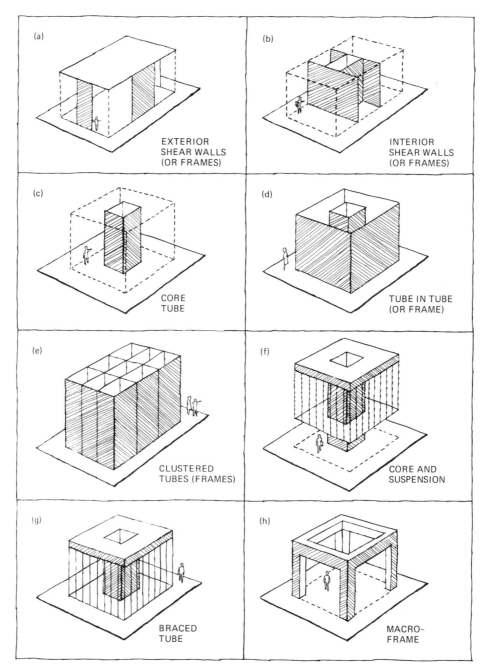

Figure 10.12 Combining vertical and horizontal subsystems in various ways to provide overall structural integrity. Reproduced by permission from Lin and Stotesbury (1988).

CREATIVE STRUCTURAL COMPOSITION

A top-down approach to composing a structural system is the way to provide structural input into the architectural concept formation. Structural opportunity can often be found in the space form requirements of the architecture. Before becoming bogged down in detail, it is helpful to use shear walls, tube forms, and braced frames to sketch out an overall structural concept (Figs.

10.12 to 10.14.) Figure 10.12 shows eight of the numerous ways shear walls, tubes, and braced frames can be configured to resist horizontal loading. Figures 10.13 and 10.14 illustrate how the emerging architectural form can be used as a concept generator for the structural system.

Lin and Stotesbury, in their book *Structural Concepts and Systems for Architects and Engineers* (1988), say that

(a)
WHEN VIEWED AS A WHOLE, A FOLDED ROOF
SUGGESTS THE POSSIBILITY OF BEING DESIGNED
TO ACT AS A FOLDED PLATE SUB-SYSTEM

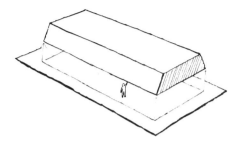

(b)
WHEN DESIGNED AS WHOLES, THE FLANGE-WEB
INTERACTION OF THE FOLDED WALLS CAN BE
MUCH STIFFER THAN FOR FLAT DESIGN ONLY

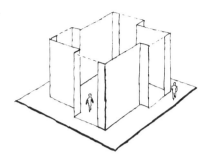

(c)
A LARGE AND CENTRALIZED VERTICAL CIRCULATION
SPACE MAY BE DESIGNED TO ACT AS A
CORE TUBE SUBSYSTEM

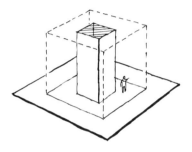

(d)
A COMBINATION OF SHEAR WALL AND MEGA-FRAME
ACTION CAN BE VISUALIZED BY CONSIDERING THAT
THE UPPERMOST HALL SPACE CAN BE DESIGNED
TO CONNECT THE SLENDER SHAFTS

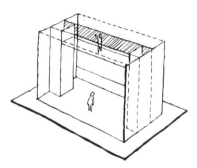

Figure 10.13 Major structural subsystem design options suggested by overall properties of space-form components. Reproduced by permission from Lin and Stotesbury (1988).

the architect must first establish, in conceptual terms, the overall space-form feasibility of basic schematic options. At this stage collaboration with specialists can be helpful, but only if in the form of overall thinking.

As the building takes more concrete form,

the architect must be able to identify the major subsystem requirements implied by the scheme and substantiate their interactive feasibility by approximating key component properties. That is, the properties of major subsystems need be worked out only in sufficient depth to verify the inherent compatibility of their basic form related and behavioral interactions. (Lin and Stotesbury 1988)

The point is to create an overall structural strategy in sympathy with the architectural intent before trying to fill in the details of the system.

APPROXIMATE SIZING AND LAYOUT OF STRUCTURAL SUBSYSTEMS

The charts that follow can be used for preliminary estimates of structural member depth and typical spacing between members. This information is for use during architectural concept formation. Detailed calculations using traditional engineering procedures need to be used for the design development and final design solutions.

The charts provide the depth of a structural member as a function of its span. Linking the use of a few charts together provides guidance on structural grid layout. The layout of a coherent structural grid that meets architectural and structural needs is an important skill to develop. The structural charts provide easy access to the information necessary for the rapid exploration of structural system alternative solutions.

(a)

(b)

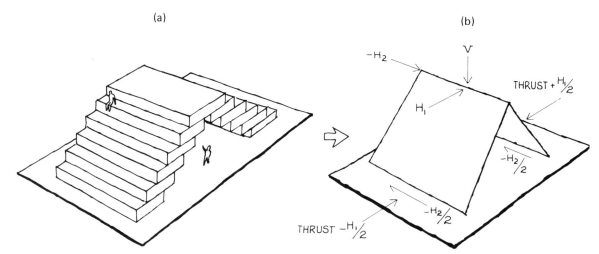

OVERALL SPACE-FORM SCHEME SUGGESTS OVERALL STRUCTURAL SYSTEM CONCEPT

(c)

(d)

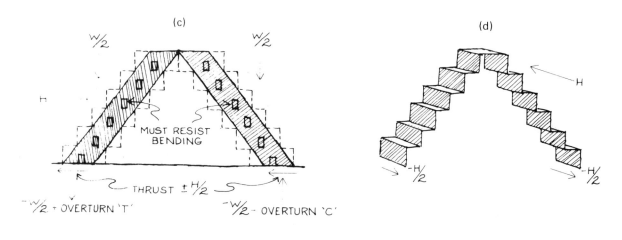

TRANSVERSE ROOM DIVIDING WALLS CAN
SERVE AS ARCH SUBSYSTEMS

LONGITUDINAL WALLS AND FLOORS
CAN SERVE AS STAGGERED
SHEAR TRANSFER SUBSYSTEM

Figure 10.14 The overall approach in dealing with unusual space form designs. Reproduced by permission from Lin and Stotesbury (1988).

The spacing of beams is dependent on the span capacity of the slab the beams support, and the spacing of the girders depends on the span capacity of the beams. Staying in the center third of the charts is a useful starting strategy when exploring structural grid options.

Also consider the underlying architectural use of the space for constraints on the structural module. For example, in a library the space needed for a stack and for the aisle space around the stack becomes a basic module. In an office environment, the minimum office size is important. In a commercial environment, the minimum rentable space width becomes a constraint.

Figure 10.15 shows the structural concept for the art museum example. Note how the overall structural strategy is described; structural detail will thus have a framework within which to develop.

Example: The layout of a concrete slab, beam, and girder system for an architectural school.

1. Start with the one-way concrete slab. The top section of Figure 10.16 suggests that a 4- to 5-inch thick slab will span 10 to 15 feet. This suggests that the concrete beams could be spaced 10 to 15 feet apart.
2. Look at the concrete beam chart (Fig. 10.16). The center third of the chart suggests that a 1.5 to 2 foot deep beam can span from 20 to 30 feet.
3. The center third of the concrete girder chart suggests that a 2 to 2.5 foot deep girder can span 20 to 30 feet.

Architectural constraints are used to choose the specific spacings of the structural members from the allowable ranges. For example, in an architectural school where 30-foot wide studios are required along with 10-foot wide faculty offices, a 4-inch slab spanning between 2-foot deep beams spaced 10 feet apart, which in turn frame into 2.5-foot deep girders spaced 30 feet apart, would provide the needed modular coordination between the structural grid and the underlying architectural space needs.

Figures 10.16 through 10.50 show structural sizing charts for concrete, steel, and wood.

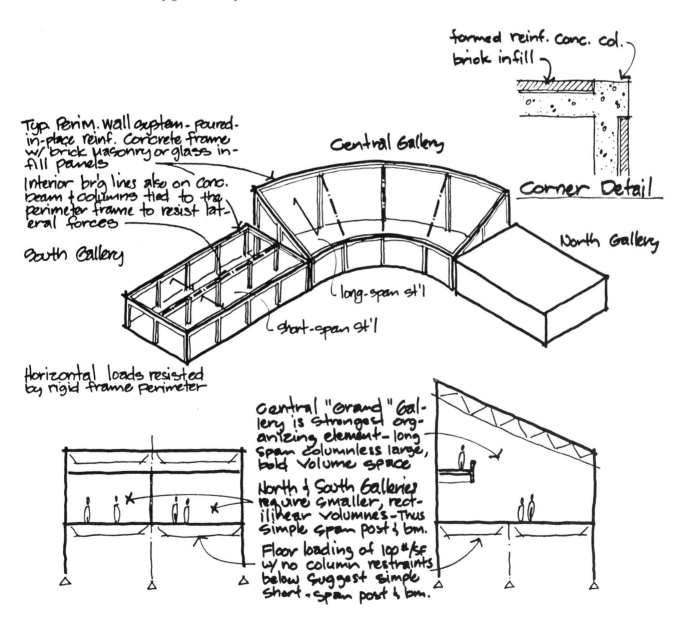

Figure 10.15 The structural concept for the art gallery example. The rectangular floor shapes of the abstract architectural plan have to be fitted into an ordered structural bay system. Building form and structural layout are tightly connected.

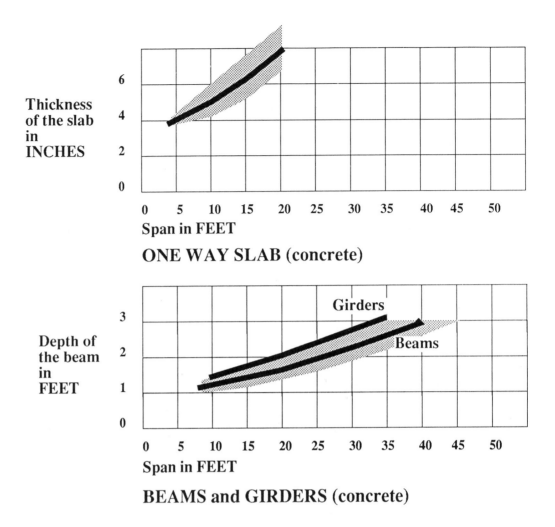

ONE WAY SLAB (concrete)

BEAMS and GIRDERS (concrete)

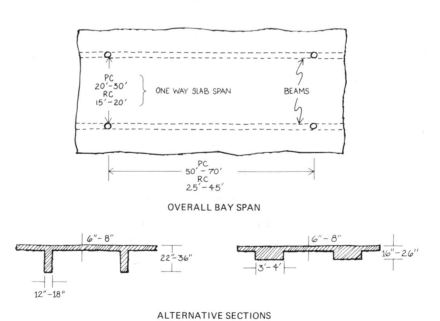

Figure 10.16 Sizing chart for a concrete beam and slab system. Chart adapted by permission from Corkill, Puderbaugh, and Sawers (1974). Example layout reproduced by permission from Lin and Stotesbury (1988).

(a) RC—(PASSIVE) BENDING REQUIRED TO BRING STEEL REINFORCEMENT INTO PLAY

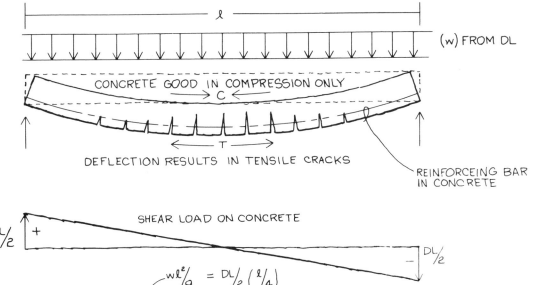

(b) PC—STEEL ACTIVATED BY PRESTRESSING

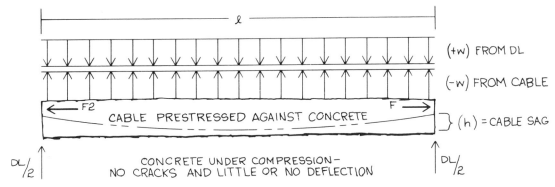

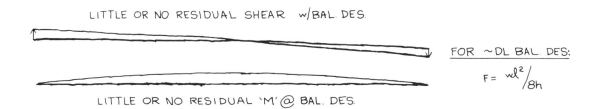

Figure 10.17 Passive versus active design for bending in concrete subsystems. RC, reinforced concrete; PC, prestressed concrete. Reproduced by permission from Lin and Stotesbury (1988).

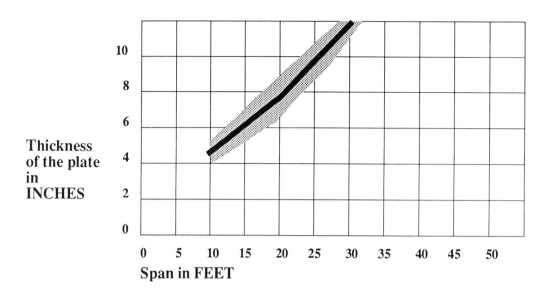

Thickness of the plate in INCHES

Span in FEET

TWO WAY FLAT PLATE (concrete)

(a) CONCRETE AND STEEL PLACEMENT FOR FLAT SLAB ON COLUMNS

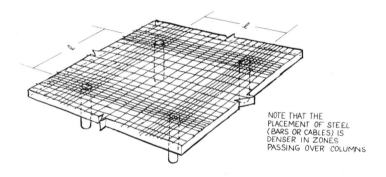

NOTE THAT THE PLACEMENT OF STEEL (BARS OR CABLES) IS DENSER IN ZONES PASSING OVER COLUMNS

(b) TYPICAL SPAN AND DEPTH FOR PC AND RC SLABS

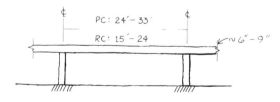

PC: 24'- 33'
RC: 15'- 24'
≈ 6"- 9"

Figure 10.18 Sizing chart for a two-way concrete flat plate. Chart adapted with permission from Corkill, Puderbaugh, and Sawers (1974). Example layout reproduced by permission from Lin and Stotesbury (1988).

(a) FLAT SLAB ON COLUMN:

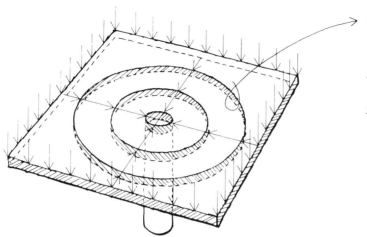

1. AS LOAD IS TRANSMITTED TO COLUMN, THE PUNCHING SHEAR RESISTANCE AREA DECREASES AND FAILURE CAN OCCUR

2. REENFORCING BARS OVER THE COLUMNS CAN HELP

3. PRESTRESSING CABLES DRAPED OVER THE COLUMNS WILL CARRY MUCH OF THE LOAD DIRECTLY TO COLUMNS

(b) LOCAL THICKENING OF SLAB MATERIAL HELPS

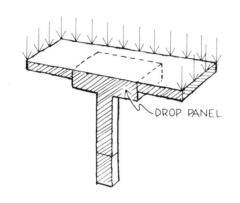

DROP PANEL

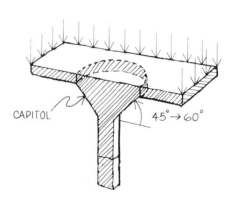

CAPITOL

$45° \rightarrow 60°$

(c) BEAMS OVER COLUMNS

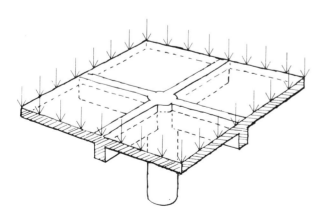

(d) WAFFLE PANEL FILLED IN

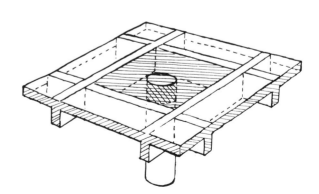

Figure 10.19 Dealing with the problem of punching shear resistance. Reproduced by permission from Lin and Stotesbury (1988).

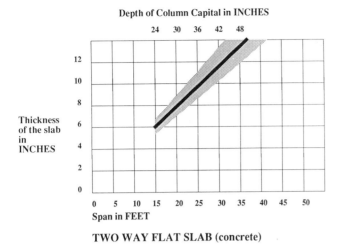

Depth of Column Capital in INCHES

TWO WAY FLAT SLAB (concrete)

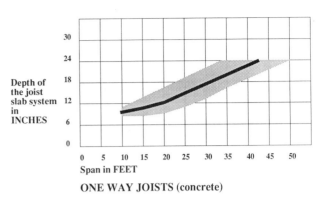

ONE WAY JOISTS (concrete)

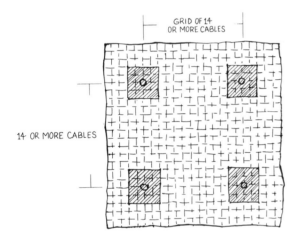

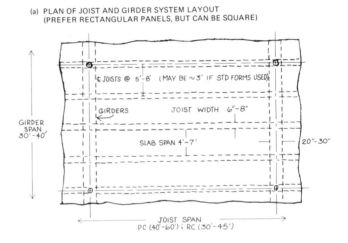

(a) PLAN OF JOIST AND GIRDER SYSTEM LAYOUT
(PREFER RECTANGULAR PANELS, BUT CAN BE SQUARE)

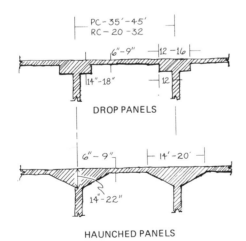

DROP PANELS

HAUNCHED PANELS

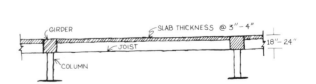

(b) SECTION THRU SLAB AND GIRDERS

Figure 10.20 Sizing chart for a two-way concrete slab. Chart adapted by permission from Corkill, Puderbaugh, and Sawers (1974). Example layout reproduced by permission from Lin and Stotesbury (1988).

Figure 10.21 Sizing chart for a one-way joist system. Chart adapted by permission from Corkill, Puderbaugh, and Sawers (1974). Example layout reproduced by permission from Lin and Stotesbury (1988).

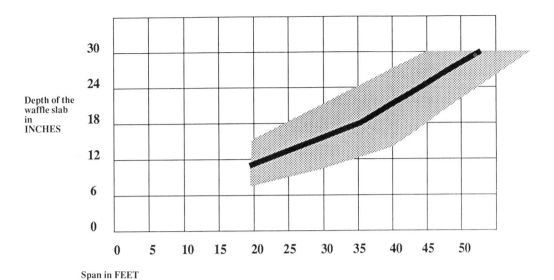

Depth of the
waffle slab
in
INCHES

Span in FEET

TWO WAY WAFFLE SLAB (concrete)

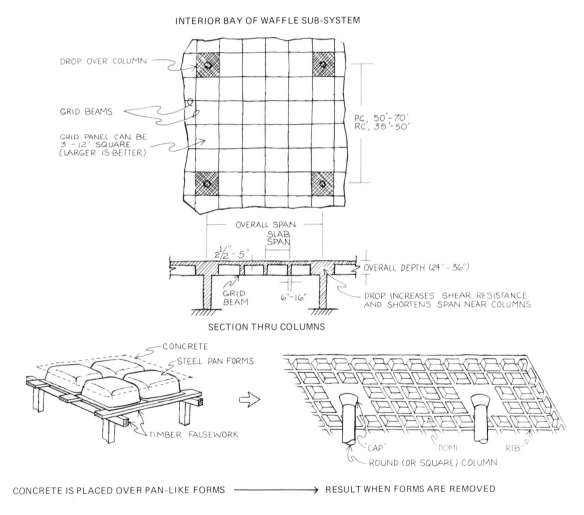

INTERIOR BAY OF WAFFLE SUB-SYSTEM

DROP OVER COLUMN

GRID BEAMS

GRID PANEL CAN BE
3'-12' SQUARE
(LARGER IS BETTER)

PC, 50'-70'
RC', 35'-50'

OVERALL SPAN

SLAB
SPAN

2½"-5"

OVERALL DEPTH (24"-36")

GRID
BEAM

6"-16"

DROP INCREASES SHEAR RESISTANCE
AND SHORTENS SPAN NEAR COLUMNS

SECTION THRU COLUMNS

CONCRETE
STEEL PAN FORMS

TIMBER FALSEWORK

"CAP"   DOME   RIB

ROUND (OR SQUARE) COLUMN

CONCRETE IS PLACED OVER PAN-LIKE FORMS ⟶ RESULT WHEN FORMS ARE REMOVED

Figure 10.22 Sizing chart for a two-way concrete waffle slab. Chart adapted by permission from Corkill, Puderbaugh, and Sawers (1974). Example layout reproduced by permission from Lin and Stotesbury (1988).

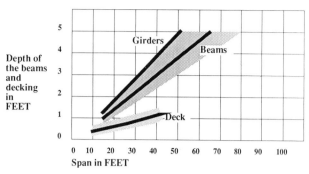

PRECAST DECK and BEAMS (concrete)

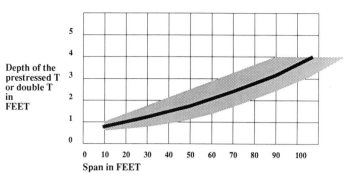

PRESTRESSED TEES and DOUBLE TEES (concrete)

(a) TYPICAL SLAB TO BEAM CONNECTIONS

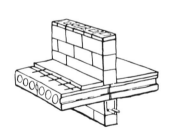

(b) TYPICAL SLAB TO WALL CONNECTIONS

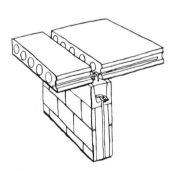

(a) SINGLE TEE

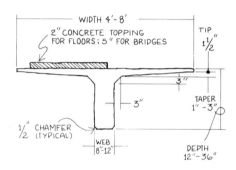

(b) DOUBLE TEE

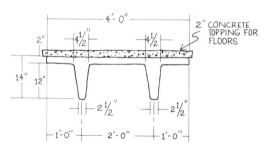

Figure 10.23 Sizing chart for precast concrete deck and beams. Chart adapted by permission from Corkill, Puderbaugh, and Sawers (1974). Example layout reproduced by permission from Lin and Stotesbury (1988).

Figure 10.24 Sizing chart for prestressed concrete tees and double tees. Chart adapted by permission from Corkill, Puderbaugh, and Sawers (1974). Example layout reproduced by permission from Lin and Stotesbury (1988).

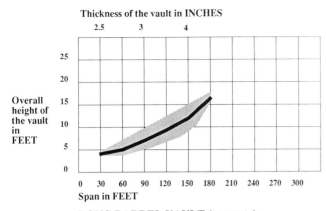

Thickness of the vault in INCHES

LONG BARREL VAULT (concrete)

(a)   LONG BARREL   SHORT BARREL

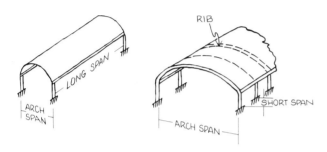

(b) MULTIPLE BARREL

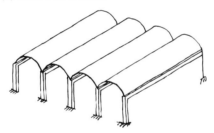

(c) STIFFENING MEMBERS REQUIRED AT ENDS AND EDGES

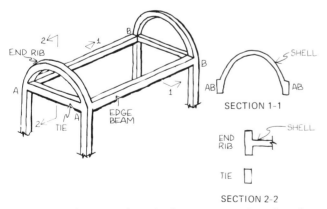

Figure 10.25 Sizing chart for long concrete barrel vaults. Chart adapted by permission from Corkill, Puderbaugh, and Sawers (1974). Example layout reproduced by permission from Lin and Stotesbury (1988).

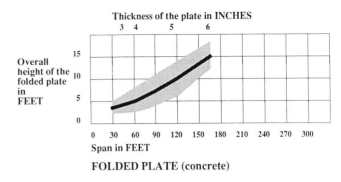

Thickness of the plate in INCHES

FOLDED PLATE (concrete)

(a) FOLDED PLATE SHELL

$$\left(\text{DESIGN LIKE} \quad \}\,\tfrac{2}{3}\,h \right)$$

$$\left(\text{FOR RC, USE } a = \tfrac{7}{8}\,h' \right)$$

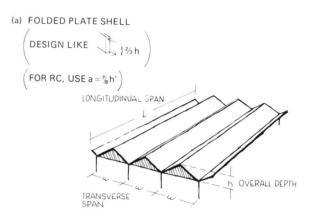

(b) FOLDED PLATE SHELL

$$\left(\text{DESIGN LIKE} \quad \}\,a \right)$$

DEPENDING ON RATIO OF FLANGE TO WEB MATERIAL, USE (0.75–0.9) h FOR a.

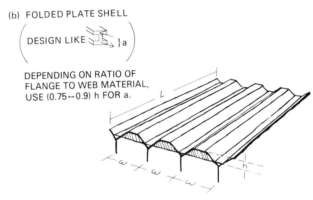

(c) CYLINDRICAL SHELL (DESIGN FOR SECTION ACCORDING TO h AND CURVATURE)

LOW ⌒, USE ⅔ h ∽ a
HIGH ⌒, USE ⅚ h ∽ a
(FOR RC, USE h' VS h)

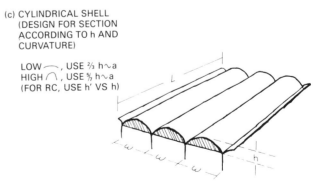

Figure 10.26 Sizing chart for concrete folded plates. Chart adapted by permission from Corkill, Puderbaugh, and Sawers (1974). Example layout reproduced by permission from Lin and Stotesbury (1988).

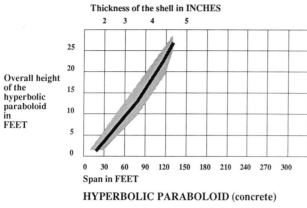

HYPERBOLIC PARABOLOID (concrete)

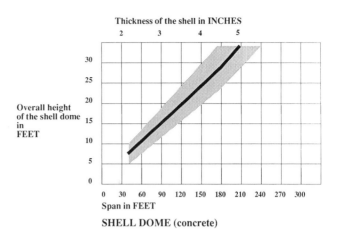

SHELL DOME (concrete)

HOOPING ACTION ALLOWS A DOME SURFACE
TO ACT AS A THIN MEMBRANE

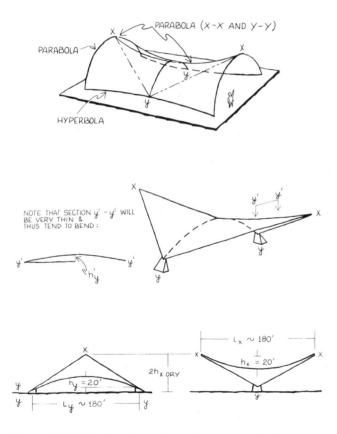

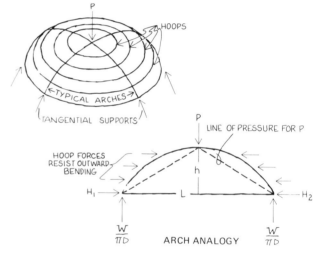

COMPOSITE SECTOR SHELLS WITH
SECTORS SHAPED ACCORDING TO
A SURFACE OF SECOND ORDER

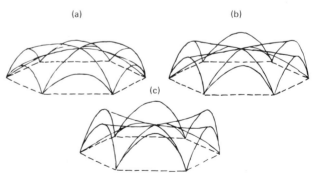

Figure 10.27 Sizing chart for concrete hyperbolic paraboloids. Chart adapted by permission from Corkill, Puderbaugh, and Sawers (1974). Example layout reproduced by permission from Lin and Stotesbury (1988).

Figure 10.28 Sizing chart for concrete shell domes. Chart adapted by permission from Corkill, Puderbaugh, and Sawers (1974). Example layout reproduced by permission from Lin and Stotesbury (1988).

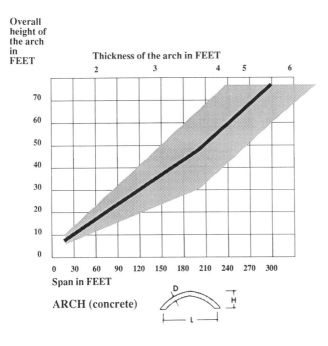

Overall
height of
the arch
in
FEET

Thickness of the arch in FEET

Span in FEET

ARCH (concrete)

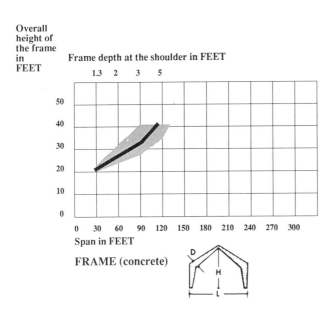

Overall
height of
the frame
in
FEET

Frame depth at the shoulder in FEET

Span in FEET

FRAME (concrete)

Figure 10.29 Sizing charts for concrete arches and single-story concrete frames. Adapted by permission from Corkill, Puderbaugh, and Sawers (1974).

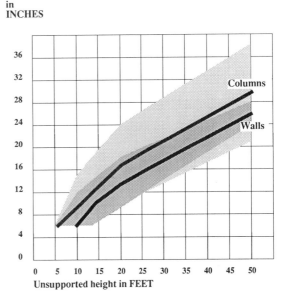

Thickness of
the column
or wall
in
INCHES

Columns

Walls

Unsupported height in FEET

SINGLE STORY COLUMNS and WALLS (concrete)

Figure 10.30 Sizing chart for single-story concrete columns and walls. Adapted by permission from Corkill, Puderbaugh, and Sawers (1974).

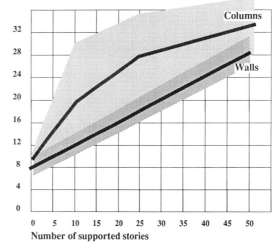

Thickness of
the column
or wall
in
INCHES

Columns

Walls

Number of supported stories

MULTISTORY COLUMNS and WALLS (concrete)

Figure 10.31 Sizing chart for multistory concrete columns and walls. Adapted by permission from Corkill, Puderbaugh, and Sawers (1974).

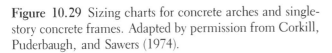

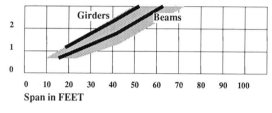

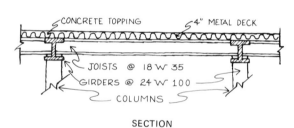

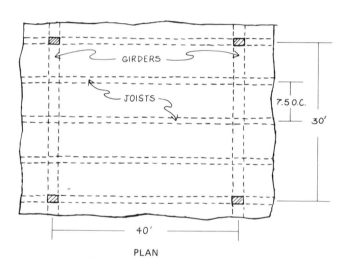

Figure 10.32 Sizing chart for steel deck, beams, and girders. Chart adapted by permission from Corkill, Puderbaugh, and Sawers (1974). Example layout reproduced by permission from Lin and Stotesbury (1988).

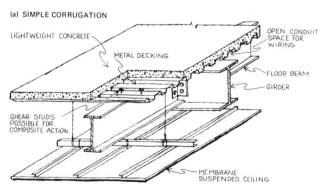

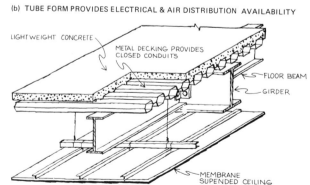

Figure 10.33 Two types of corrugated metal decking forms for steel beam and girder framing systems. Reproduced by permission from Lin and Stotesbury (1988).

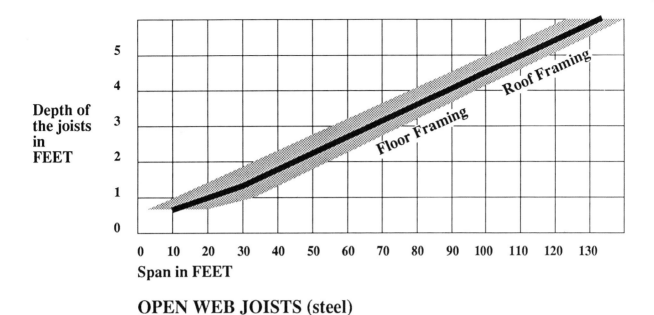

OPEN WEB JOISTS (steel)

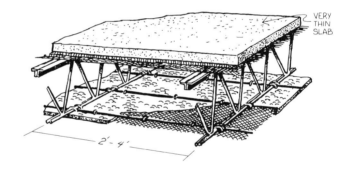

(a) LIGHTWEIGHT STEEL JOIST SUB-SYSTEM WITH CONCRETE SLAB

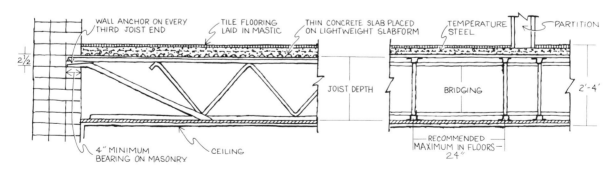

(b) SECTION SHOWING TYPICAL FLOOR CONSTRUCTION

Figure 10.34 Sizing chart for open web steel joists. Chart adapted by permission from Corkill, Puderbaugh, and Sawers (1974). Example layout reproduced by permission from Lin and Stotesbury (1988).

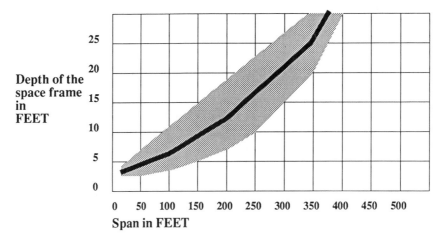

SPACE FRAME (steel or aluminum)

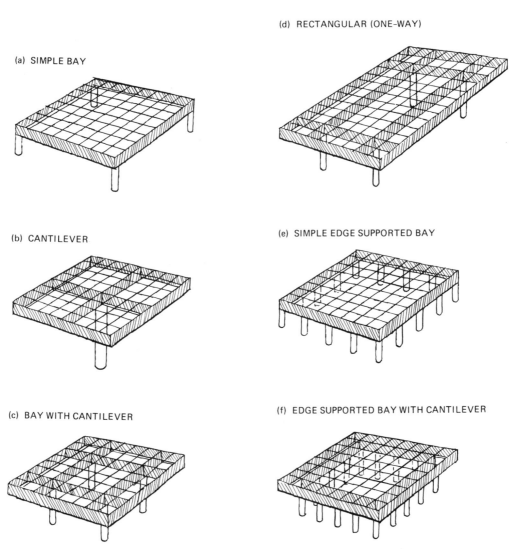

(a) SIMPLE BAY

(b) CANTILEVER

(c) BAY WITH CANTILEVER

(d) RECTANGULAR (ONE-WAY)

(e) SIMPLE EDGE SUPPORTED BAY

(f) EDGE SUPPORTED BAY WITH CANTILEVER

Figure 10.35 Sizing chart for steel or aluminum space frames. Chart adapted by permission from Corkill, Puderbaugh, and Sawers (1974). Example layout reproduced by permission from Lin and Stotesbury (1988).

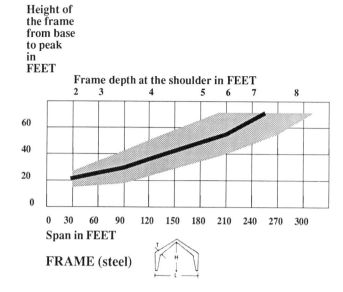

Depth of
the truss
in
FEET

FLAT TRUSS (steel)

FRAME (steel)

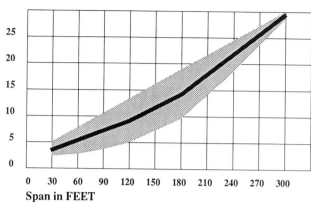

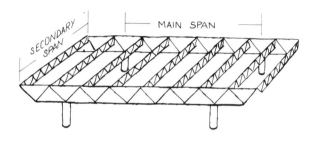

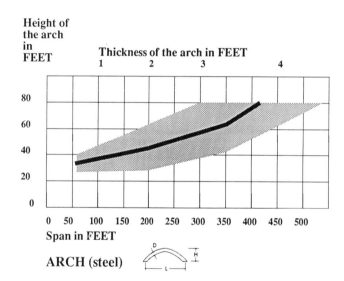

Height of
the arch
in
FEET

ARCH (steel)

Figure 10.37 Sizing charts for steel frames and steel arches. Adapted by permission from Corkill, Puderbaugh, and Sawers (1974).

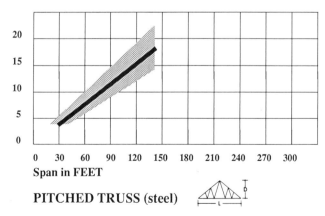

Depth of
the truss
from the peak
in
FEET

PITCHED TRUSS (steel)

Figure 10.36 Sizing charts for steel trusses. Chart adapted by permission from Corkill, Puderbaugh, and Sawers (1974). Example layout reproduced by permission from Lin and Stotesbury (1988).

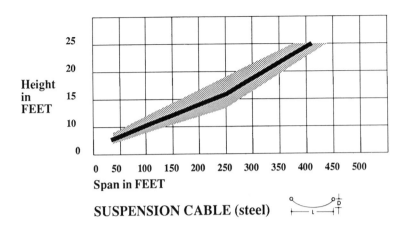

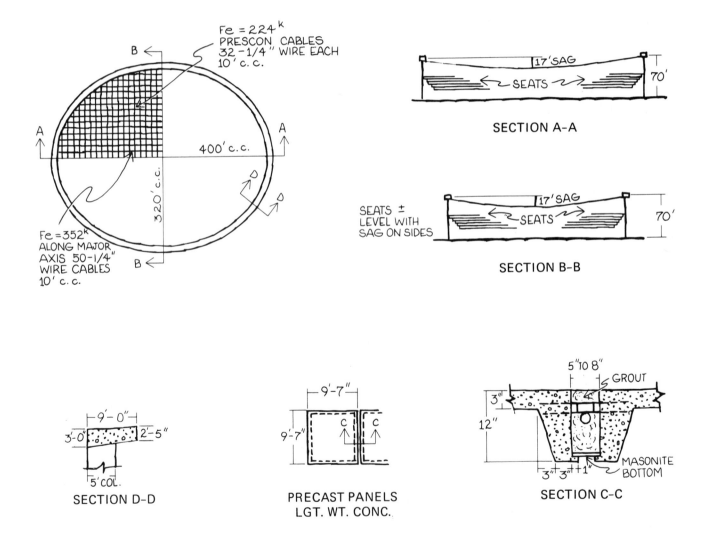

Figure 10.38 Sizing chart for steel suspension cable roofs. Chart adapted by permission from Corkill, Puderbaugh, and Sawers (1974). Example layout reproduced by permission from Lin and Stotesbury (1988).

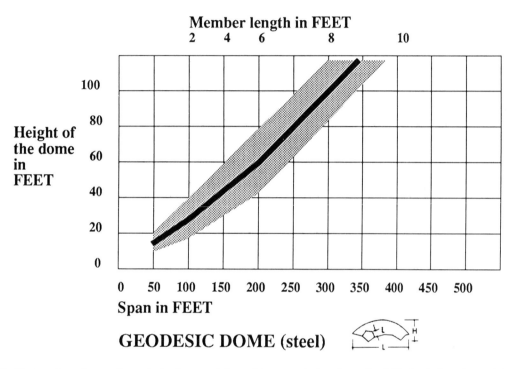

Figure 10.39 Sizing chart for steel geodesic domes. Adapted by permission from Corkill, Puderbaugh, and Sawers (1974).

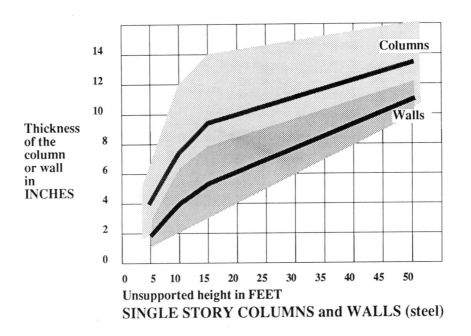

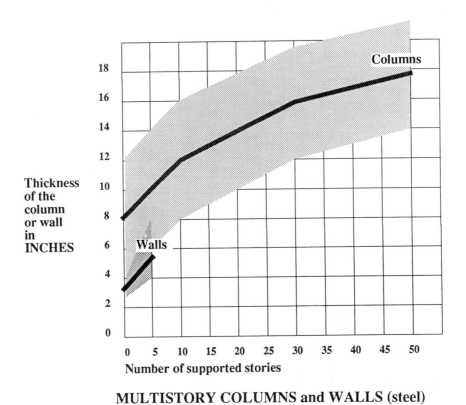

Figure 10.40 Sizing chart for single-story steel columns and walls. Adapted by permission from Corkill, Puderbaugh, and Sawers (1974).

Figure 10.41 Sizing chart for multistory steel columns and walls. Adapted by permission from Corkill, Puderbaugh, and Sawers (1974).

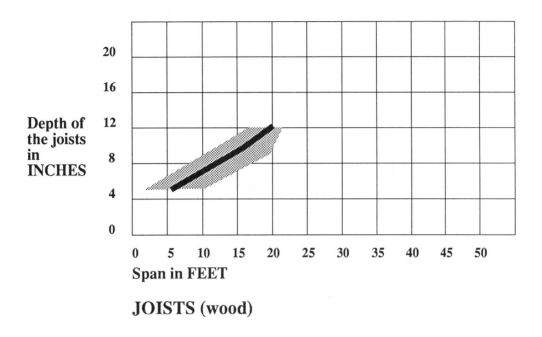

Depth of the joists in INCHES

Span in FEET

JOISTS (wood)

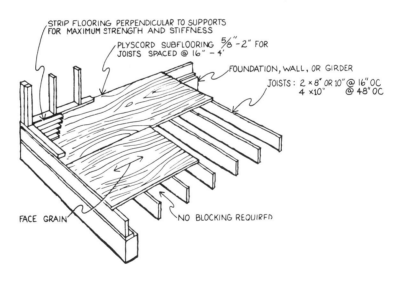

STRIP FLOORING PERPENDICULAR TO SUPPORTS FOR MAXIMUM STRENGTH AND STIFFNESS

PLYSCORD SUBFLOORING 5/8"-2" FOR JOISTS SPACED @ 16"- 4'

FOUNDATION, WALL, OR GIRDER

JOISTS : 2 × 8" OR 10" @ 16" OC
4 × 10" @ 48" OC

FACE GRAIN

NO BLOCKING REQUIRED

Figure 10.42 Sizing chart for wood joist systems. Chart adapted by permission from Corkill, Puderbaugh, and Sawers (1974). Example layout reproduced by permission from Lin and Stotesbury (1988).

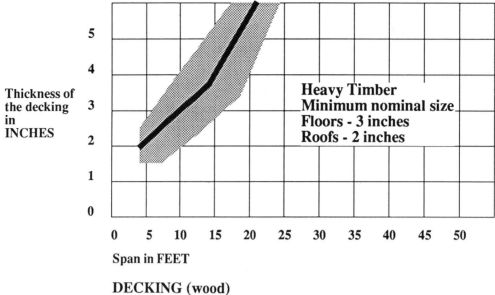

DECKING (wood)

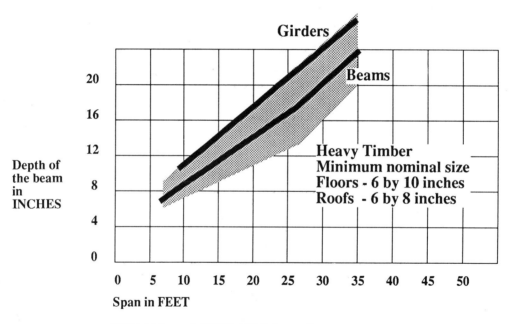

BEAMS and GIRDERS (wood)

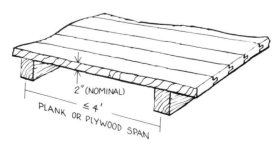

Figure 10.43 Sizing chart for wood decking, beams, and girders. Chart adapted by permission from Corkill, Puderbaugh, and Sawers (1974). Example layout reproduced by permission from Lin and Stotesbury (1988).

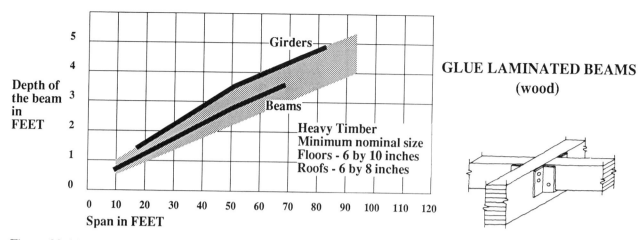

GLUE LAMINATED BEAMS
(wood)

Figure 10.44 Sizing chart for wood glue-laminated beams. Adapted by permission from Corkill, Puderbaugh and Sawers (1974).

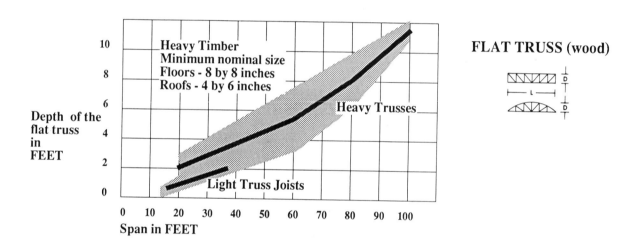

FLAT TRUSS (wood)

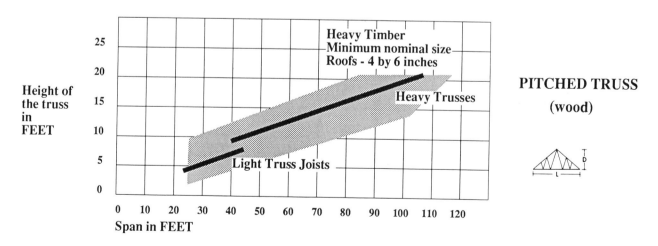

PITCHED TRUSS
(wood)

Figure 10.45 Sizing charts for wood trusses. Adapted by permission from Corkill, Puderbaugh, and Sawers (1974).

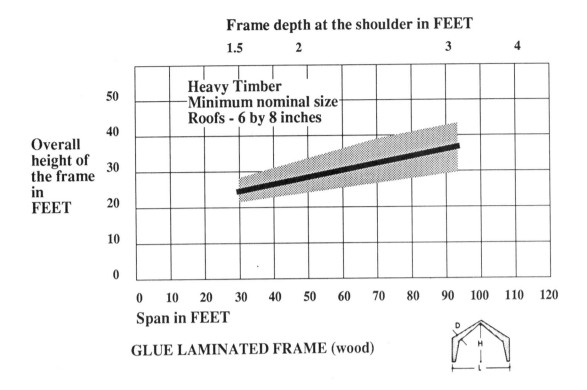

GLUE LAMINATED FRAME (wood)

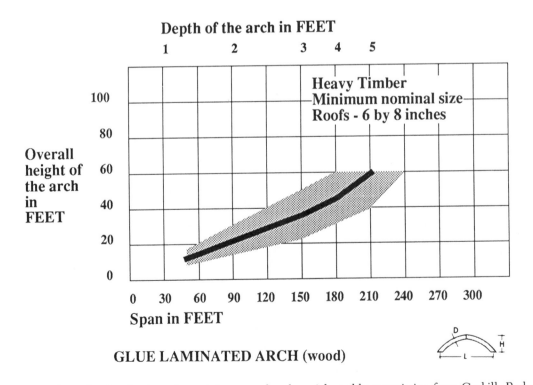

GLUE LAMINATED ARCH (wood)

Figure 10.46 Sizing charts for glue-laminated wood frames and arches. Adapted by permission from Corkill, Puderbaugh, and Sawers (1974).

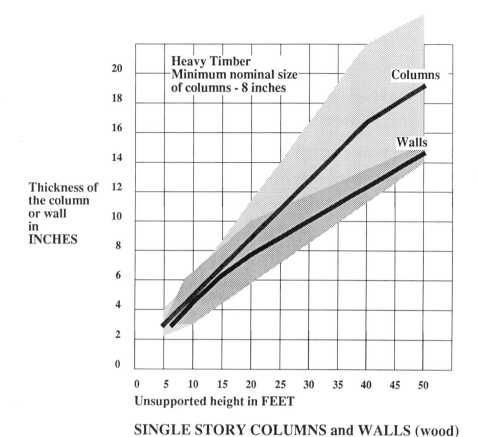

SINGLE STORY COLUMNS and WALLS (wood)

Figure 10.47 Sizing chart for single-story wood columns and walls. Adapted by permission from Corkill, Puderbaugh, and Sawers (1974).

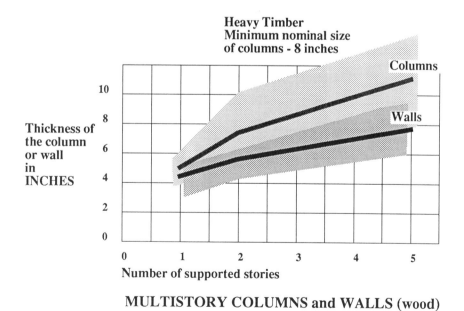

MULTISTORY COLUMNS and WALLS (wood)

Figure 10.48 Sizing chart for multistory wood columns and walls. Adapted by permission from Corkill, Puderbaugh, and Sawers (1974).

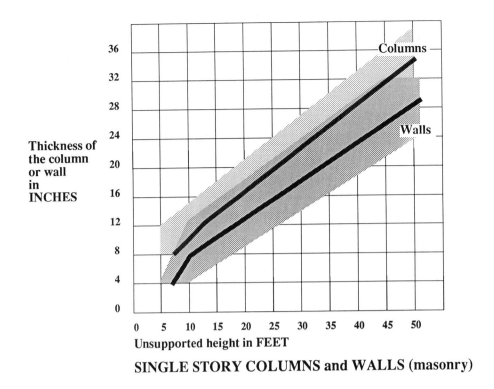

SINGLE STORY COLUMNS and WALLS (masonry)

Figure 10.49 Sizing chart for single-story masonry columns and walls. Adapted by permission from Corkill, Puderbaugh, and Sawers (1974).

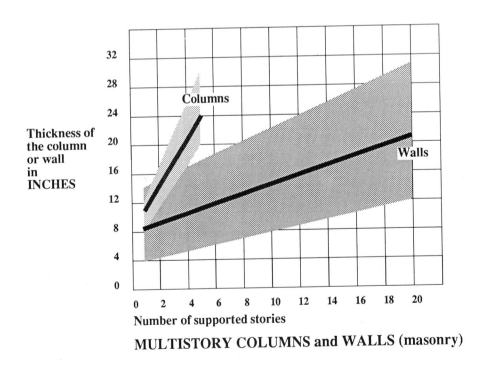

MULTISTORY COLUMNS and WALLS (masonry)

Figure 10.50 Sizing chart for multistory masonry columns and walls. Adapted by permission from Corkill, Puderbaugh, and Sawers (1974).

11

The HVAC System

The heating, ventilating, and air-conditioning (HVAC) system has many components, some of which take up a large area. For the creative manipulation of the HVAC implications in architectural design the architect needs to consider the relationship between spatial organization, structural requirements, and the HVAC needs in an overall way. In order for this to happen at the highest levels of design intent, detail must be suppressed and strategic concept emphasized.

MAJOR HVAC SYSTEM COMPONENTS

The purpose of the HVAC system is to produce thermal comfort inside the building. The major components of the HVAC system are the centrally located equipment—the chiller and boiler, the cooling tower, and the air handlers—and the delivery equipment—the air duct and/or water pipe delivery system and the diffusers.

The chiller and boiler produce heat and cold, usually in the form of hot and chilled water. The system uses the hot and chilled water to heat or cool the air inside the building. This is done with an air handler, which consists of a filter, heating and cooling coils, and a fan housed in an insulated sheet metal enclosure. Air handlers can be large and centrally located, serving a major portion of the building, or they can be local and serve only a small part of the building. Local air handlers (fan coil units and induction units) will have minimal to no duct distribution system. Large centralized air handlers will have a bulky duct distribution system delivering tempered air to the building area served. The large systems will need to create smaller subzones with reheat boxes, variable air volume boxes, or mixing boxes, depending on the distribution system type. Figure 11.1 is a generic diagram of the major components of an HVAC system serving a single large zone.

CENTRALLY LOCATED EQUIPMENT

The chiller, boiler, and air handlers are large pieces of equipment that serve the whole building and are often grouped together into a mechanical room located for convenient distribution of HVAC services to the building. The cooling tower is located outside to reject heat to the environment. Figures 11.2 through 11.4 show how these elements function within the HVAC system.

Boiler and Chiller   The boiler produces the hot water and the chiller produces the chilled water (Fig. 11.2). These two pieces of equipment with their accompanying hot and chilled water pumps are often grouped together in a room. The outputs from this room are the hot and chilled water supply and return insulated pipes (6 to 10 inches in diameter including the insulation). Because these pipes take up very little room and can extend long distances, the room containing the chiller and boiler can be located fairly freely.

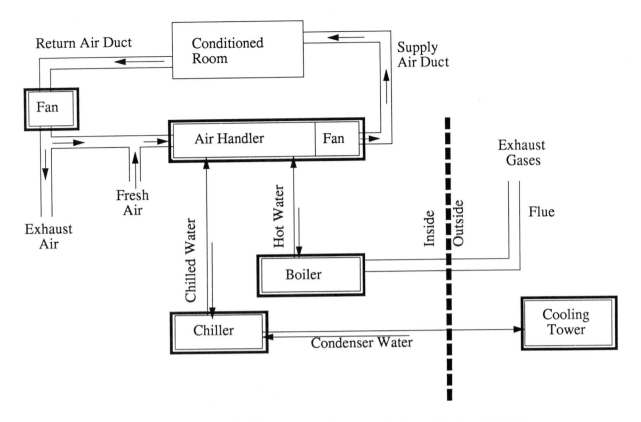

Figure 11.1 Major components of a centralized heating, ventilating, and air conditioning (HVAC) system.

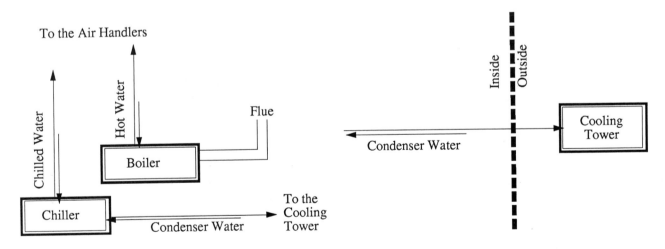

Figure 11.2 The chiller and boiler. Hot and chilled water are produced.

Figure 11.3 The cooling tower. Heat from the condenser water is ejected to the outside environment.

Two percent of the building floor area served by the boiler and chiller will provide a room large enough for the chiller and boiler and their accompanying pumps. The room must be 12 feet high with a minimum width of 30 to 40 feet, with access to the outside for replacement of large pieces of equipment. It should be located away from critical noise areas. The boiler will require an exhaust flue up through the building. Hot and chilled water from one boiler and chiller can serve all the air handlers in the building.

Boiler sizes vary but can be approximated as:

5 feet by 8 feet by 5 feet high (650,000 Btu/hr)
6 feet by 10 feet by 6 feet high (1,650,000 Btu/hr)
6 feet by 15 feet by 6 feet high (3,350,000 Btu/hr)

Chiller sizes also vary:

10 feet by 3 feet by 5 feet high (50 tons)
15 feet by 6 feet by 6 feet high (100 tons)
15 feet by 8 feet by 7 feet high (500 tons)
27 feet by 8 feet by 12 feet high (1000 tons)

Commercial buildings need approximately 1 ton of refrigeration for every 300 square feet of floor area.

The Cooling Tower   The chiller moves heat out of the building, ejecting it to the outside environment (Fig. 11.3) by pumping water from the condenser side of the chiller to the cooling tower. The cooling tower is a cascade of water evaporatively rejecting heat to the environment. The cooling tower is noisy, ugly, and can spit water droplets.

The cooling tower requires 1 square foot of plan area per 300 square feet of building floor area served. This area will be large enough for the cooling tower and the necessary access space around it. The tower must be located in the outside air to reject heat to the environment and away from people, because of noise and splatter. Cooling tower sizes vary but can be approximated as:

5 feet by 5 feet by 7 feet high (50 tons)
8 feet by 5 feet by 8 feet high (100 tons)
9 feet by 10 feet by 15 feet high (500 tons)
25 feet by 10 feet by 15 feet high (1000 tons)

Air Handlers   The air handler operates by means of a fan that draws air through heating and cooling coils and then pushes it into a supply duct system for its trip to the rooms that are to be conditioned. There is also a return fan that draws air back from the conditioned rooms, exhausts some of it to the outside, and takes in an equal amount of fresh outside air (Fig. 11.4).

During information ordering, the building program areas are broken up into groupings with similar sched-

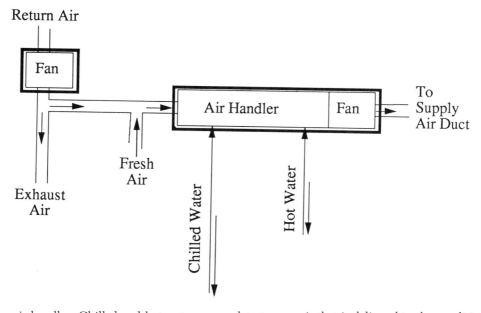

Figure 11.4 The air handler. Chilled and hot water are used to temper air that is delivered to the conditioned space.

ules, temperature set points, ventilation and air quality requirements, internal heat generation, and needs for heating, cooling, and/or ventilation. To produce an energy-efficient and comfortable building these separate groupings should be served by separate air handlers. This arrangement will allow the thermal response of the HVAC system to be tuned closely to the thermal requirements of the building.

Large areas of building might be served by more than one air handler to reduce the size of the main supply and return ducts. For example, a low-velocity duct serving 10,000 square feet of floor area will have a diameter of about 3 feet—big enough to make horizontal duct runs difficult.

A fan coil unit or an induction unit is a very small air handler serving a small floor area. If the area is one room, there will be no need for a duct distribution system. With a slightly larger area, like one apartment, there will be a duct distribution system.

A room large enough for the air handler will be provided by 4% of the building floor area served. The room should have a minimum ceiling height of 12 feet (less if only one air handler is in the room), and a minimum width of 8 to 12 feet depending on the equipment. The room must provide access to an outside wall for fresh air and equipment replacement.

Air handlers can be grouped together in one room or spread around the building in separate rooms. In a multistory building, they are often stacked above each other. They are best located near the center of the area they serve so that the main supply duct can be divided into two branches, thus reducing the diameter of the ducting.

Air handler sizes vary but can be approximated as:

5 feet by 15 feet by 4 feet high (2,000 cfm)
8 feet by 20 feet by 5 feet high (10,000 cfm)
12 feet by 25 feet by 7 feet high (20,000 cfm)

Return fan sizes also vary:

A 4 foot cube (2,000 cfm)
A 5 foot cube (10,000 cfm)
A 7 foot cube (20,000 cfm)

Commercial buildings require approximately 1 cubic foot per minute (cfm) of air flow into the space for every square foot of floor area.

DELIVERY SYSTEMS THAT USE ONLY AIR

HVAC delivery systems that use air as the principal means of delivering cooling or heating to the zones they serve are referred to as all-air systems. The large interior spaces of commercial buildings will most commonly be served by an all-air system of some form. Different types of ducts and all-air systems are discussed below.

Air Ducts   The air ducts used in these all-air systems are sufficiently large to require strategic care in their placement (Fig. 11.5). How they thread under or through the structural system and how they are expressed or hidden in the architectural composition are matters of architectural concern.

High-velocity ducts are under higher pressure and thus are capable of pushing more air through a smaller cross-sectional area. The high pressure is reduced to low-pressure levels and thus low velocity at the subzone boxes downstream in the distribution system. The return duct is always a low-velocity duct.

The main supply and return ducts are very often run in the ceiling space above the main hallways of the building because additional ceiling space is often available and the hallways provide a natural path of easy access to the majority of the building spaces.

High-velocity ducts require 0.5 square feet of cross-sectional area per 1000 square feet of building floor area served.

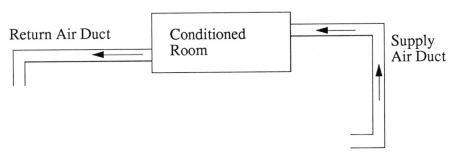

Figure 11.5 Air ducts. The function of the ducts is to supply air to the conditioned space and return it to the air handler.

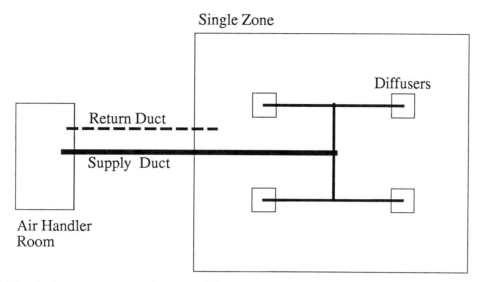

Figure 11.6 The single-zone constant-volume air delivery system.

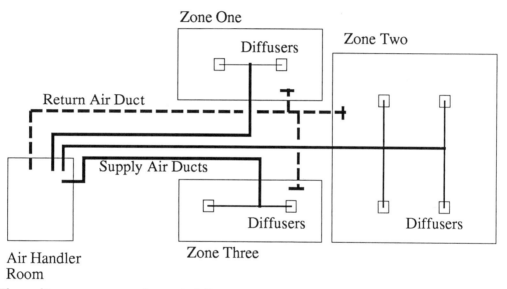

Figure 11.7 The multi-zone constant-volume air delivery system.

Low-velocity ducts require 1 square foot of cross-sectional area per 1000 square feet of building floor area served.

The Single-Zone Constant-Volume System   The single-zone constant-volume system (Fig. 11.6) serves only one zone. This system is used for large open-space rooms without diverse exterior exposure. A thermostat in the zone controls the temperature of the air delivered to the zone. The main supply duct leaving the air handler divides into smaller ducts to deliver the air directly to diffusers that spread the air over the zone. This is a low-velocity duct system.

The Multi-Zone Constant-Volume System   The multi-zone system can serve up to eight separately controlled zones (Fig. 11.7). It is used in modest sized buildings where there is diversity of exterior exposure and/or diversity of interior loading.

A thermostat in each zone tells the air handler how to mix hot and cold air together to create the necessary air temperature to temper the zone properly. Each zone is served by a separate supply duct leaving the air handler. Thus if there are eight zones, there are eight separate supply ducts leaving the air handler. A particular zone's main supply duct divides into smaller ducts to spread air directly to diffusers that deliver the air to the zone.

These are low-velocity duct systems. The return ducts, coming back from the separate zones, will converge together into one large return duct.

Subzone Boxes   The three all-air systems described below use subzone boxes that branch off the main supply duct to create as many separate zones as the building requires. Like the main supply ducts, these boxes are bulky pieces of equipment that require strategic concern for their placement. The size of the subzone boxes can be related approximately to the floor area they serve.

For 500 to 1500 square feet of floor area, a subzone box 4 feet long, 3 feet wide, and 1.5 feet high is needed.

For 1500 to 5000 square feet, a box 5 feet long, 4 feet wide, and 1.5 feet high is required.

The Constant-Volume Reheat System   The constant-volume reheat system modifies a system that is meant to serve one zone so that it serves more than one (Fig. 11.8). This system is not often used since it wastes energy and does not produce substantially better performance than the variable air-volume system.

A thermostat in each subzone determines how much heat is added at the reheat box to the cool air that the air handler is delivering down the main supply duct. Each reheat box creates a separate subzone. Distribution ducts then leave the reheat box to deliver air to the diffusers that spread the air over the space.

The main supply duct can be a high-velocity duct with the subzone boxes stepping down the pressure for low-velocity delivery to the diffusers through the distribution ducts coming out of the box. The return duct is a low-velocity duct.

The Variable Air-Volume System   The variable air-volume (VAV) system (Fig. 11.9) can serve as many subzones as are desired. This system is the dominant choice in many commercial office building projects because of its flexibility in handling many zones and its excellent energy-saving features. Variable air volume systems are most effectively used for interior areas of buildings where there is a variation of cooling load and no need for heat. Hot water or electric reheat coils incorporated into the VAV boxes can be used on perimeter zones where heating and cooling are required.

The main supply duct feeds cool air to all the VAV boxes. If a subzone is being overcooled, a thermostat in the subzone tells its VAV box to reduce the amount of cool air that is being delivered to the space through the

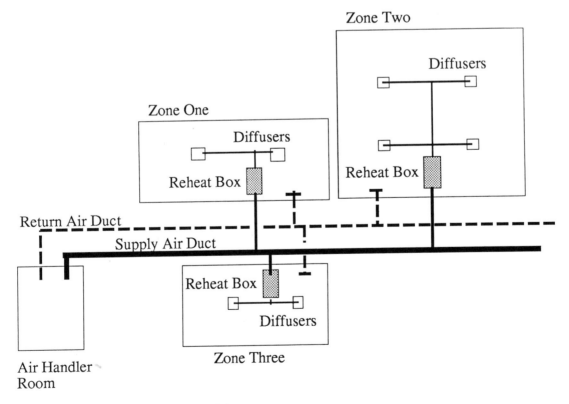

Figure 11.8 The constant-volume reheat air delivery system.

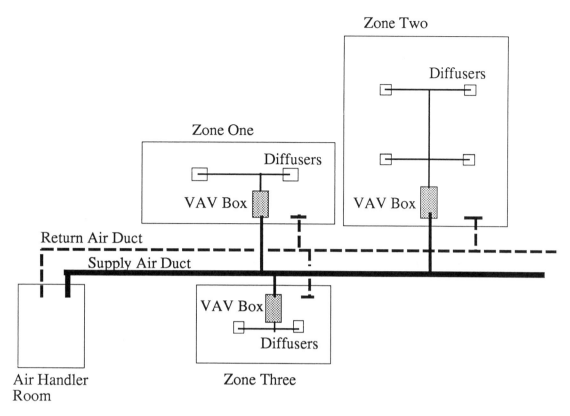

Figure 11.9 The variable air-volume air delivery system.

box. If this amount still provides too much cooling for the space needs of the subzone, reheat can be added to the VAV box. Reheat is only necessary for exterior zones that will require some heating in the winter. Each VAV box creates a separate subzone of the system. Distribution ducts then leave the VAV box to deliver air to the diffusers that spread the air over the space.

During partial loading conditions, when many of the VAV boxes have reduced air flows, a pressure sensor in the main air duct tells the fan at the air handler to produce less pressure in the main duct. This reduces the fan energy used. VAV systems save energy by minimizing both reheat energy and fan energy.

The main supply duct can be a high-velocity duct with the subzone boxes stepping down the pressure for low-velocity delivery to diffusers through the distribution ducts coming out of the box. The return duct is a low-velocity duct.

The Double Duct System   The double duct system can serve as many subzones as desired (Fig. 11.10). The

double duct system is a good choice where air quality control is very important. An example would be a biology or chemistry lab building with fume hoods, where the air flow into the zones needs to be constant. The double duct system supplies this constant flow of air.

The air handler creates a supply stream of hot air and a supply stream of cold air. There are two supply ducts running through the building (double duct). A thermostat in the subzone tells its mixing box the proportion of hot and cold air to mix together to create the delivered air temperature the subzone needs to condition itself correctly. Each mixing box creates a separate subzone. Distribution ducts then leave the mixing box to deliver air to the diffusers that spread the air through the space.

The two main supply ducts can be high-velocity ducts with the subzone boxes stepping down the pressure for low-velocity delivery to the diffusers through the distribution ducts coming out of the box. The return duct is a low-velocity duct.

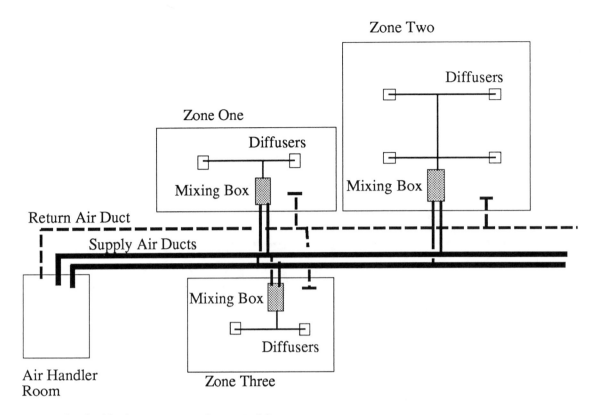

Figure 11.10 The double-duct constant-volume air delivery system.

DELIVERY SYSTEMS THAT USE BOTH AIR AND WATER

In these systems a stream of air is tempered at an air handler that is remote from the zones being served. This stream of air, which is only 10 to 25 percent of the quantity used by all-air systems, makes up the fresh outside air requirement for the spaces served. The heating or cooling of the zones is achieved by hot or chilled water circulated through an induction or fan coil unit in the zone being served.

Since the air duct carries only fresh air, it can be sized at 0.2 square feet of cross-sectional area per 1000 square feet of building floor area served. The main hot and cold water pipes will be 4 to 8 inches in diameter including the insulation.

The Induction System   An induction system is often used for the perimeter offices of high-rise office buildings to provide the individual control of heating or cooling needed by these spaces (Fig. 11.11). It is a fairly expensive system to install.

Tempered air is produced at a centrally located air handler. The amount of air is set to meet the outside air requirements (about 0.2 cfm/sq. ft.). This air is delivered to the spaces through a high-velocity duct system. Hot and cold water is also delivered to the spaces. The high-velocity air is used to draw room air through a coil that has chilled or hot water in it depending on the need for cooling or heating. The water does most of the heating or cooling work.

The return air stream will be 100 percent exhaust air, which can be drawn out locally with many separate exhaust fans or centrally with one large exhaust fan and a return duct system.

Each induction unit creates a separate zone and is usually located along the outside wall and at the base of exterior windows. A thermostat in the zone regulates how much hot or cold water flows through the coil in the induction unit. The air flow through the unit remains constant.

Induction units are 6 to 12 inches deep. Height varies from 1 to 3 feet to meet requirements of the architectural setting, and length also varies to meet requirements.

The Fan Coil System with Supplementary Air A fan coil system with supplementary air is used where there are many small rooms that need separate control (Fig. 11.12). The fan coil units receive chilled and hot water that is circulated through a coil. A fan draws room air through the coil to heat or cool the space. A separate supply of ventilation air (0.2 cfm/sq. ft.), produced at a central air handler, is introduced to the room through diffusers.

The return air stream, which is 100 percent exhaust air, can be removed locally with many separate exhaust fans or centrally by means of one large exhaust fan and a return duct system.

Each fan coil unit creates a separate zone. The unit is usually located along the outside wall and at the base of exterior windows. A thermostat in the zone regulates the amount of hot or cold water that flows through the coil in the fan coil unit. The air flow through the fan coil unit can usually be set by the user to high, medium, or low.

Horizontal fan coil units are 6 to 12 inches deep; their height varies from 1 to 3 feet to meet the requirements of the particular architectural setting. Length also varies to meet requirements. Fan coil units are also manufactured in a vertical shape to fit in a closet space. The units are approximately 2 feet by 2 feet and 6 feet high. This type of fan coil unit might have a duct distribution system to serve a group of rooms, as in an apartment. They are often stacked vertically above each other up through a tall building so that the water piping can run straight up and down.

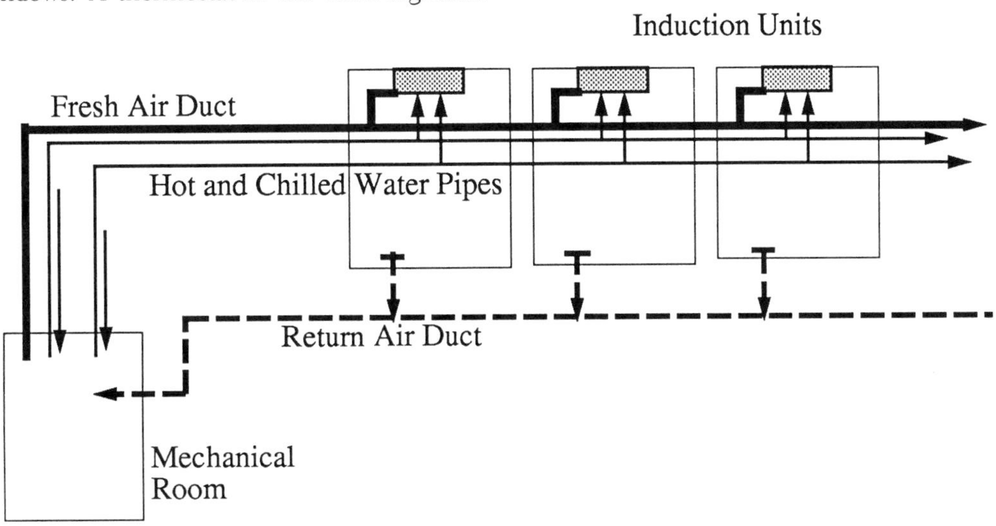

Induction Units

Figure 11.11 The induction air/water delivery system.

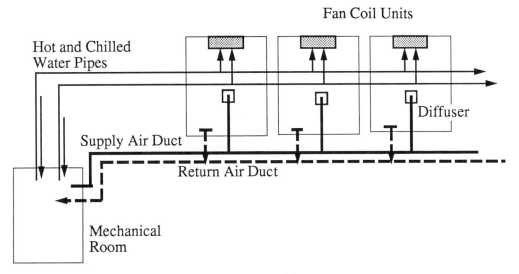

Figure 11.12 A fan coil unit with supplementary air air/water delivery system.

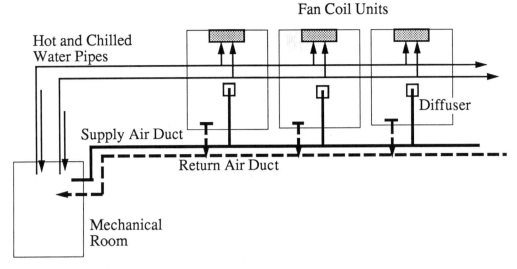

Figure 11.13 The fan coil unit water delivery system.

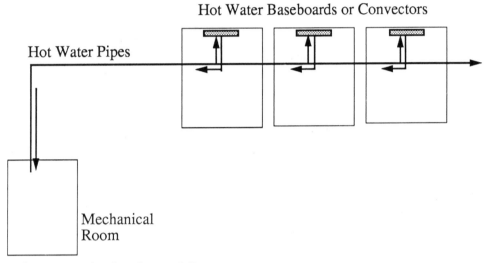

Figure 11.14 The hot water baseboard water delivery system.

DELIVERY SYSTEMS THAT USE ONLY WATER

All-water delivery systems are those that have no central air handler supplying fresh air. The heating or cooling is achieved by circulating hot or chilled water to the zones.

Fan Coil Units   Fan coil units are an example of this kind of system (Fig. 11.13). Hot or chilled water is circulated to the fan coil units in the zones. Fresh air is introduced locally through openable windows or an outdoor air intake through the fan coil unit.

Hot Water Baseboards   Another all-water delivery system uses hot water baseboards (Fig. 11.14). This delivery system supplies only heat. It is often used in conjunction with a cooling-only variable air volume delivery system to provide the heating necessary at the perimeter of the building.

Hot water baseboards are 6 inches high by 5 inches deep and as long as is necessary. Hot water convectors can be made higher to fit in the area under the sill of a window.

DIFFUSER CHOICE AND LAYOUT

The diffusers are the interface between the HVAC system and the design of the interior of the building. Their choice and layout will have an important effect on both the visual impact and the thermal comfort of the space.

From a thermal standpoint the diffusers should be located in a uniformly distributed pattern over the ceiling to spread the tempered air over the entire space (Fig. 11.15). The spacing between diffusers should be approximately equal to the ceiling height.

Diffusers come in many sizes and styles and can deliver air down from the ceiling, out from the wall, or up from the floor (Fig. 11.16). Coordinating diffuser spacing with the lighting system is a major ceiling design consideration. Some light fixtures incorporate air diffusers into the design of the fixture, an arrangement that simplifies ceiling layout.

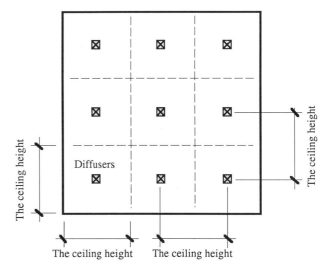

Figure 11.15 Diffuser layout for good air distribution over the entire space.

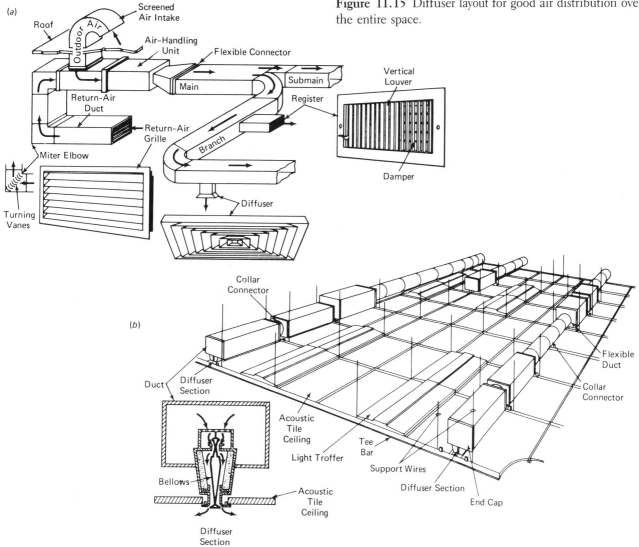

Figure 11.16 Diffuser types. (a) Ducts discharging air through vertical and horizontal rectangular diffusers; (b) ducts discharging air through linear diffusers. Reproduced by permission from Merritt and Ambrose (1990).

CHOOSING AN APPROPRIATE HVAC SYSTEM

The choice of a HVAC system is a qualitative one. Each of the major thermal zones into which an architectural program is divided may have different HVAC characteristics. The problem now is to choose the type of HVAC system that will accommodate these needs most efficiently.

Qualitative Scales   The five characteristics listed below are the basis for qualitative scales covering the many dimensions of the HVAC system choice problem.

Ability to minimize reheat
Ability to produce good air quality
Ability to create many zones
Ability to adapt to future changes
Ability to deliver heat effectively

Each of these scales has a five-step range from low to high with the end points defined. Figures 11.17 through 11.21 rate the various types of HVAC systems according to their performance on these qualitative scales.

Qualitative Linear Programming   Using the same qualitative scale to order the relative importance of the performance scales themselves, a subset of potential HVAC systems can be split and pruned down to a small set of semi-optimal systems. Figure 11.22 shows the interaction of two qualitative specifications. Note that the constraint equations are represented with a region of fuzzy acceptability. This provision allows solutions in the immediate neighborhood of the specified constraint to be left in contention, thus carrying some vagueness through the analysis. Vagueness is included in the analysis because qualitative scales are vague by nature.

Generating HVAC System Choices   The qualitative linear programming method can be used to determine a subset of optimal HVAC system types. This can be achieved through the simple mechanism of ordering the performance objectives along the same five-element

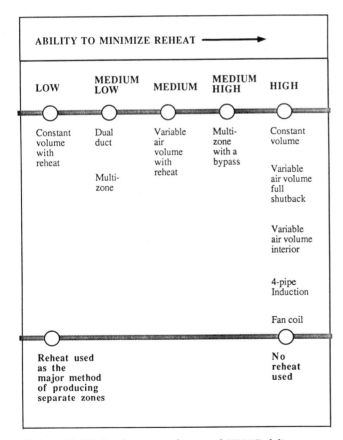

Figure 11.17 Qualitative ordering of HVAC delivery systems according to their ability to minimize reheat.

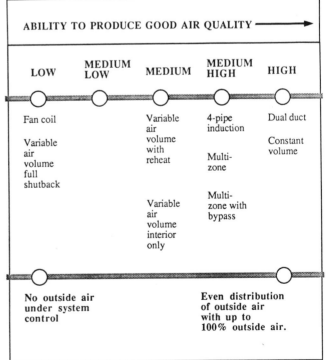

Figure 11.18 Qualitative ordering of HVAC delivery systems according to their ability to produce good air quality.

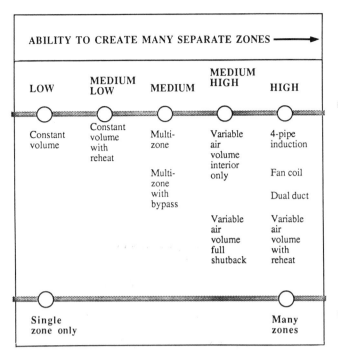

Figure 11.19 Qualitative ordering of HVAC delivery systems according to their ability to create many separate zones.

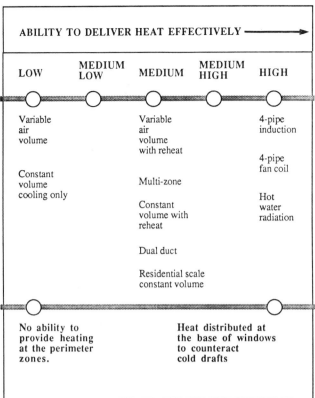

Figure 11.21 Qualitative ordering of HVAC delivery systems according to their ability to deliver heat effectively.

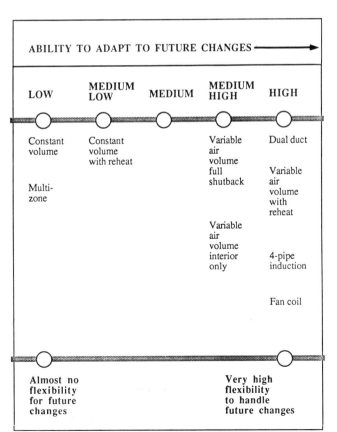

Figure 11.20 Qualitative ordering of HVAC delivery systems according to their ability to adapt to future changes.

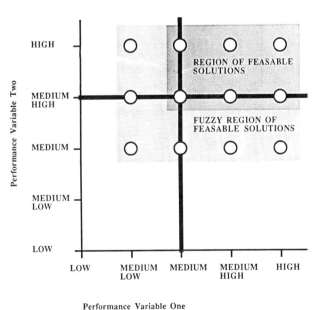

Figure 11.22 Qualitative linear programming to produce a subset of acceptable system types.

scale from low to high. Start with the highest priority performance scale. The subset of HVAC systems that meet this qualitative priority can be read off the performance objective scales. Remember to include the fuzzy boundary area. All other systems will not meet this qualitative specification and are therefore pruned from the search. Then proceed to the next highest priority objective. The intersection of the subset of HVAC systems that meet this second performance specification with the subset of HVAC systems from the first performance specification becomes the further pruned down list of possible HVAC systems. Continue this process through all the performance specifications.

Figures 11.23 and 11.24 are examples of performance specifications with their resultant HVAC system choices. Note that in the examples the qualitative analysis does not produce a single answer. The tighter the specification the smaller the range of allowable choices. The point of the method is to prune out the vast majority of systems that do not fit the performance specification, leaving a small range of HVAC system choices for the designer to investigate.

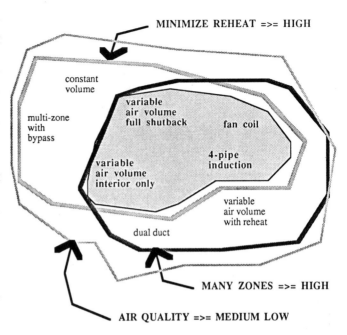

Figure 11.23 An example of HVAC delivery systems chosen by a performance specification that might apply to a university building where the campus architect insists that reheat not be used.

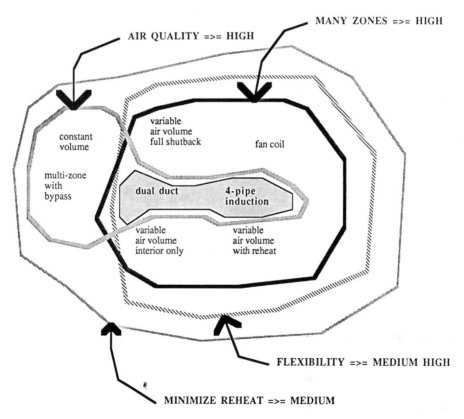

Figure 11.24 An example of HVAC delivery systems chosen by a performance specification that might apply to a biology research building where air quality control is very important.

PACKAGED VERSUS CUSTOM SYSTEMS

HVAC systems can be divided into four major parts. First, the boiler and chiller are used to create heat and cold for the system to use. Second, the cooling tower or air-cooled condenser has to be located outside the building somewhere to exhaust its heat to the outside. Third, the air handlers transfer the heat and cold to air that is to be blown into the building zones. Fourth, the ducts, control boxes, and diffusers deliver the conditioned air to the spaces.

Packaged Systems   In a packaged system the manufacturer puts everything but the ducts, control boxes, and diffusers together into a single piece of equipment that usually ends up being placed on the roof of a building (Fig. 11.25). These units come in sizes up to about 70 tons of cooling, which limits their use to building areas of about 20,000 square feet. Of course the designer could use multiple units to serve a larger building area.

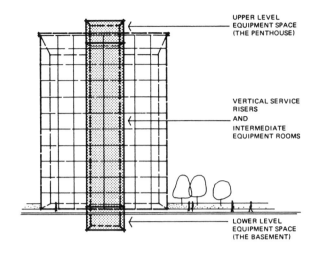

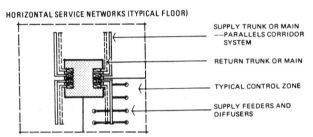

Figure 11.26 Typical plan of a custom HVAC system, which requires space for equipment inside the building.

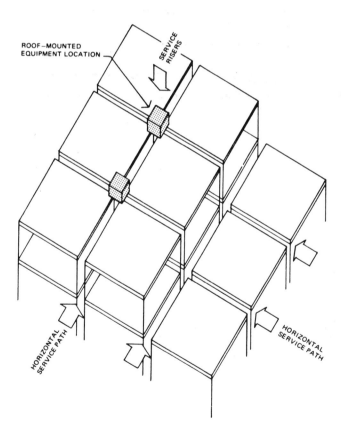

Figure 11.25 A packaged HVAC system. Such systems are most often mounted on the roof with ducts feeding down into the building.

A unit providing 5 to 10 tons of refrigeration serves 1,500 to 4,500 square feet of space with a single-zone constant-volume delivery system. The unit will be approximately 10 feet long, 7 feet wide, and 5 feet high. Four feet of service clearance all around is required.

A unit supplying 15 to 75 tons of refrigeration serves 4,500 to 22,500 square feet of space. More than one zone can be served with a variable air volume distribution system. The unit will be approximately 25 feet long, 9 feet wide, and 6 feet high. The service clearance requirement is 4 feet all around.

Custom Systems   Custom systems require that the designer reserve enough space in the building to house the boiler and chiller (the mechanical room), and the air handlers (the air handler room or rooms) (Fig. 11.26). In addition enough room must be reserved for a cooling tower somewhere outside the building.

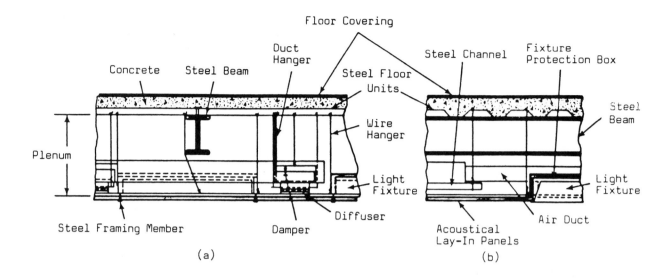

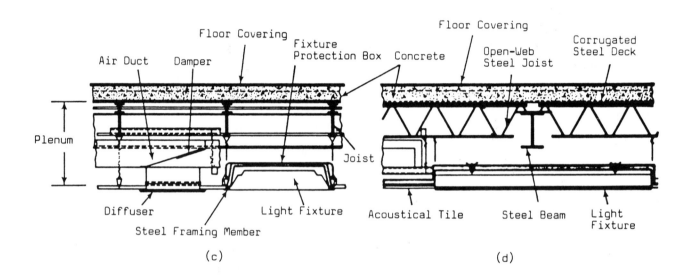

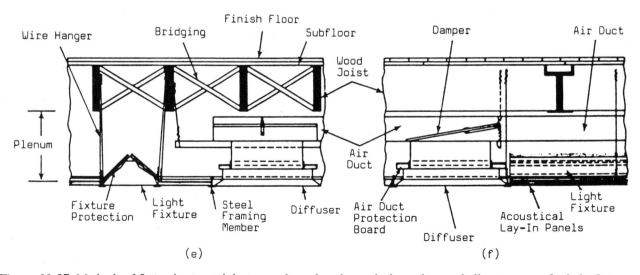

Figure 11.27 Methods of fitting horizontal duct runs through or beneath the ceiling and allowing room for light fixtures.

TALL BUILDINGS

In tall buildings the HVAC distribution system can become stretched through too long a distance. This problem can be dealt with by creating mechanical floors. Air handlers can move air up and down from a mechanical floor through 10 to 15 floors. Thus mechanical floors are spaced 20 to 30 floors apart. A decentralized chiller and boiler could be located on the intermediate mechanical floors serving the air handlers on that floor. (Remember that the boiler needs a flue for exhaust gases.)

An alternative to having mechanical floors is to place the chiller and boiler at the base or top of the building. One or more air handlers on each floor can distribute air. The hot and chilled water runs up and down the building feeding the air handlers. The air handlers will have to get fresh air through louvers located on every floor of the building.

The cooling tower needs to be located outside. In a crowded city environment this means the roof of the building.

HORIZONTAL DUCT RUNS

The duct distribution system must spread horizontally through the building. The main supply ducts are large and require strategic placement in order to fit between or through the structural system (Fig. 11.27).

Main ducts can be run above hallways where the ceiling can be lower thus providing more space for the ducts. Girders or beams may be slightly oversized to allow for penetration of ducts through the girder or beam. Main ducts can run parallel to the main structural members with the secondary distribution ducts running below or through the structure where necessary.

The following duct sizes will fit in the triangular openings left by open web steel joists:

8-inch joist depth: 4-inch diameter round duct
12-inch joist depth: 6-inch diameter round duct
18-inch joist depth: 10-inch diameter round duct
24-inch joist depth: 12-inch diameter round duct

In a high-rise building, minimizing ceiling cavity height is an important economic venture. Six inches of extra height at every floor of a 50-story building is 25 feet of extra material or two floors of lost rentable space.

The diffuser pattern needs to be coordinated with the light fixture pattern.

INCORPORATING THE HVAC SYSTEM INTO THE ABSTRACT MODEL

The HVAC partition discussed in Chapter 4 needs to be overlaid on the emerging design of the building. Figure 11.28 shows the blocked out building areas grouped according to HVAC needs. This provides the designer with a view of the design problem from the standpoint

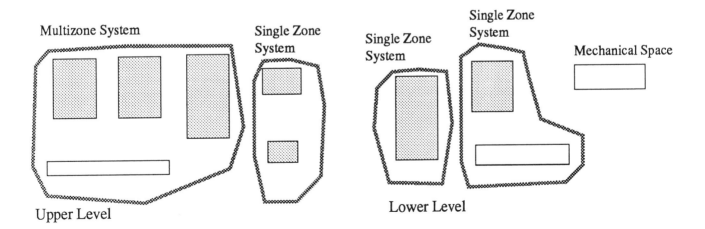

Figure 11.28 Building areas grouped according to HVAC system needs, with possible HVAC system types noted.

of the HVAC system needs. Each of these groupings will be served by a separate air handler and therefore the spaces included in a group should be located near each other in the design solution. In addition, as the spaces of the building are being blocked out, the location of the mechanical equipment room or rooms that hold the chiller, boiler, and air handlers should be located. Vertical duct chases should be located. The cooling tower can also be located. Figure 11.29 shows this blocking out of the major spaces needed by the HVAC system for the art museum project.

Figure 11.30 shows the strategic layout of the major duct runs located on the abstract model of a building floor plan. Adjustments will have to be made to the strategy as the design develops, but an overall framework has been laid down. The HVAC strategy can be compared with the structural strategy and any conflicts resolved before more detailed development takes place.

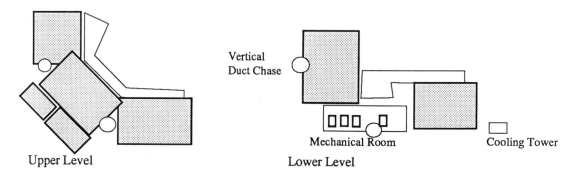

Figure 11.29 Sketching of the HVAC system over the abstract architectural layout. Block out the mechanical room or rooms, the vertical duct chases, and the cooling tower.

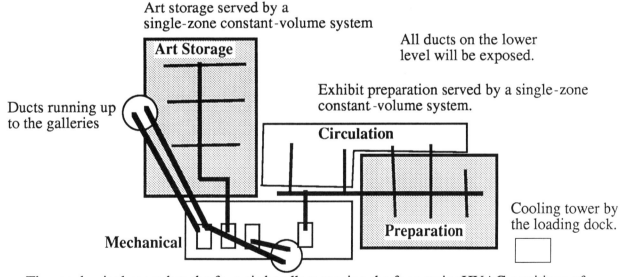

In the north gallery the ducts will run in a ceiling space hidden from view.

Gallery

The ducts in the central gallery will be exposed along with the steel bar joists that make up the high sloping ceiling.

Circulation

The circulation space will feed off the adjacent gallery system.

Restrooms

Gallery

In the restrooms and administrative areas the ducts will be hidden in a ceiling space.

Administration

Gallery

In the south gallery the ducts will be hidden in a ceiling space.

Upper Level HVAC Concept Diagram
Scale 1"= 60'

Art storage served by a single-zone constant-volume system

Art Storage

All ducts on the lower level will be exposed.

Exhibit preparation served by a single-zone constant-volume system.

Circulation

Ducts running up to the galleries

Cooling tower by the loading dock.

Preparation

Mechanical

The mechanical room has the four air handlers serving the four major HVAC partitions of the building. The chiller and boiler are in an extension of the same room.

Lower Level HVAC Concept Diagram
Scale 1"= 60'

Figure 11.30 Strategic layout of the major duct runs located on the abstract architectural layout.

12

The Lighting System

The design of the lighting system is often left to the end of the design process. This is a mistake. Our sensitivity to brightness makes the lighting system one of the most prominent features of a building. Whether it is a splash of daylight, display highlighting, or the grid of fluorescent lights illuminating an open office area, the brightness will attract attention. The architect needs to compose this brightness pattern along with other architectural design features for optimal effect. As with the other technical systems considered in this book, the intent in concept formation should be to sketch out a strategy and avoid getting lost in detail.

LIGHTING TERMINOLOGY

What we call light is a small segment of the electromagnetic radiation spectrum. Solar radiation is a mix of frequencies ranging from ultraviolet radiation through visible light to infrared radiation. The visible light from the sun is a mix of frequencies and appears white in color (Fig. 12.1). If the frequencies of visible light are separated they appear blue at the high-energy end of the spectrum ranging through green, yellow, and orange to red at the low-energy end of the spectrum. To render color well, a light source must have a complete range of frequencies.

Since our eyes are only sensitive to part of the solar

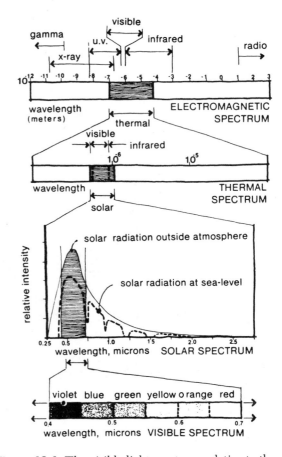

Figure 12.1 The visible light spectrum relative to the electromagnetic, thermal, and solar spectrums. Reproduced by permission from Moore (1985).

106

spectrum, the usual energy term, *watts*, cannot be used as a quantifier of visible light. The following concepts and terms are used to define the quantity of light and how it flows out of fixtures.

· Visible light flux is measured in lumens. It is related to the overall energy that the light source is using through the ratio lumens/watts, which is called efficacy.
· One lumen of light flux spread over one square foot of area illuminates that area to one footcandle. Footcan-

dles are the unit used to specify the amount of light necessary to see well enough to perform a task (Fig. 12.2).

· Light hitting a surface at an angle will illuminate the surface less than light hitting perpendicular to the surface. The cosine of the incident angle is used to make the correction.
· Electric light sources and light fixtures have their directional luminous intensity, in candelas, defined in a polar graph called a candlepower diagram. The candlepower diagram shows the light intensity com-

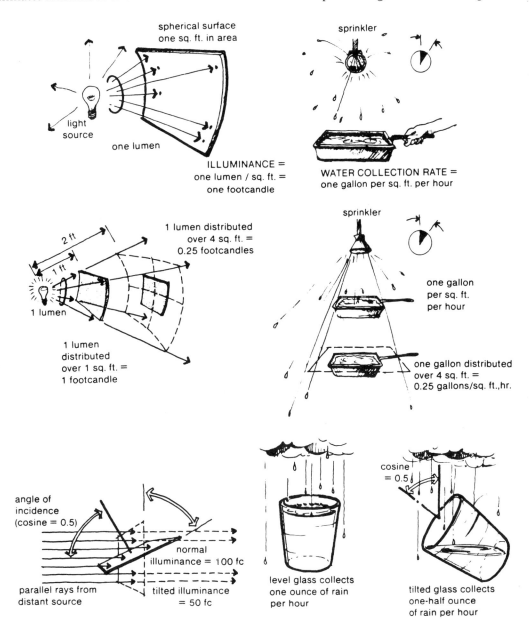

Figure 12.2 Calculations of illuminance (with their conceptual parallels in rainwater collection). Reproduced by permission from Moore (1985).

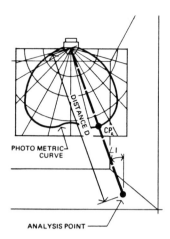

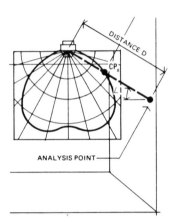

Figure 12.3 Candlepower diagrams for a downlight. Reproduced by permission from Flynn, Segil, and Steffy (1985).

ing out of the fixture as a function of direction. A downlight would only show candelas going down (Fig. 12.3). An uplight would only have them going up. A diffuse globe light would have candelas going in all directions. The relationship between the candlepower diagram and illumination at a point on a surface below the fixture is given by the following equation.

Footcandles = [(candelas)/(distance)^2] [cos(incident angle)]

· The lumens per square foot of light reflecting off a surface is called footlamberts of luminance or brightness. The relationship between the light striking a surface and the light reflected off a surface is the reflectance of the surface (Fig. 12.4).
· Reflected light can be specular or diffuse. The same is true for light transmitted through a material like glass.

DAYLIGHTING

Daylighting, even more than artificial lighting, needs to be considered early in the design process. It is the form of the building itself that will govern the quality of the daylighting. A useful conceptual approach to conceiving a daylighting scheme is to think in terms of

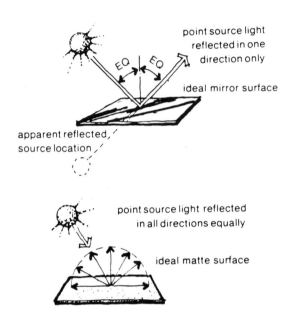

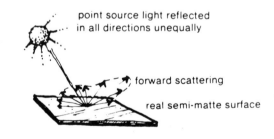

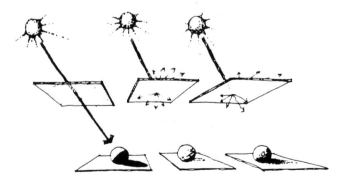

Figure 12.4 Reflected and transmitted light. Reproduced by permission from Moore (1985).

bouncing the daylight off interior surfaces onto the area to be illuminated (Moore 1985). Direct skylight and sunlight are almost always too bright to work under. After a daylighting scheme has been conceived, a physical model should be made that is large enough to allow observation of daylighting effects. If an artificial sky is not available for observing the model, the model should be examined out of doors.

Clear Skies   A clear sky is very bright around the position of the sun and relatively dark around a point 90 degrees away from the sun—a 10 to 1 variation in luminance. This variation and the movement of the bright spot make daylight calculations from a clear sky very difficult (Fig. 12.5).

The clear sky has a luminous efficacy of 150 lumens/watts. A clear blue northern sky has the following brightness values in footlamberts, which will produce an equivalent amount of illumination on a horizontal surface in footcandles (Flynn, Segil, and Steffy 1988):

Winter: 500 footcandles
Spring and fall: 800 footcandles
Summer: 1000 footcandles

Direct solar illumination in footcandles is:

Winter illumination at noon

On a horizontal surface: 3000 footcandles
Perpendicular to the sun's rays: 6500 footcandles

Spring and fall illumination at noon

On a horizontal surface: 6000 footcandles
Perpendicular to the sun's rays: 8000 footcandles

Summer illumination at noon

On a horizontal surface: 8000 footcandles
Perpendicular to the sun's rays: 9000 footcandles

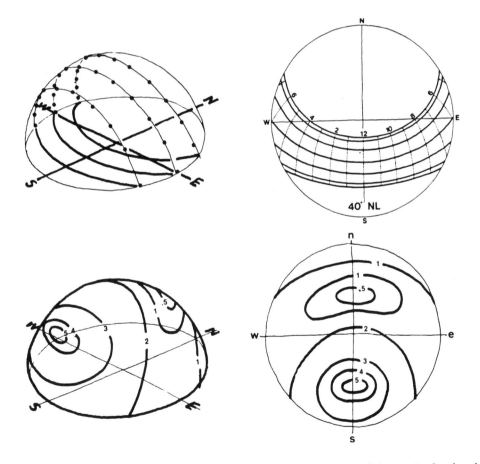

Figure 12.5 Clear sky brightness variation. The upper drawings show the position of the sun in the sky; the lower drawings show relative sky brightness. The figures on the left are 3-dimensional images of the sky dome; the figures on the right are projections of the sky dome onto a plane, as seen from above. Reproduced by permission from Moore (1985).

Overcast Skies   An overcast sky is three times as bright at the zenith as it is around the horizon. The clouds diffuse the solar illumination into a fairly even distribution around the sky dome and throughout the day. This even distribution makes straightforward daylight calculations possible because the illumination from all directions and through most of the day is a constant (Fig. 12.6). Determination of the daylight factor is based on an overcast sky.

An overcast sky has the following brightness values at noon in footlamberts, which will produce an equivalent amount of illumination on a horizontal surface in footcandles (Flynn, Segil, and Steffy 1988):

Winter: 1000 footlamberts
Spring and fall: 1800 footlamberts
Summer: 3000 footlamberts

The Daylight Factor   The daylight factor is a method of defining the quantity of daylight inside a building. The daylight factor is a fraction defined as the illumination in footcandles at a point inside a building divided by the illumination in footcandles outside the building under the open overcast sky. It is usually stated as a percent rather than a decimal fraction. The daylight factors for locations inside a building can be calculated if an overcast sky is assumed. However, it is easier to determine the daylight factor experimentally with a light meter and a model of the building. The model is placed outside under an overcast sky, and the light meter is used to measure the illumination from the unobstructed sky. The illumination is then measured at various points inside the model. The daylight factor for each point within the model is calculated as follows:

Daylight factor = (footcandles inside)/(footcandles outside)

(Daylight factors do not apply to clear sky conditions but they still can be used as an approximately correct quantification method.)

Building a Daylighting Concept   In a daylighting scheme that works by bouncing the light off interior surfaces toward the area to be illuminated, there are several elements to be considered. The amount of illumination that will arrive at the receiving point from the reflecting surface is affected by the amount of light entering, the size of the reflecting surface, the distance from the receiving point, and the tilt of the reflecting

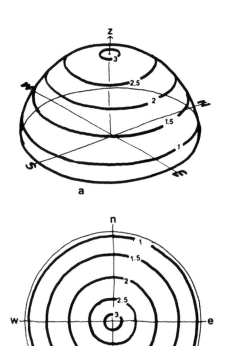

Figure 12.6 Overcast sky brightness variation. (a) A 3-dimensional image of the sky dome; (b) projection of the sky dome information onto a plane, as seen from above. Reproduced by permission from Moore (1985).

surface (Fig. 12.7). A good source of design inspiration for daylighting ideas is the work of Alvar Alto, who was a master of bouncing light off interior surfaces (Fig. 12.8).

Sky brightness values combined with the cosine effect of orientation can be used to estimate surface brightness levels. Building a study model is easier and produces more information, however, since the designer can view the results and make modifications to achieve his or her goals while letting the sun provide information for the calculations. In addition, viewing the daylight results provides qualitative information that calculations cannot.

The following list, adapted in part from *Daylight in Architecture* (Evans 1981), can be used as a guide to laying out a daylighting concept.

· Direct skylight and sunlight on critical task areas should be avoided.
· Direct skylight and sunlight should be used sparingly in noncritical areas.

- Daylight should be bounced off surrounding surfaces.
- Daylight should be brought in high and let down softly.
- Daylight can be filtered through drapes, screens, trees, and plants.
- North light should be used where soft, cool, uniform illumination is needed.
- South light should be allowed only where intense, warm, variable illumination is appropriate.
- Skylights and clerestories can be used to deliver light deep into the interior of a building.
- Daylight from one side of a room can cause a glare

problem. Daylight admitted from two or more sides will tend to balance the light in the room and thus control glare.
- Southern orientations are relatively easy to shield from direct solar penetrations with horizontal louvers or overhangs.
- Northern orientations will receive only minor direct solar penetration in the early morning and late afternoon in summer.
- Eastern and western orientations are almost impossible to protect from direct solar penetrations and at the same time provide a view out the window.

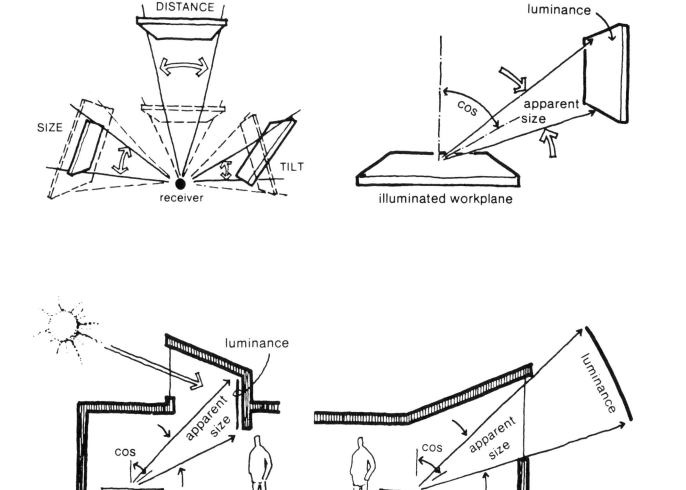

Figure 12.7 Interacting daylighted surfaces. Reproduced by permission from Moore (1985).

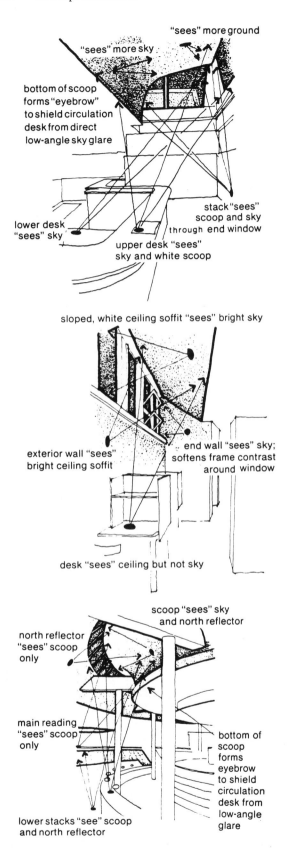

"sees" more ground

"sees" more sky

bottom of scoop
forms "eyebrow"
to shield circulation
desk from direct
low-angle sky glare

lower desk
"sees" sky

stack "sees"
scoop and sky
through end window

upper desk "sees"
sky and white scoop

sloped, white ceiling soffit "sees" bright sky

exterior wall "sees"
bright ceiling soffit

end wall "sees" sky;
softens frame contrast
around window

desk "sees" ceiling but not sky

scoop "sees" sky
and north reflector

north reflector
"sees" scoop
only

main reading
"sees" scoop
only

bottom of
scoop
forms
eyebrow
to shield
circulation
desk from
low-angle
glare

lower stacks "see" scoop
and north reflector

Figure 12.8 Examples of Alvar Alto's use of interacting day-lighted surfaces. Reproduced by permission from Moore (1985).

Using Sun Path Diagrams and Sundials   Sun path diagrams provide an analytic method for exploring the geometry of shading devices and window openings to provide controlled exposure to sky and sun (Figs. 12.9 and 12.10). A sundial for the appropriate latitude can be mounted on a study model and taken outside where the sun will do the shading calculations for you. The study model, which is not intended as a finished model, should be simply built and easily modified.

Sizing Window Areas for Daylighting   Daylighting is a pleasant amenity if there is not too much of it. Too much daylight can create glare and overheating problems. Daylight can be used to reduce the need for electric lighting, but too much daylight causes the air-conditioning load of the building to rise. The following list provides a useful guide to determining the approximate daylight aperture areas that will balance lighting and air-conditioning requirements.

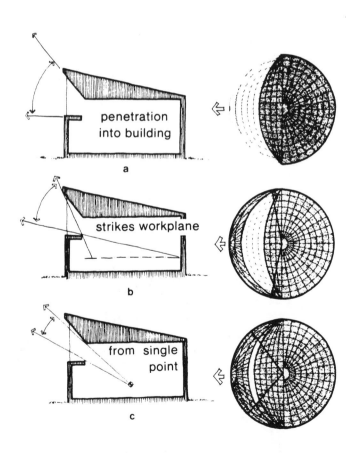

penetration
into building

a

strikes workplane

b

from single
point

c

Figure 12.9 Using the sun path diagram for daylight access. Reproduced by permission from Moore (1985).

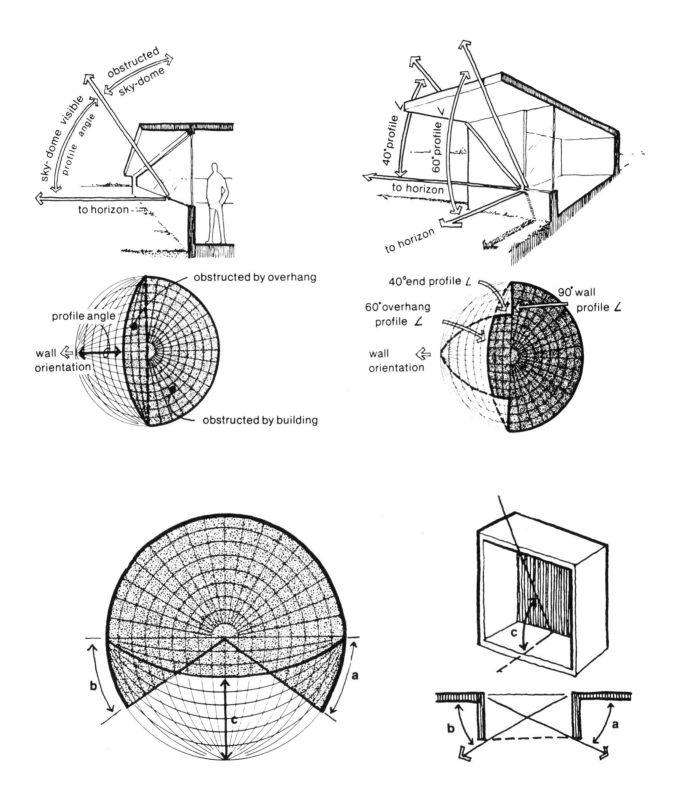

Figure 12.10 Using the sun path diagram for overhang design. Labels a, b, and c indicate how angles measured on a shading device are plotted on the sun path projection diagrams. Reproduced by permission from Moore (1985).

Sidelighting

Window openings: 25% of the floor area
Room depth: 2 times the window height

Toplighting

Window opening: 5% for skylights, 10% for
    clerestories
Spacing: 1.5 times the ceiling height

Examples of daylighting designs allowing no direct solar penetration are shown in Figures 12.11 and 12.12.

ARTIFICIAL LIGHTING

One helpful method of approaching lighting design is to think of lighting as information. Good lighting reinforces the message of the building. Bad lighting hides or destroys the message. The compositional components of the artificial lighting design problem are a combination of light source characteristics and lighting fixture characteristics. Light fixtures can provide even illumination over the working plane, illuminate wall surfaces, outline and reinforce architectural shapes, and highlight the architectural composition.

Light Source Characteristics Light sources can be divided into two major groups, incandescent and gaseous discharge. Incandescent lamps are inexpensive and easy to use but have limited lumen output per watt of energy. The gaseous discharge lamps are more expensive and difficult to use since they need a ballast, but they produce higher lumen output per watt of energy and last longer than incandescent lamps.

Incandescent Lamps. Incandescent light is produced by the incandesing (glowing) of an electric resistance element.

Normal voltage incandescent lamps produce a point source of light. The glowing filament is relatively small compared to the size of the light fixture. The light from an incandescent lamp is therefore easily focused by the fixture into a beam of light. Good color rendering results from a continuous frequency spectrum, but there is more energy in the warm (red) end of the spectrum. Incandescent lamps can be easily dimmed. Because the lumens of light produced per watt of energy are low (20–40 lumens/watt), operating costs are high. The purchase price is small and the life of the lamp relatively short. Incandescent lamps come in many shapes, but the most common shapes are the A, R, and PAR shapes shown in Figure 12.13.

Low-voltage incandescent lamps produce a very small point of intense brightness that can be focused

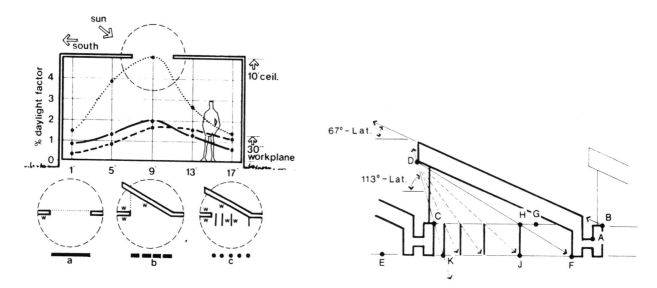

Figure 12.11 South-facing roof monitor design with no direct solar penetration. (a) Horizontal translucent skylight; (b) vertical translucent glazing; (c) clear glazing with diffusing baffles. Reproduced by permission from Moore (1985).

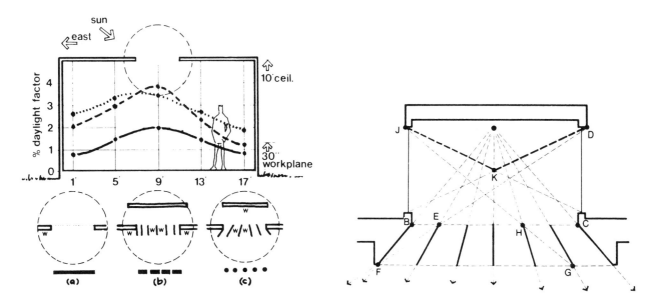

Figure 12.12 East-west-facing roof monitor with no direct solar penetration. (a) Horizontal translucent skylight; (b) clear glazing with vertical diffusing baffles; (c) clear glazing with sloping diffusing baffles. Reproduced by permission from Moore (1985).

The **A shape** is the standard incandescent lamp shape.

The **R shape** lamp incorporates a reflecting surface inside the lamp to produce a beam of light.

The **PAR shape** is constructed from two separate pieces. The parabolic reflector is formed and the incandescent filament is carefully placed at the focus of the parabola. Then the front lens in connected onto the lamp. This process produces a more precise beam of light than the R shape can produce.

Figure 12.13 Incandescent lamp shapes.

into a precise narrow beam of light. This type of lamp is useful in highlighting merchandise or art. Low-voltage incandescent lamps are either a PAR shape or are designed to fit in a parabolic reflector.

Gaseous Discharge Lamps. Gaseous discharge lamps produce light by passing electricity through a gas. The atoms of the gas are excited and give off radiant energy. In some cases the radiant energy needs to be modified by phosphors on the inside surface of the lamp to produce visible light and control the color rendering characteristics of the lamp.

Gaseous discharge lamps require a ballast to get the lamp started and then to control the current flowing through the lamp while it is on.

Fluorescent lamps produce a wide, linear, diffuse light source that is well suited to spreading light downward to the working surfaces of desks or displays in a commercial environment with normal ceiling heights (8 to 12 feet). The deluxe lamps have good color rendering characteristics and can be chosen to favor the cool (blue) or the warm (red) end of the spectrum. Dimmers for fluorescent lamps are expensive. Fluorescent lamps produce more light per watt of energy (50–80 lumens/ watt) than incandescent lamps; thus operating costs are low. The purchase price and length of life of fluorescent lamps are greater than for incandescent lamps and less than for high-intensity discharge lamps.

High-intensity discharge lamps (HID) produce a

glowing glob of gas—about the size of the end of your little finger—that can be focused into a fairly good beam of light. These lamps matched with an appropriate fixture are well suited to beaming light down to the working plane from a high ceiling. The color rendering from the high-pressure sodium (warm), and metal halide (cool) lamps is almost as good as the deluxe fluorescent lamps. Dimming HID lamps is difficult. The lamps are expensive but produce a lot of light and last a long time. High-pressure sodium produces 100 lumens/watt; metal halide produces 80 lumens/watt.

Low-pressure sodium lamps produce the most lumens per watt of energy used (150 lumens/watt), but they do not render color well since all the light is produced over a narrow frequency band. All colors appear as shades of gray. They are useful for parking lot and roadway lighting where color rendering is of minimal importance.

If there is an electric power interruption, HID lamps will go out and cannot come on again for about 10 minutes while they cool down. Therefore, in an installation of HID lamps, a few incandescent or fluorescent lamps are needed to provide backup lighting.

Light Fixture Characteristics The following discussion is intended to provide a conceptual bridge between a lighting vocabulary and the lighting fixtures that are necessary to implement the vocabulary. A useful beginning lighting vocabulary can be organized into four concepts:

1. Even illumination over a large horizontal working plane
2. Illumination of vertical wall surfaces
3. Outlining and reinforcing architectural shapes
4. Highlighting the composition

Even Illumination on the Working Plane. A large proportion of commercial interior space requires even illumination over the working plane of desk surfaces, workbenches, or sales counters. Even illumination is achieved by balancing a number of factors.

The first element to consider is the *spacing to mounting height ratio* (S/MH). This ratio is used to calculate the appropriate space between light fixtures. For fluorescent fixtures the ratio is about 1.5; for medium-beam downlights, about 0.8; and for narrow-beam downlights, about 0.5. (The manufacturer's literature will give exact ratios for their lighting fixtures.)

The mounting height is the height from the working plane (2.5 feet above the floor) to the level of the light fixtures. (The light fixtures are often on the ceiling but they can be mounted below the ceiling on pendants.) Proper spacing is then calculated as

$$\text{Spacing} = (\text{S/MH}) \times (\text{Mounting Height})$$

Wide-beam diffuse downlight is an important component in even illumination. In commercial interiors, it is produced very well by fluorescent lamp fixtures located on the ceiling with all their light directed downward. Fluorescent fixtures can also be hung slightly below the ceiling with a small amount of light directed upward providing some direct illumination of the ceiling. Both fixture types efficiently spread light down from the ceiling to the working plane and, if spaced correctly, create even illumination. This diffuse spreading of light works well for normal ceiling heights (8 to 12 feet). The fixtures will produce a repetitive two-dimensional pattern that becomes the most prominent feature of the ceiling plane.

Figure 12.14 shows a wide range of fluorescent fixture types. Figure 12.15 shows a high-end parabolic baffled recessed fluorescent fixture.

Table 12.1 can be used to quickly determine the number of fluorescent fixtures needed for a given workspace.

Medium-beam downlighting is produced with a fixture located in or on the ceiling that creates a beam of light directed downward. This form of lighting is used to achieve even illumination where the ceiling height is relatively high. The beamed light is effectively projected down onto the working plane by these fixtures. For large areas HID lamps are usually selected. (Figures 12.16 and 12.17 provide information about HID downlights.) In the circulation and lobby areas of a building, medium-beam downlight fixtures with incandescent lamps are often used to create a warmly lighted low-brightness environment. Figures 12.18 and 12.19 provide information about recessed downlights.

In both of these cases, because the light is in the form of a conical beam, scallops of light will be produced on wall surfaces where the grid of fixtures approaches the wall. The scallops should relate to the architectural rhythms of the wall.

Table 12.2 shows the areas illuminated by various types of downlighting lamps. Note how the compact flourescent downlights use considerably less energy than the incandescent downlights.

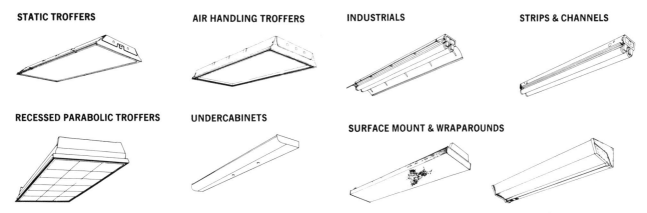

STATIC TROFFERS   **AIR HANDLING TROFFERS**   **INDUSTRIALS**   **STRIPS & CHANNELS**

RECESSED PARABOLIC TROFFERS   **UNDERCABINETS**   **SURFACE MOUNT & WRAPAROUNDS**

Figure 12.14 Fluorescent fixture types. Adapted with permission from *USI Lighting Catalogues*, © 1989, USI Lighting, 1251 Doolittle Drive, San Leandro, CA.

TABLE 12.1. Footcandles of illumination on the working plane from flourescent fixtures mounted in a 9-foot high ceiling

2′ × 4′, 3-Lamp Parabolume Fixtures, S/MH (across = 1.6, along = 1.2)						
			12 × 8			
Spacing[b]	8 × 8	10 × 8	12 × 8	offset[c]	10 × 10	12 × 10	12 × 12
Footcandles	108	88	74	74	71	60	51
Watts/sq. ft.	2.3	1.8	1.5	1.5	1.4	1.2	1.0

2′ × 4′, 2-Lamp Parabolume Fixtures, S/MH (across = 1.7, along = 1.2)					
				12 × 8	
Spacing[b]	10 × 6	8 × 8	10 × 8	12 × 8	offset[c]	10 × 10
Footcandles	81	75	60	50	50	49
Watts/sq. ft.	1.5	1.4	1.2	1.0	1.0	0.9

1′ × 4′, 1-Lamp Parabolume Fixtures, S/MH (across = 1.7, along = 1.2)			
Spacing[b]	5 × 5	8 × 4	10 × 4	12 × 4
Footcandles	96	75	60	50
Watts/sq. ft.	1.8	1.4	1.2	1.0

1′ × 4′, 2-Lamp Parabolume Fixtures, S/MH (across = 1.6, along = 1.2)				
		10 × 5			
Spacing[b]	10 × 5	offset[c]	8 × 8	9 × 8	10 × 8
Footcandles	87	86	68	61	55
Watts/sq. ft.	1.8	1.8	1.4	1.3	1.2

2′ × 2′, 2U-Lamp Parabolume Fixtures, S/MH (across = 1.3, along = 1.2)			
		10 × 5		
Spacing[b]	8 × 6	offset[c]	8 × 8	10 × 8
Footcandles	92	86	68	55
Watts/sq. ft.	1.9	1.8	1.4	1.2

[a]Assuming a large open room (60 by 60 feet). For a smaller room (30 by 30 feet) the illumination levels drop approximately 15%.
[b]The first number in the spacing definition is the distance in feet between rows of fixtures; the second number is the distance in feet between fixtures along a row. Both distances are from the centerline of the fixture.
[c]Offset refers to a checkerboard layout of fixtures.
S/MH, space-to-mounting-height ratio.

Parabolume

2'x4' 3-Lamp

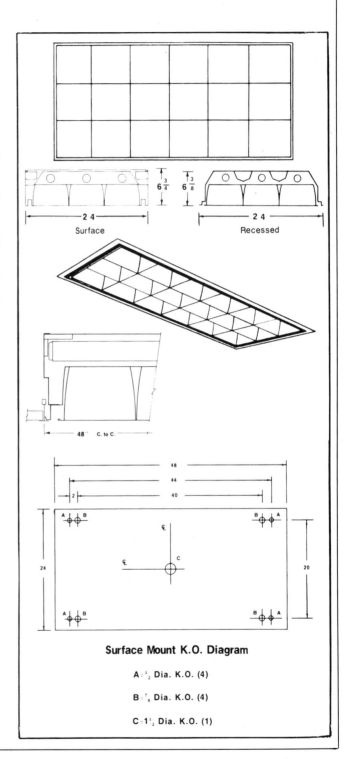

Description: Critical power consumption applications are particularly satisfied by this luminaire. The 3-lamp saves on both initial and re-lamping costs while maintaining footcandle levels comparable to 4-lamp lensed fixtures. Large cell, low brightness appearance is esthetically pleasing in all interiors. Provides a recognized balance of lifetime comfort, quality and economy.

Air Handling: All recessed models are available with U.L. labels as air supply units; air return units; with heat extract functions; or static. Heat Extract option (removing room air through lamp compartment) must be specified. Compatible air diffusers by Columbia, Anemostat, Barber Colman, Krueger, Titus or Tuttle & Bailey. For air supply information, see Columbia catalog Page 92-31.

Surface or Pendant Mount: Attractive surface mount luminaires - designed for compatibility with comparable recessed models - are also available as standard stock. Construction features completely enclosed steel housing finished in baked white enamel or custom finishes to meet your needs. These luminaires require only minimal maintenance and match the performance of recessed Parabolumes.

Average Maintained Footcandles Shown On Table Below Based On:

1. **Task Illumination:** Does not include non-work areas adjacent to walls.
2. **Reflectances:** .80 - .50 - .20
3. **Maintenance Factor:** .85
4. **Lamps:** Warm White (for CW. multply readings by .98)

Average Maintained Footcandles

Square foot area per luminaire	RCR										Watts Per Sq.Ft.
	1	2	3	4	5	6	7	8	9	10	
25	262	239	215	196	177	161	145	129	118	106	5.76
32	205	187	169	153	138	126	114	101	92	83	4.5
36	183	166	149	136	122	112	101	89	82	73	4.0
48	137	125	112	102	92	84	76	68	61	55	3.0
50	131	119	108	98	88	80	72	64	58	53	2.88
60	110	99	90	81	74	67	61	54	49	44	2.4
64	103	93	84	77	69	62	56	50	46	42	2.25
72	91	83	75	68	61	56	50	44	41		2.0
80	82	74	67	62	55	50	45	41			1.8

```
COEFFICIENTS OF UTILIZATION - ZONAL CAVITY METHOD

EFFECTIVE FLOOR CAVITY REFLECTANCE 0.20

RC        80              70              50          30
RW    70 50 30 10     70 50 30 10     50 30 10    50 30 10

 1    69 67 65 63     67 65 64 62     63 61 60    61 59 58
 2    64 61 58 55     63 60 57 54     58 55 53    56 54 52
 3    60 55 51 48     59 54 51 48     53 50 47    51 48 46
 4    56 50 46 42     55 49 45 42     48 44 42    46 43 41
 5    52 45 40 37     50 44 40 37     43 39 37    42 39 36
 6    48 41 36 33     47 40 36 33     39 35 32    38 35 32
 7    44 37 32 29     43 36 32 29     35 31 28    35 31 28
 8    41 33 28 25     40 33 28 25     32 28 25    31 27 25
 9    37 30 25 22     37 29 25 22     29 24 22    28 24 21
10    35 27 22 19     34 27 22 19     26 22 19    25 22 19
```

Surface Mount K.O. Diagram

A = ½ Dia. K.O. (4)

B = ⅞ Dia. K.O. (4)

C = 1½ Dia. K.O. (1)

Figure 12.15 Typical fluorescent fixture data. The 2" × 4", three-lamp fixture can be wired with two wall switches. One switch turns on the center lamp over the entire room. The other switch turns on the two outside lamps over the entire room. This arrangement provides three possible illumination levels evenly distributed over the room. Adapted with permission from *USI Lighting Catalogues,* © 1989, USI Lighting, 1251 Doolittle Drive, San Leandro, CA.

PRESCOLITE H.I.D. CYLINDERS
Featuring vandal resistance, wet location approval, and high efficiencies. For exterior or indoor use.

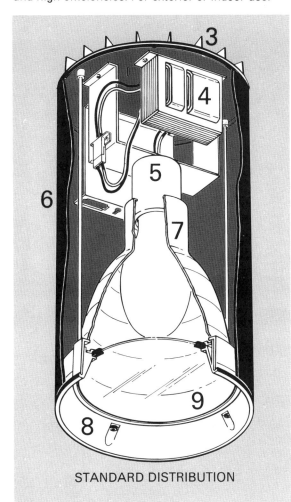

STANDARD DISTRIBUTION

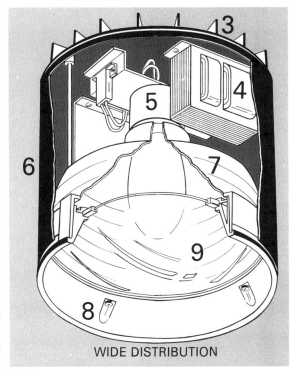

WIDE DISTRIBUTION

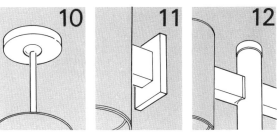

DESIGN FEATURES

1. **MOUNTING STRAP:** (not shown) 1½″ × 9/16″ steel channel w/½″ I.P. nipple

2. **CANOPY:** (not shown) .062 aluminum

3. **TOP:** Diecast aluminum with heat dissipating radial fins.

4. **BALLAST:** Integral and accessible through lamp compartment. Mercury Vapor and Metal Halide ballasts are high power factor (CWA) -20°F; High Pressure Sodium ballasts are high power factor—Lag -20°F. 120V, 208V, 240V, and 347V (Canada) are available —Specify.

5. **SOCKET:** Porcelain medium base for R-40 lamps; Mogul base for E and BT lamps. Nickel plated screw shell.

6. **HOUSING:** Heavy gauge, seamless aluminum with baked enamel finish. Diecast aluminum trim carrier clamped to top with (2) ¼″ internal tie rods.

7. **REFLECTOR:** Specular clear Alzak®

8. **TRIM FRAME:** Diecast aluminum, regressed, secured neatly to trim carrier by (4) vandal resistance hex socket screws. Torsion relamping springs provided.

9. **LENS:** Tempered 3/16″ (clear on R-40 units, stippled on Mogul lamp units, clear convex on wide distribution). Sealed by a molded EPDM high temperature rubber gasket and continuously clamped to the trim frame for vandal resistance.

10. **PENDANT MOUNT UNITS:** Supplied with a stem kit consisting of an 18″ × ½″ I.P. stem, 45° hang-straight, lockable swivel and canopy.

11. **WALL MOUNT UNITS:** Supplied with mounting plate and welded arm canopy assembly.

12. **ARM TO POLE UNITS:** Supplied with a 6½″ extruded aluminum arm and tie rods which adapt to Prescolite poles shown in the Prescolite Outdoor Catalog #P-5, pages, 38 & 39.

    U.L. Approved for wet locations.

Figure 12.16 Typical high-intensity discharge lamp cylindrical fixtures. The standard distribution fixture is good for high bay spaces where the light needs to be pushed down to the working plane. Adapted with permission from *USI Lighting Catalogues,* © 1989, USI Lighting, 1251 Doolittle Drive, San Leandro, CA.

Standard Distribution HID Cylinders
13″ Diameter

250W Clear Metal Halide E-28

	250W	175W
Ceiling Mount	HD13C07	HD13C06
Wall Mount	HD13W07	HD13W06
Pendant Mount	HD13P07	HD13P06
Arm to Pole Mount	HD13A07	HD13A06

SINGLE UNIT

BEAM ANGLE* **71°**

DIAMETER* LIGHTED	INITIAL FT-C
22′ - 1″	121
25′ - 0″	95
27′ - 10″	77
30′ - 8″	63
33′ - 6″	53

FIXTURE OPENING TO WORKPLANE

15′ - 6″	
17′ - 6″	
19′ - 6″	
21′ - 6″	
23′ - 6″	

MULTIPLE INSTALLATION

AVERAGE INITIAL FOOTCANDLES†

MAXIMUM SPACING (FEET)	ROOM CAVITY RATIO		
	1	5	9
9′- 9″	181	150	127
11′- 0″	142	118	100
12′- 3″	114	95	80
13′- 7″	94	78	66
14′-10″	79	65	55

*BEAM ANGLE & DIA TO 10% MAX C P   †FOOTCANDLES BASED ON 80/50/20 REFLECTANCE

250W CLEAR M.H., BT-28   RATED LUMENS - 20500   LUMINAIRE SPACING CRITERION — .63
For 175W Clear M.H., BT-28 multiply FT-C and C.P. values by .68

CANDLEPOWER DISTRIBUTION

250W

3000	85°
6000	75°
9000	65°
12000	55°
15000	
18000	45°
21000	
24000	35°
27000	
30000	5° 15° 25°

COEFFICIENTS OF UTILIZATION Zonal Cavity Method

ROOM CAVITY RATIO	% EFFECTIVE CEILING CAVITY REFLECTANCE														
	80%			70%			50%			30%			10%		
	20% EFFECTIVE FLOOR CAVITY REFLECTANCE														
	% WALL REFLECTANCE														
	70	50	30	10	70	50	30	10	50	30	10	50	30	10	50 30 10
1	.85	.84	.82	.81	.84	.82	.81	.80	.79	.78	.77	.76	.76	.75	.74 .73 .73
2	.82	.80	.77	.75	.81	.78	.76	.75	.76	.74	.73	.74	.73	.71	.72 .71 .70
3	.80	.76	.73	.71	.78	.75	.73	.71	.73	.71	.70	.72	.70	.69	.70 .69 .68
4	.77	.73	.70	.68	.76	.72	.69	.67	.71	.68	.66	.69	.67	.66	.68 .66 .65
5	.74	.70	.67	.64	.73	.69	.66	.64	.68	.65	.63	.67	.65	.63	.66 .64 .62
6	.72	.67	.64	.62	.71	.67	.64	.61	.66	.63	.61	.65	.62	.61	.64 .62 .60
7	.69	.64	.61	.59	.69	.64	.61	.59	.63	.60	.58	.62	.60	.58	.62 .59 .58
8	.67	.62	.59	.56	.66	.61	.58	.56	.61	.58	.56	.60	.58	.56	.59 .57 .55
9	.65	.59	.56	.54	.64	.59	.56	.54	.58	.56	.54	.58	.55	.53	.57 .55 .53
10	.63	.57	.54	.52	.62	.57	.54	.52	.56	.54	.52	.56	.53	.51	.56 .53 .51

TEST NO. - B1318D

250W Coated Metal Halide E-28

	250W	175W
Ceiling Mount	HD13C07	HD13C06
Wall Mount	HD13W07	HD13W06
Pendant Mount	HD13P07	HD13P06
Arm to Pole Mount	HD13A07	HD13A06

SINGLE UNIT

BEAM ANGLE* **103°**

DIAMETER* LIGHTED	INITIAL FT-C
23′ - 11″	111
28′ - 11″	76
33′ - 11″	55
39′ - 0″	42
44′ - 0″	33

FIXTURE OPENING TO WORKPLANE

9′ - 6″	
11′ - 6″	
13′ - 6″	
15′ - 6″	
17′ - 6″	

MULTIPLE INSTALLATION

AVERAGE INITIAL FOOTCANDLES†

MAXIMUM SPACING (FEET)	ROOM CAVITY RATIO		
	1	5	9
10′-1″	152	119	95
12′-2″	103	81	65
14′-4″	75	59	47
16′-5″	57	45	36
18′-7″	45	35	28

*BEAM ANGLE & DIA TO 10% MAX C P   †FOOTCANDLES BASED ON 80/50/20 REFLECTANCE

250W METAL HALIDE, BT-28 COATED   RATED LUMENS - 20500   LUMINAIRE SPACING CRITERION — 1.06
For 175W Coated M.H., BT-28 multiply FT-C and C.P. values by .68

CANDLEPOWER DISTRIBUTION

250W

1500	85°
3000	75°
4500	65°
6000	55°
7500	
9000	45°
10500	
12000	35°
13500	
15000	5° 15° 25°

COEFFICIENTS OF UTILIZATION Zonal Cavity Method

ROOM CAVITY RATIO	% EFFECTIVE CEILING CAVITY REFLECTANCE														
	80%			70%			50%			30%			10%		
	20% EFFECTIVE FLOOR CAVITY REFLECTANCE														
	% WALL REFLECTANCE														
	70	50	30	10	70	50	30	10	50	30	10	50	30	10	50 30 10
1	.76	.75	.73	.72	.75	.73	.72	.71	.71	.69	.68	.68	.67	.66	.66 .65 .64
2	.73	.70	.68	.66	.72	.69	.77	.65	.67	.65	.64	.65	.64	.62	.63 .62 .61
3	.70	.66	.64	.61	.69	.66	.63	.61	.64	.62	.60	.62	.61	.59	.61 .59 .58
4	.67	.63	.59	.57	.66	.62	.59	.57	.60	.58	.56	.59	.57	.55	.58 .56 .55
5	.64	.59	.56	.53	.63	.58	.55	.53	.57	.55	.52	.56	.54	.52	.55 .53 .52
6	.61	.56	.52	.50	.60	.55	.52	.50	.55	.52	.49	.54	.51	.49	.53 .50 .49
7	.59	.53	.49	.47	.58	.53	.49	.47	.52	.49	.46	.51	.48	.46	.50 .48 .46
8	.56	.50	.46	.44	.55	.49	.46	.44	.49	.46	.44	.48	.45	.43	.48 .45 .43
9	.53	.47	.43	.41	.52	.47	.43	.41	.46	.43	.41	.45	.42	.40	.45 .42 .40
10	.49	.42	.38	.36	.48	.42	.38	.36	.41	.38	.35	.41	.38	.35	.40 .37 .35

TEST NO. - B1318B

Figure 12.17 Illumination data for 13-inch-diameter standard distribution HID cylinders. Adapted with permission from *USI Lighting Catalogues,* © 1989 USI Lighting, 1251 Doolittle Drive, San Leandro, CA.

Incandescent

Available with a varied selection of narrow trims and wide trims which provide maximum finish opening coverage. Available in matte white, satin aluminum, satin brass, and polished brass finishes (as noted).

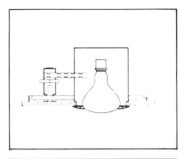

Incandescent. . .
High Performance

Specular Alzak® reflectors provide precise, highly efficient illumination.

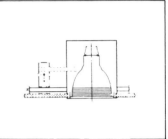

Compact Fluorescent

Uses high efficacy, long life, delux color compact fluoresent lamps.

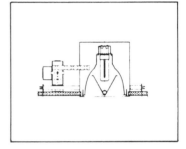

Low Voltage

Patented transformer module converts standard housing to low voltage for use with either MR-16 or PAR-36 lamps. Small aperture trims for MR-16 lamps also available.

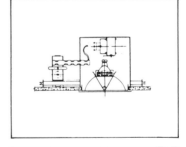

H.I.D.

Economy and off-the-shelf availability. Shallow housing (7½" depth) enables use in 2 x 8" construction. Encased and potted ballast ensures extended ballast life and quiet operation.

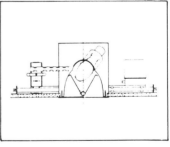

Figure 12.18 Recessed downlight fixture types. Adapted with permission from *USI Lighting Catalogues,* © 1989, USI Lighting, 1251 Doolittle Drive, San Leandro, CA.

Open Fixed

Clear Alzak Reflector
Champagne Gold Alzak
Reflector
Black Alzak Reflector

Baffle

Black Diecast
Milligroove Baffle

Figure 12.19 Open recessed downlights come with clear aluminum reflectors and with black milligroove baffles. The aluminum reflector type emits approximately 30 percent more light than the black baffle type. Adapted with permission from *USI Lighting Catalogues*, © 1989, USI Lighting, 1251 Doolittle Drive, San Leandro, CA.

Uplighting is also used to promote even illumination. It is produced by fixtures that direct their light up to the ceiling. The light reflects back into the room in a very diffuse, shadowless fashion. The fixtures can be pendant types hung from the ceiling or can be located on a furniture or building feature. Where the intent is to produce even, shadowless light over large areas, the fixtures will use fluorescent or HID lamps. Fluorescent fixtures tend to be long tubular forms; HID fixtures tend to be round or square forms. Figure 12.20 shows a fluorescent fixture providing half uplighting and half direct lighting.

Illumination of Vertical Wall Surfaces. Illuminating wall surfaces produces the impression of a well-lighted interior since our vision is usually directed perpendicular to the walls. Bright wall surfaces give a sense of definition to a lighted space and also offer a means of organizing the flow of attention within it.

TABLE 12.2.   Square feet per open downlight luminaire[a]

				Initial Footcandles			
	S/MH	10	20	30	40	50	60
Incandescent lamps							
100-watt A-19 lamp	1.1	130	66	44	32	25	21
Watts/sq. ft.		0.8	1.5	2.3	3.1	4.0	4.8
150-watt A-21 lamp	1.2	225	115	75	55	45	38
Watts/sq. ft.		0.7	1.3	2.0	2.7	3.3	3.9
300-watt PS-25 lamp	1.3	500	250	170	130	100	85
Watts/sq. ft.		0.6	1.2	1.8	2.7	3.0	3.5
Compact flourescent lamps							
18-watt lamp	1.4	90	45	30	23	18	15
Watts/sq. ft.		0.2	0.4	0.6	0.8	1.0	1.2
26-watt lamp	1.4	151	76	50	38	30	25
Watts/sq. ft.		0.2	0.3	0.5	0.7	0.9	1.1
Two 18-watt lamps	1.4	168	84	56	42	34	28
Watts/sq. ft.		0.2	0.4	0.6	0.9	1.1	1.3
Two 26-watt lamps	1.4	227	113	76	57	45	38
Watts/sq. ft.		0.2	0.5	0.7	0.9	1.2	1.4
High-pressure sodium lamps							
70-watt lamp	0.9	356	178	119	89	71	59
Watts/sq. ft.		0.2	0.4	0.6	0.8	1.0	1.2

[a]Assuming a room cavity ratio between 1 and 2, and a clear aluminum reflector. If a black multigroove baffle is used the area per fixture needs to be reduced by approximately 30%.
S/MH, spacing-to-mounting-height ratio.

Pendalume/ Pendacurve

Description: Pendalume/Pendacurve is an innovative suspended lighting system that maximizes luminaire efficiency. The indirect lighting reflects in a wide pattern reducing overall ceiling contrast associated with most purely indirect systems. Pendalume features the crisp straight lines of extruded aluminum, while the Pendacurve has soft rounded extruded sides. Trim profile, low brightness Parabolume louvers and variable patterns; make Pendalume/Pendacurve the ideal fluorescent luminaires for retrofit or new construction.

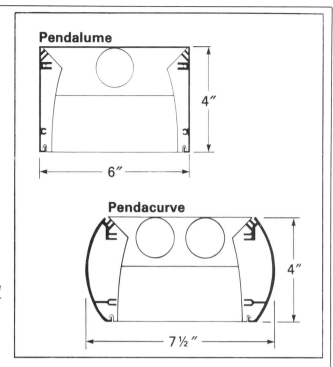

Pendalume

4″

6″

Pendacurve

4″

7 ½ ″

T12 Lamps

Pendalume/Pendacurve 1-Lamp

Cat. No:	PDP1-43-411
	and PCP1-43-411
Test No:	LSI 4616
Date:	4/1/85
Eff:	88.1
S/MH Ratio:	1.9

Zonal Summary

Zone	Lumens	Lamp	Fixt.
0- 30	311	9.7	11.0
0- 40	582	18.2	20.7
0- 60	1080	33.8	38.3
0- 90	1163	36.4	41.3
40- 90	581	18.2	20.6
60- 90	83	2.6	3.0
90-180	1655	51.7	58.7
0-180	2819	88.1	100.0

Coefficients of Utilization

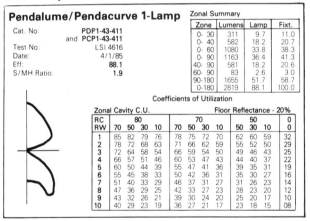

Zonal Cavity C.U.   Floor Reflectance - 20%

RC	80				70				50			0
RW	70	50	30	10	70	50	30	10	50	30	10	0
1	85	82	79	76	78	75	72	70	62	60	59	32
2	78	72	68	63	71	66	62	59	55	52	50	29
3	72	64	58	54	66	59	54	50	49	46	43	25
4	66	57	51	46	60	53	47	43	44	40	37	22
5	60	50	44	39	55	47	41	36	39	35	31	19
6	55	45	38	33	50	42	36	31	35	30	27	16
7	51	40	33	29	46	37	31	27	31	26	23	14
8	47	36	29	25	42	33	27	23	28	23	20	12
9	43	32	26	21	39	30	24	20	25	20	17	10
10	40	29	23	19	36	27	21	17	23	18	15	08

Pendalume/Pendacurve 2-Lamp

Cat. No:	PDP1-43-421
	and PCP1-43-421
Test No:	LSI 4617
Date:	4/1/85
Eff:	85.2
S/MH Ratio:	1.7

Zonal Summary

Zone	Lumens	Lamp	Fixt.
0- 30	724	11.3	13.3
0- 40	1215	19.0	22.3
0- 60	2082	32.5	38.2
0- 90	2208	34.5	40.5
40- 90	993	15.5	18.2
60- 90	126	2.0	2.3
90-180	3244	50.7	59.5
0-180	5453	85.2	100.0

Coefficients of Utilization

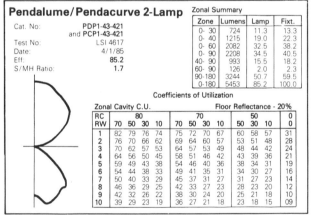

Zonal Cavity C.U.   Floor Reflectance - 20%

RC	80				70				50			0
RW	70	50	30	10	70	50	30	10	50	30	10	0
1	82	79	76	74	75	72	70	67	60	58	57	31
2	76	70	66	62	69	64	60	57	53	51	48	28
3	70	62	57	53	64	57	53	49	48	44	42	24
4	64	56	50	45	58	51	46	42	43	39	36	21
5	59	49	43	38	54	46	40	36	38	34	31	19
6	54	44	38	33	49	41	35	31	34	30	27	16
7	50	40	33	29	45	37	31	27	31	27	23	14
8	46	36	29	25	42	33	27	23	28	23	20	12
9	42	32	26	22	38	30	24	20	25	21	18	10
10	39	29	23	19	36	27	21	18	23	18	15	09

T8 Lamps

Pendalume/Pendacurve 1-Lamp

Cat. No:	T8 PDP1-42-414
	and T8 PCP1-42-414
Test No:	LSI 4618
Date:	3/27/85
Eff:	89.0
S/MH Ratio:	2.1

Zonal Summary

Zone	Lumens	Lamp	Fixt.
0- 30	255	8.8	9.9
0- 40	518	17.9	20.1
0- 60	1042	35.9	40.4
0- 90	1095	37.8	42.4
40- 90	576	19.9	22.3
60- 90	52	1.8	2.1
90-180	1486	51.3	57.6
0-180	2581	89.0	100.0

Coefficients of Utilization

Zonal Cavity C.U.   Floor Reflectance - 20%

RC	80				70				50			0
RW	70	50	30	10	70	50	30	10	50	30	10	0
1	87	83	80	77	79	76	74	71	63	61	60	34
2	79	74	69	64	73	68	63	60	56	53	51	30
3	73	65	59	55	67	60	55	51	50	47	44	26
4	67	58	51	46	61	53	48	43	45	41	37	23
5	61	51	44	39	56	47	41	37	40	35	32	19
6	56	46	39	34	51	42	36	32	35	31	27	17
7	51	41	34	29	47	37	31	27	32	27	23	14
8	47	36	29	25	43	33	27	23	28	23	20	12
9	43	32	25	21	39	30	24	20	25	20	17	10
10	40	29	22	18	36	27	21	17	22	18	15	08

Pendalume/Pendacurve 2-Lamp

Cat. No.	T8 PDP1-42-424
	and T8 PCP1-42-424
Test No:	LSI 4619
Date:	3/27/85
Eff:	86.3
S/MH Ratio:	2.1

Zonal Summary

Zone	Lumens	Lamp	Fixt.
0- 30	649	11.2	13.0
0- 40	1117	19.3	22.3
0- 60	2046	35.3	40.9
0- 90	2131	36.8	42.6
40- 90	1014	17.5	20.3
60- 90	84	1.5	1.7
90-180	2871	49.5	57.4
0-180	5002	86.3	100.0

Coefficients of Utilization

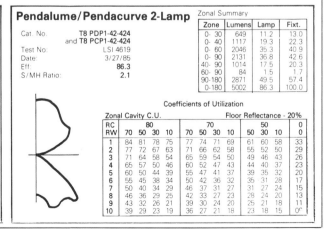

Zonal Cavity C.U.   Floor Reflectance - 20%

RC	80				70				50			0
RW	70	50	30	10	70	50	30	10	50	30	10	0
1	84	81	78	75	77	74	71	69	61	60	58	33
2	77	72	67	63	71	66	62	58	55	52	50	29
3	71	64	58	54	65	59	54	50	49	46	43	26
4	65	57	50	46	60	52	47	43	44	40	37	23
5	60	50	44	39	55	47	41	37	39	35	32	20
6	55	45	38	34	50	42	36	32	35	31	27	17
7	50	40	34	29	46	37	31	27	31	27	24	15
8	46	36	29	25	42	33	27	23	28	24	20	13
9	43	32	26	21	39	30	24	20	25	21	18	11
10	39	29	23	19	36	27	21	18	23	18	15	0*

Figure 12.20 Typical pendant-mounted direct-indirect fluorescent fixture. Adapted with permission from *USI Lighting Catalogues,* © 1989, USI Lighting, 1251 Doolittle Drive, San Leandro, CA.

Wallwashing illuminates the entire surface of a wall with an even amount of light that hides the texture of the wall. The bright wall creates a strong directional one-sided focus. The lamp type is often incandescent or HID because the light beam can be controlled; however, fluorescent lamps can also be used. Figure 12.21 provides information on placement and illumination produced by an incandescent wall wash figure; note that the fixtures are mounted 3 feet out from the wall. Figure 12.22 provides information on a fluorescent wall wash fixture.

Grazing directs light downward along a wall surface.

Figure 12.21 Typical incandescent recessed wall wash fixture. This type of wall wash fixture is also available with compact fluorescent lamps and HID lamps. Adapted with permission from *USI Lighting Catalogues*, © 1989, USI Lighting, 1251 Doolittle Drive, San Leandro, CA.

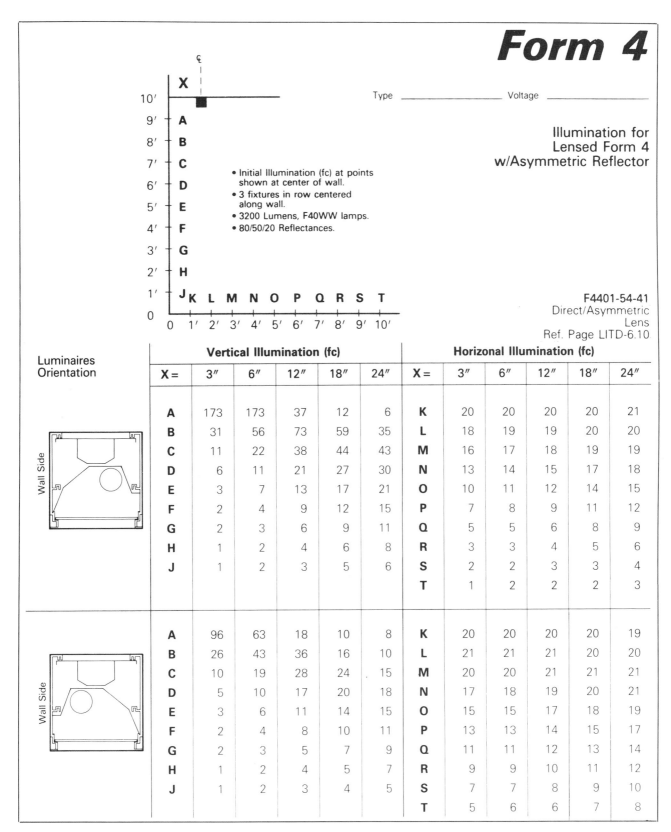

Form 4

Type _____ Voltage _____

Illumination for Lensed Form 4 w/Asymmetric Reflector

- Initial Illumination (fc) at points shown at center of wall.
- 3 fixtures in row centered along wall.
- 3200 Lumens, F40WW lamps.
- 80/50/20 Reflectances.

F4401-54-41
Direct/Asymmetric
Lens
Ref. Page LITD-6.10

Luminaires Orientation	Vertical Illumination (fc)					Horizonal Illumination (fc)					
	X =	3″	6″	12″	18″	24″	X =	3″	6″	12″	18″	24″
	A	173	173	37	12	6	K	20	20	20	20	21
	B	31	56	73	59	35	L	18	19	19	20	20
	C	11	22	38	44	43	M	16	17	18	19	19
	D	6	11	21	27	30	N	13	14	15	17	18
	E	3	7	13	17	21	O	10	11	12	14	15
	F	2	4	9	12	15	P	7	8	9	11	12
	G	2	3	6	9	11	Q	5	5	6	8	9
	H	1	2	4	6	8	R	3	3	4	5	6
	J	1	2	3	5	6	S	2	2	3	3	4
							T	1	2	2	2	3
	A	96	63	18	10	8	K	20	20	20	20	19
	B	26	43	36	16	10	L	21	21	21	20	20
	C	10	19	28	24	15	M	20	20	21	21	21
	D	5	10	17	20	18	N	17	18	19	20	21
	E	3	6	11	14	15	O	15	15	17	18	19
	F	2	4	8	10	11	P	13	13	14	15	17
	G	2	3	5	7	9	Q	11	11	12	13	14
	H	1	2	4	5	7	R	9	9	10	11	12
	J	1	2	3	4	5	S	7	7	8	9	10
							T	5	6	6	7	8

Figure 12.22 Illumination data for a fluorescent wall wash fixture. This fixture can be mounted out from the wall to produce even illumination over the surface of the wall. Adapted with permission from *USI Lighting Catalogues*, © 1989, USI Lighting, 1251 Doolittle Drive, San Leandro, CA.

This produces scallops of light that march along the wall and emphasizes the texture of the wall through shadows. Like wallwashing, grazing can create a large bright vertical surface, bringing attention to the one illuminated wall over the others in the space. A rhythm is set up by the scallops of light that form on a grazed wall. The fixtures are mounted close to the wall and aimed straight down so the scallop beam will intersect the wall. Figure 12.23 provides information on placement and illumination levels for a fluorescent wall grazing fixture; note how the fixture is mounted right at the wall surface.

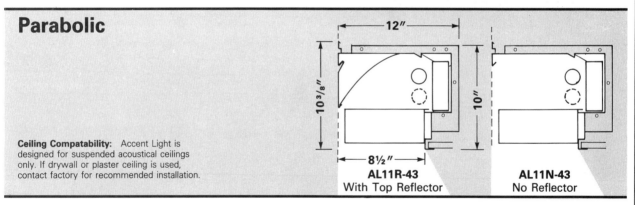

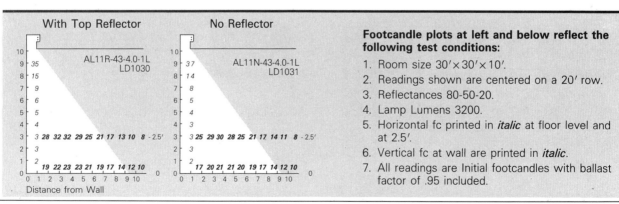

Figure 12.23 Information on a fluorescent accent light fixture. The fixture grazes the wall with light and is brighter at the top. Adapted with permission from *USI Lighting Catalogues*, © 1989, USI Lighting, 1251 Doolittle Drive, San Leandro, CA.

Outlining and Reinforcing of Architectural Shapes. The lines of the architecture can be emphasized by light to bring out the aesthetic intent of the shapes used. These lines and planes of light can direct attention and create a layered order in a space through the use of structural lighting and neon lamps.

Designer fixtures are specialty fixtures that are intended to help the architect create aesthetically coordinated interiors. They are predominantly linear in form and come in recessed and pendant mounted types. Arranged in long continuous lines they guide the eye and emphasize the depth of an area. Arranged in patterns they can complement or stand against other architectural features. Arranged across an area they create a progression. A variety of light distributions is available, from direct through direct-indirect to indirect light. Figures 12.24 and 12.25 are examples of pendant mounted linear fluorescent fixture forms. Figures 12.26 and 12.27 are examples of recessed linear fluorescent fixture forms. Figure 12.28 is an example of a luminous ceiling creating a planer shape.

Structural lighting is a term used for light fixtures hidden behind building features like cornices. This reinforces the lines of the architecture while providing soft ambient illumination. All types of lamps can be used. Incandescent and HID lamps will produce a rhythmic effect because of the point light source, while fluorescent fixtures will produce a more even line of light. Figure 12.29 provides information on staggered fluorescent light strips. Staggering the strips provides a continuous light source effect. The lamps need to be mounted below the ceiling at a distance approximately equal to ⅙ the span of the ceiling to be lighted. They should also be shielded from the view of people in the room. Only the indirect lighting effect should be seen.

Neon lamps can be used to produce long, unbroken low-illumination lines of light to reinforce architectural form. The ambient spill light from this form of lighting is very small. Neon lamps are also referred to as cold cathode fluorescent lamps.

Highlighting the Composition. Most interiors require some form of even illumination to provide light for the task that is being performed there. The lighting system, however, should go beyond purely functional illumination and provide diverse visual interest. Methods of highlighting include spotlighting, the use of sconces, and "sparkle."

Spotlighting produces a spot of relatively bright illumination that is often used to draw attention to paintings, directional signs, interesting wall or ceiling features, free-standing sculpture, or other design features that should stand out from the general background. It can also produce enough reflected light for ambient circulation needs, for example, in a hallway used as a picture gallery. Most spotlighting uses incandescent lamps. Low-voltage incandescent lamps can be used where precise control of the light beam is desirable. Spotlight fixtures come in a variety of sizes and shapes and are often mounted on a track for flexibility of placement. Figure 12.30 shows some of the styles of spotlight that are available. Figure 12.31 provides beam spread and illumination levels at various aiming angles for a range of incandescent PAR lamps; Figure 12.32 shows the use of recessed low-voltage incandescent lamps; and Figures 12.33 and 12.34 provide beam spread and illumination information for a range of low-voltage MR and PAR lamps.

Sconces are wall-mounted fixtures that produce a pool of light on the surface on which they are mounted. The lamp type is incandescent or compact flourescent. The light can be thrown up, up and down, or down only. This form of lighting is very good for reinforcing the rhythm of the architectural design. Sconces are often used along circulation areas where even illumination is unnecessary or monotonous.

Sparkle is a means of using light to produce small bits of pleasing brightness. This effect is usually achieved with low-brightness exposed filament incandescent lamps and is used sparingly.

Composing the Lighting Plan A *lighting plan* is an overlay drawing done on top of the architectural floor plan showing the location of the light fixtures on the ceiling above (Fig. 12.35, on p. 139). It should also give some indication of how the light fixtures are switched. Exploring the lighting design can also take the form of a one-point interior perspective with the light fixtures located in dark bold pen strokes so they stand out in the drawing. Because of their brightness, light fixtures will attract attention. The patterns the fixtures create, whether intended or not, will be a dominant feature of the interior layout.

One very important feature to consider is the interaction between the light fixture pattern and the HVAC system diffuser pattern. They are governed by different principles and will clash with each other unless the designer takes command of the situation. There are two effective approaches. The first is to coordinate light fixtures with diffusers to create a single pattern of units.

Supertube 6

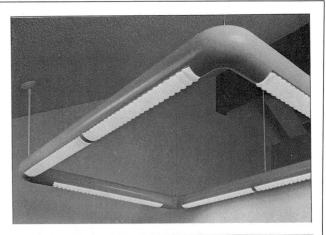

Description

Supertube 6 is an extruded aluminum luminaire designed to use long-life fluorescent lamps. It is designed for use in commercial and institutional interiors with numerous options to extend its flexiblity in room applications. A wide spectrum of color options will complement any traditional architectural styling.

Each fixture may be installed in the direct or indirect lighting positon without on-site modification to the fixture.

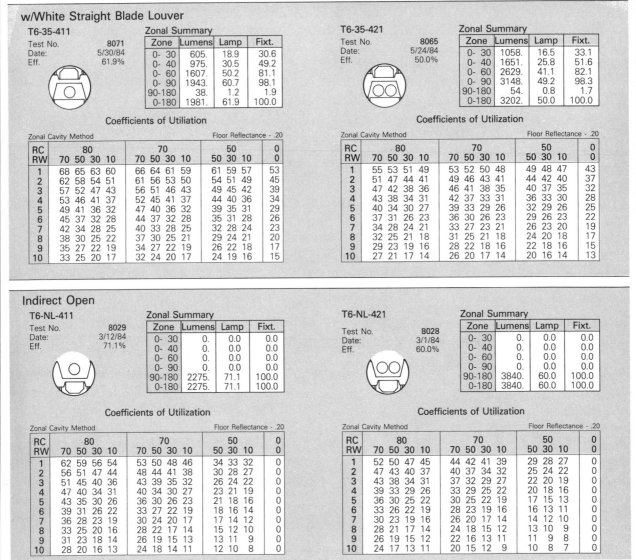

w/White Straight Blade Louver

T6-35-411

Test No. 8071
Date: 5/30/84
Eff. 61.9%

Zonal Summary

Zone	Lumens	Lamp	Fixt.
0- 30	605.	18.9	30.6
0- 40	975.	30.5	49.2
0- 60	1607.	50.2	81.1
0- 90	1943.	60.7	98.1
90-180	38.	1.2	1.9
0-180	1981.	61.9	100.0

Coefficients of Utiliation

Zonal Cavity Method — Floor Reflectance - .20

RC RW	80				70				50			0
	70	50	30	10	70	50	30	10	50	30	10	0
1	68	65	63	60	66	64	61	59	61	59	57	53
2	62	58	54	51	61	56	53	50	54	51	49	45
3	57	52	47	43	56	51	46	43	49	45	42	39
4	53	46	41	37	52	45	41	37	44	40	36	34
5	49	41	36	32	47	40	36	32	39	35	31	29
6	45	37	32	28	44	37	32	28	35	31	28	26
7	42	34	28	25	40	33	28	25	32	28	24	23
8	38	30	25	22	37	30	25	21	29	24	21	20
9	35	27	22	19	34	27	22	19	26	22	18	17
10	33	25	20	17	32	24	20	17	24	19	16	15

T6-35-421

Test No. 8065
Date: 5/24/84
Eff. 50.0%

Zonal Summary

Zone	Lumens	Lamp	Fixt.
0- 30	1058.	16.5	33.1
0- 40	1651.	25.8	51.6
0- 60	2629.	41.1	82.1
0- 90	3148.	49.2	98.3
90-180	54.	0.8	1.7
0-180	3202.	50.0	100.0

Coefficients of Utilization

Zonal Cavity Method — Floor Reflectance - .20

RC RW	80				70				50			0
	70	50	30	10	70	50	30	10	50	30	10	0
1	55	53	51	49	53	52	50	48	49	48	47	43
2	51	47	44	41	49	46	43	41	44	42	40	37
3	47	42	38	36	46	41	38	35	40	37	35	32
4	43	38	34	31	42	37	33	31	36	33	30	28
5	40	34	30	27	39	33	29	26	32	29	26	25
6	37	31	26	23	36	30	26	23	29	26	23	22
7	34	28	24	21	33	27	23	21	26	23	20	19
8	32	25	21	18	31	25	21	18	24	20	18	17
9	29	23	19	16	28	22	18	16	22	18	16	15
10	27	21	17	14	26	20	17	14	20	16	14	13

Indirect Open

T6-NL-411

Test No. 8029
Date: 3/12/84
Eff. 71.1%

Zonal Summary

Zone	Lumens	Lamp	Fixt.
0- 30	0.	0.0	0.0
0- 40	0.	0.0	0.0
0- 60	0.	0.0	0.0
0- 90	0.	0.0	0.0
90-180	2275.	71.1	100.0
0-180	2275.	71.1	100.0

Coefficients of Utilization

Zonal Cavity Method — Floor Reflectance - .20

RC RW	80				70				50			0
	70	50	30	10	70	50	30	10	50	30	10	0
1	62	59	56	54	53	50	48	46	34	33	32	0
2	56	51	47	44	48	44	41	38	30	28	27	0
3	51	45	40	36	43	39	35	32	26	24	22	0
4	47	40	34	31	40	34	30	27	23	21	19	0
5	43	35	30	26	36	30	26	23	21	18	16	0
6	39	31	26	22	33	27	22	19	18	16	14	0
7	36	28	23	19	30	24	20	17	17	14	12	0
8	33	25	20	16	28	22	17	14	15	12	10	0
9	31	23	18	14	26	19	15	13	13	11	9	0
10	28	20	16	13	24	18	14	11	12	10	8	0

T6-NL-421

Test No. 8028
Date: 3/1/84
Eff. 60.0%

Zonal Summary

Zone	Lumens	Lamp	Fixt.
0- 30	0.	0.0	0.0
0- 40	0.	0.0	0.0
0- 60	0.	0.0	0.0
0- 90	0.	0.0	0.0
90-180	3840.	60.0	100.0
0-180	3840.	60.0	100.0

Coefficients of Utilization

Zonal Cavity Method — Floor Reflectance - .20

RC RW	80				70				50			0
	70	50	30	10	70	50	30	10	50	30	10	0
1	52	50	47	45	44	42	41	39	29	28	27	0
2	47	43	40	37	40	37	34	32	25	24	22	0
3	43	38	34	31	37	32	29	27	22	20	19	0
4	39	33	29	26	33	29	25	22	20	18	16	0
5	36	30	25	22	30	25	22	19	17	15	13	0
6	33	26	22	19	28	23	19	16	16	13	11	0
7	30	23	19	16	26	20	17	14	14	12	10	0
8	28	21	17	14	24	18	15	12	13	10	9	0
9	26	19	15	12	22	16	13	11	11	9	8	0
10	24	17	13	11	20	15	12	9	10	8	7	0

Figure 12.24 "Supertube 6" fluorescent fixture data. Pendant-mounted tubular fluorescent fixtures can be used to reinforce architectural lines and rhythms. Adapted with permission from *USI Lighting Catalogues*, © 1989, USI Lighting, 1251 Doolittle Drive, San Leandro, CA.

Form 4

Description

Form 4 is designed as a complementary lighting source for distinctive architectural interiors. Trim lines, cast aluminum endcaps, precisely formed and fitted components are its trademark. They are constructed in a variety of contemporary finishes combined with the versatility of various mounting methods and possible fixture patterns. Form 4 offers high efficiency in fluorescent lighting.

Lighting Distribution

Many lighting distribution options are available with Form 4. As a direct lighting source it may be surface, pendant, bracket or wall-to-wall mounted with any finish or lighting diffuser listed. It is also available as an indirect source or in combination as a direct/indirect fixture.

Where the architectural design requires a wall wash or ceiling accent, specify Form 4 with an asymmetric reflector.

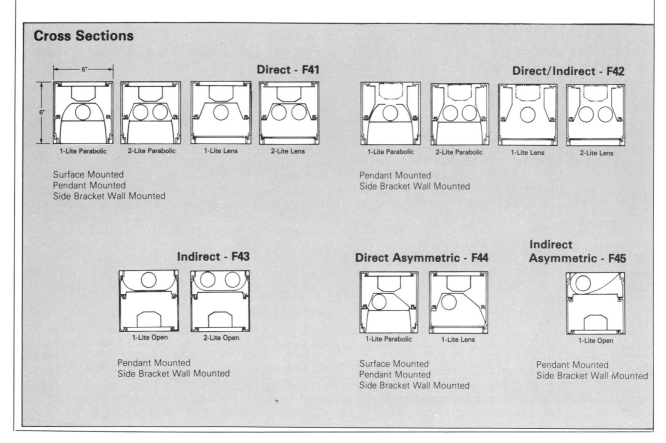

Figure 12.25 "Form 4" fluorescent fixture data. Adapted with permission from *USI Lighting Catalogues*, © 1989, USI Lighting, 1251 Doolittle Drive, San Leandro, CA.

Line 6
1-Lite

Description

Line 6 is a six inch wide recessed fluorescent luminaire designed specifically for mounting in rows. It provides long uninterrupted lines of light with control, comfort and the architectural richness of continuous lines of Parabolume louver. Anodized aluminum louvers are available in natural semi-specular or specular, and with champagne or ferric gold finishes.

Line 6 is also available with prismatic or translucent opal lenses or straight cross-blade louvers in baked white enamel. Lenses are lay-in type and may be ordered to fit flush with ceiling or regressed 1¾″ above the ceiling plane.

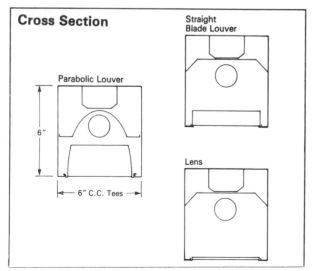

Cross Section

Parabolic Louver

6″

6″ C.C. Tees

Straight Blade Louver

Lens

Photometry

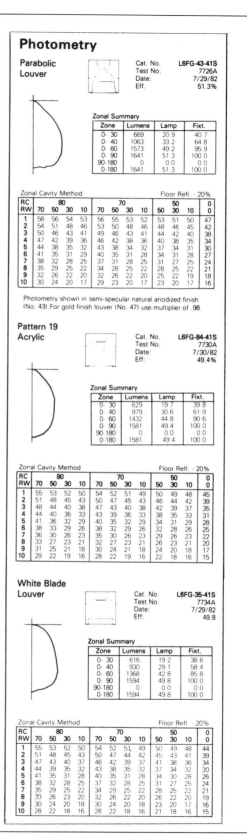

Parabolic Louver

Cat. No. L6FG-43-41S
Test No. 7726A
Date: 7/29/82
Eff: 51.3%

Zonal Summary

Zone	Lumens	Lamp	Fixt.
0- 30	669	20.9	40.7
0- 40	1063	33.2	64.8
0- 60	1573	49.2	95.9
0- 90	1641	51.3	100.0
90-180	0	0.0	0.0
0-180	1641	51.3	100.0

Zonal Cavity Method — Floor Refl. - 20%

RC RW	80				70				50			0
	70	50	30	10	70	50	30	10	50	30	10	0
1	58	56	54	53	56	55	53	52	53	51	50	47
2	54	51	48	46	53	50	48	46	48	46	45	42
3	50	46	43	41	49	46	43	41	44	42	40	38
4	47	42	39	36	46	42	38	36	40	38	35	34
5	44	38	35	32	43	38	34	32	37	34	31	30
6	41	35	31	29	40	35	31	28	34	31	28	27
7	38	32	28	25	37	31	28	25	31	27	25	24
8	35	29	25	22	34	28	25	22	28	25	22	21
9	32	26	22	20	32	26	22	20	25	22	19	18
10	30	24	20	17	29	23	20	17	23	20	17	16

Photometry shown in semi-specular natural anodized finish (No. 43). For gold finish louver (No. 47) use multiplier of .98.

Pattern 19 Acrylic

Cat. No. L6FG-84-41S
Test No. 7730A
Date: 7/30/82
Eff: 49.4%

Zonal Summary

Zone	Lumens	Lamp	Fixt.
0- 30	629	19.7	39.8
0- 40	979	30.6	61.9
0- 60	1432	44.8	90.6
0- 90	1581	49.4	100.0
90-180	0	0.0	0.0
0-180	1581	49.4	100.0

Zonal Cavity Method — Floor Refl. - 20%

RC RW	80				70				50			0
	70	50	30	10	70	50	30	10	50	30	10	0
1	55	53	52	50	54	52	51	49	50	49	48	45
2	51	48	45	43	50	47	45	43	46	44	42	39
3	48	44	40	38	47	43	40	38	42	39	37	35
4	44	40	36	33	43	39	36	33	38	35	33	31
5	41	36	32	29	40	35	32	29	34	31	29	28
6	38	33	29	26	38	32	29	26	32	28	26	25
7	36	30	26	23	35	30	26	23	29	26	23	22
8	33	27	23	21	32	27	23	21	26	23	21	20
9	31	25	21	18	30	24	21	18	24	20	18	17
10	29	22	19	16	28	22	19	16	22	18	16	15

White Blade Louver

Cat. No. L6FG-35-41S
Test No. 7734A
Date: 7/29/82
Eff: 49.8

Zonal Summary

Zone	Lumens	Lamp	Fixt.
0- 30	616	19.2	38.6
0- 40	930	29.1	58.4
0- 60	1368	42.8	85.8
0- 90	1594	49.8	100.0
90-180	0	0.0	0.0
0-180	1594	49.8	100.0

Zonal Cavity Method — Floor Refl. - 20%

RC RW	80				70				50			0
	70	50	30	10	70	50	30	10	50	30	10	0
1	55	53	52	50	54	52	51	49	50	49	48	44
2	51	48	45	43	50	47	44	42	45	43	41	39
3	47	43	40	37	46	42	39	37	41	38	36	34
4	44	39	35	32	43	38	35	32	37	34	32	30
5	41	35	31	28	40	35	31	28	34	30	28	26
6	38	32	28	25	37	32	28	25	31	27	25	24
7	35	29	25	22	34	29	25	22	28	25	22	21
8	33	26	23	20	32	26	22	20	26	22	20	19
9	30	24	20	18	30	24	20	18	23	20	17	16
10	28	22	18	16	28	22	18	16	21	18	16	15

Figure 12.26 "Line 6" one-light fluorescent fixture data. Adapted with permission from *USI Lighting Catalogues*, © 1989, USI Lighting, 1251 Doolittle Drive, San Leandro, CA.

Line 6
2-Lite

Description

Line 6 is a six inch wide recessed fluorescent luminaire designed specifically for mounting in rows. It provides long uninterrupted lines of light with control, comfort and the architectural richness of continuous lines of Parabolume louver. Anodized aluminum louvers are available in natural semi-specular or specular, and with champagne or ferric gold finishes.

Cross Section

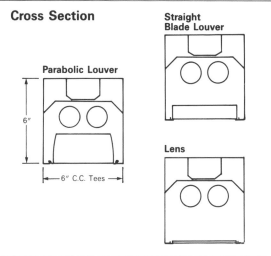

Parabolic Louver

6"

← 6" C.C. Tees →

Straight Blade Louver

Lens

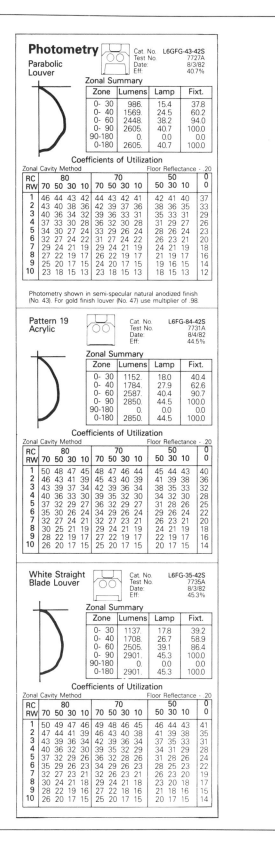

Photometry

Parabolic Louver

Cat. No. L6GFG-43-42S
Test No. 7727A
Date: 8/3/82
Eff: 40.7%

Zonal Summary

Zone	Lumens	Lamp	Fixt.
0- 30	986.	15.4	37.8
0- 40	1569.	24.5	60.2
0- 60	2448.	38.2	94.0
0- 90	2605.	40.7	100.0
90-180	0.	0.0	0.0
0-180	2605.	40.7	100.0

Coefficients of Utilization

Zonal Cavity Method — Floor Reflectance - .20

RC RW	80				70				50			0
	70	50	30	10	70	50	30	10	50	30	10	0
1	46	44	43	42	44	43	42	41	42	41	40	37
2	43	40	38	36	42	39	37	36	38	36	35	33
3	40	36	34	32	39	36	33	31	35	33	31	29
4	37	33	30	28	36	32	30	28	31	29	27	26
5	34	30	27	24	33	29	26	24	28	26	24	23
6	32	27	24	22	31	27	24	22	26	23	21	20
7	29	24	21	19	29	24	21	19	24	21	19	18
8	27	22	19	17	26	22	19	17	21	19	17	16
9	25	20	17	15	24	20	17	15	19	16	15	14
10	23	18	15	13	23	18	15	13	18	15	13	12

Photometry shown in semi-specular natural anodized finish (No. 43). For gold finish louver (No. 47) use multiplier of .98.

Pattern 19 Acrylic

Cat. No. L6FG-84-42S
Test No. 7731A
Date: 8/4/82
Eff: 44.5%

Zonal Summary

Zone	Lumens	Lamp	Fixt.
0- 30	1152.	18.0	40.4
0- 40	1784.	27.9	62.6
0- 60	2587.	40.4	90.7
0- 90	2850.	44.5	100.0
90-180	0.	0.0	0.0
0-180	2850.	44.5	100.0

Coefficients of Utilization

Zonal Cavity Method — Floor Reflectance - .20

RC RW	80				70				50			0
	70	50	30	10	70	50	30	10	50	30	10	0
1	50	48	47	45	48	47	46	44	45	44	43	40
2	46	43	41	39	45	43	40	39	41	39	38	36
3	43	39	37	34	42	39	36	34	38	35	33	32
4	40	36	33	30	39	35	32	30	34	32	30	28
5	37	32	29	27	36	32	29	27	31	28	26	25
6	35	30	26	24	34	29	26	24	29	26	24	22
7	32	27	24	21	32	27	23	21	26	23	21	20
8	30	25	21	19	29	24	21	19	24	21	19	18
9	28	22	19	17	27	22	19	17	22	19	17	16
10	26	20	17	15	25	20	17	15	20	17	15	14

White Straight Blade Louver

Cat. No. L6FG-35-42S
Test No. 7735A
Date: 8/3/82
Eff: 45.3%

Zonal Summary

Zone	Lumens	Lamp	Fixt.
0- 30	1137.	17.8	39.2
0- 40	1708.	26.7	58.9
0- 60	2505.	39.1	86.4
0- 90	2901.	45.3	100.0
90-180	0.	0.0	0.0
0-180	2901.	45.3	100.0

Coefficients of Utilization

Zonal Cavity Method — Floor Reflectance - .20

RC RW	80				70				50			0
	70	50	30	10	70	50	30	10	50	30	10	0
1	50	49	47	46	49	48	46	45	46	44	43	41
2	47	44	41	39	46	43	40	38	41	39	38	35
3	43	39	36	34	42	39	36	34	37	35	33	31
4	40	36	32	30	39	35	32	29	34	31	29	28
5	37	32	29	26	36	32	28	26	31	28	26	24
6	35	29	26	23	34	29	26	23	28	25	23	22
7	32	27	23	21	32	26	23	21	26	23	20	19
8	30	24	21	18	29	24	21	18	23	20	18	17
9	28	22	19	16	27	22	18	16	21	18	16	15
10	26	20	17	15	25	20	17	15	20	17	15	14

Figure 12.27 "Line 6" two-light fluorescent fixture data. Adapted with permission from *USI Lighting Catalogues*, © 1989, USI Lighting, 1251 Doolittle Drive, San Leandro, CA.

Description: Custom Parabolume luminous ceilings allow you design freedom to differentiate those special areas and set them apart from the building lighting standard. This special effect may work best in a lobby, a board room or any area requiring a distinctive illuminated appearance. Lamps are an intergral part of ceiling design with each different fluorescent color providing its own hue on the "neutral" aluminum reflecting surface. A translucent overlay of .040 opaline acrylic is available as an option when needed to mask unsightly overhead structures. Specify Parabolume ceilings for the rich, low brightness, different look.

Parabolume

Luminous Ceilings

Standard Modules *

2' x 2'

9 Cell   16 Cell

3' x 3'

16 Cell   36 Cell

4' x 4'

36 Cell   64 Cell

* Other Sizes Available

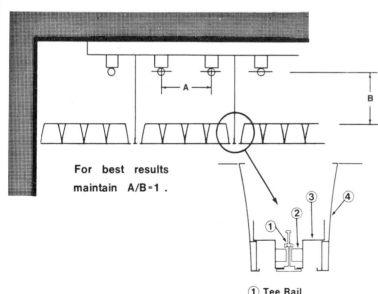

**For best results
maintain A/B=1 .**

① Tee Rail
② Bend Lock Tabs
③ Lay-in Frame
④ Parabolic Baffle

Dimensions A and B are required for proper illumination. Dimension A is the center to center distance between lamps. Dimension B is from the centerline of the lamps to the back side of the baffle blades. To provide even illumination and prevent dark or shaded areas from appearing in your luminous ceiling observe this "rule of thumb": maintain a **1** to **1** ratio between A and B.

Figure 12.28 "Parabolume" luminous ceiling data. Adapted with permission from *USI Lighting Catalogues*, © 1989, USI Lighting, 1251 Doolittle Drive, San Leandro, CA.

Staggered Strips

Description

A sturdy and quality constructed staggered fluorescent striplight with an easy and flexible means of adjusting to fit actual job-site conditions. The channel is offset at each end to accept adjoining fixtures. The 3″ overlapping adjacent lamps provide continuous uniform illumination without shadows in one or two lamp models.

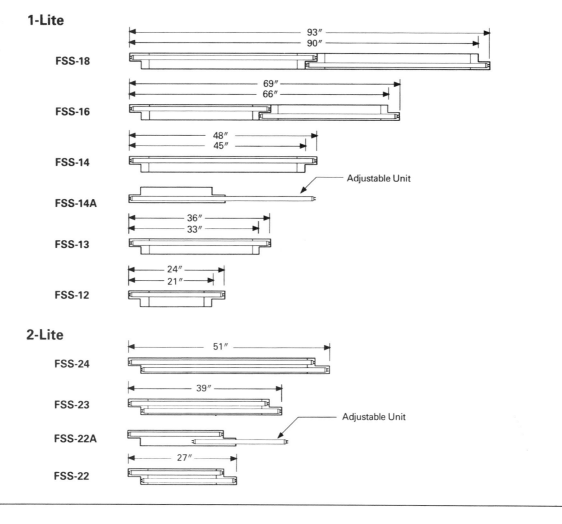

1-Lite

FSS-18 — 93″ / 90″

FSS-16 — 69″ / 66″

FSS-14 — 48″ / 45″

FSS-14A — Adjustable Unit

FSS-13 — 36″ / 33″

FSS-12 — 24″ / 21″

2-Lite

FSS-24 — 51″

FSS-23 — 39″

FSS-22A — Adjustable Unit

FSS-22 — 27″

Figure 12.29 Data on staggered fluorescent light strips. Staggered strips can be used in custom-designed ceiling coffer lighting. When light is coming from two sides the fluorescent strips should be mounted approximately (⅙)* (the horizontal dimension across the coffer) below the coffer ceiling surface. Adapted with permission from *USI Lighting Catalogues*, © 1989, USI Lighting, 1251 Doolittle Drive, San Leandro, CA.

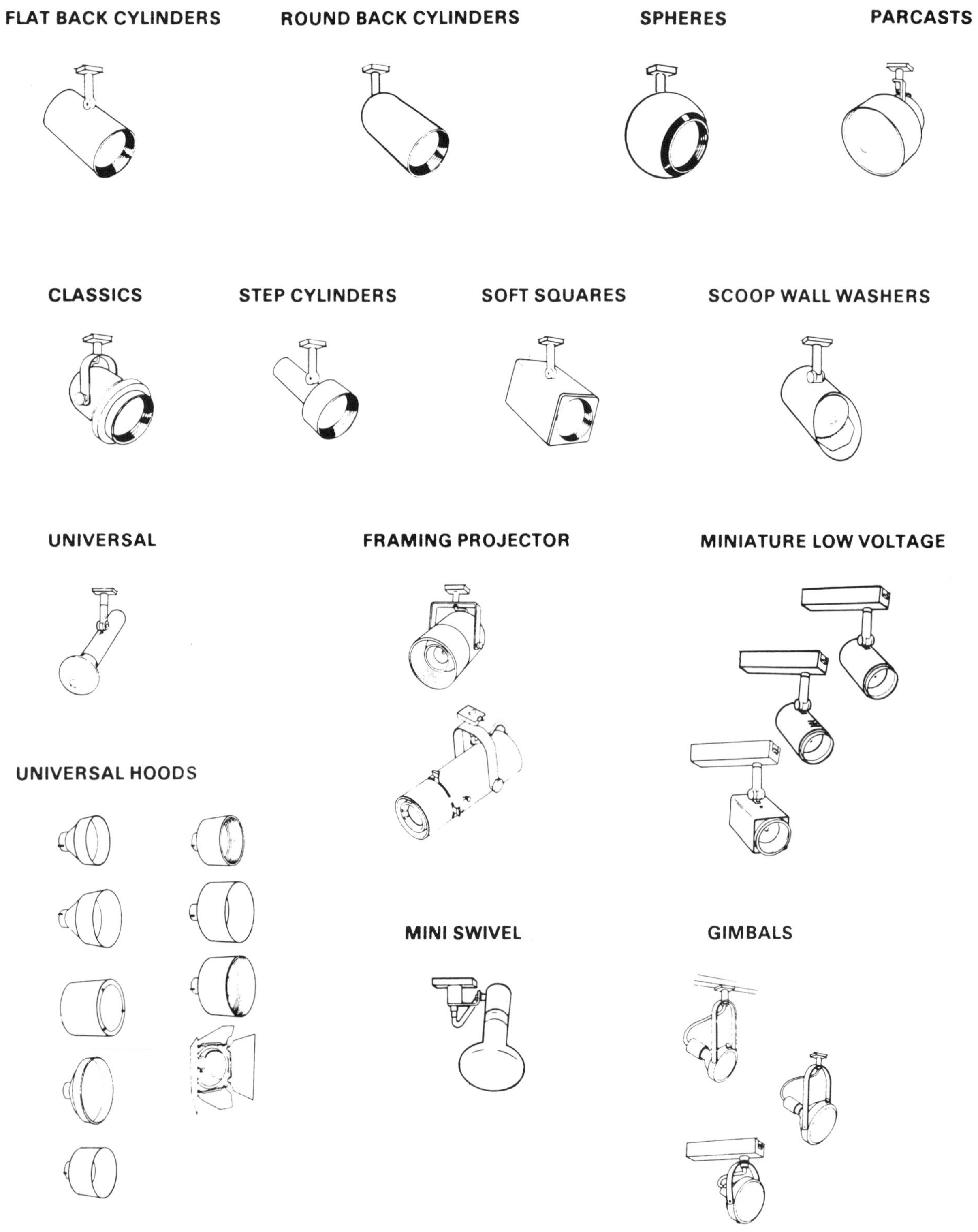

FLAT BACK CYLINDERS

ROUND BACK CYLINDERS

SPHERES

PARCASTS

CLASSICS

STEP CYLINDERS

SOFT SQUARES

SCOOP WALL WASHERS

UNIVERSAL

FRAMING PROJECTOR

MINIATURE LOW VOLTAGE

UNIVERSAL HOODS

MINI SWIVEL

GIMBALS

Figure 12.30 Typical spotlight fixture types. They can be mounted on an exposed or recessed track light system. Adapted with permission from *USI Lighting Catalogues*, © 1989, USI Lighting, 1251 Doolittle Drive, San Leandro, CA.

Listed below are a few of the many lamps suitable for use with Prescolite's new recessed adjustable pulldown series.

D   Distance to fixture from wall or floor
FC Initial footcandles at center of beam
L   Beam Length
W   Beam Width
S   Maximum spacing for even illumination

Lamp Performance Data			0° Aiming Angle					30° Aiming Angle					45° Aiming Angle					60° Aiming Angle				
Lamp	Rated Life	Beam Spread	D	FC	L	W	S	D	FC	L	W	S	D	FC	L	W	S	D	FC	L	W	S
50W PAR-20 NSP *	2,000	12°	6	128	1	1	1	5	120	1	1	1	4	102	2	1	1	3	64	3	1	1
			8	72	2	2	2	7	61	2	2	2	6	45	3	2	2	5	23	4	2	2
			10	46	2	2	2	9	37	3	2	2	8	25	3	2	2	7	12	6	3	3
50W PAR-20 NFL *	2,000	32°	6	35	3	3	3	5	32	4	3	3	4	28	5	3	3	3	17	9	3	3
			8	20	5	5	5	7	17	6	5	5	6	12	7	5	5	5	6	15	6	6
			10	13	6	6	6	9	10	7	6	6	8	7	10	6	6	7	3	21	8	8
50W PAR-30 NSP *	2,000	12°	8	102	2	2	2	7	86	2	2	2	6	64	3	2	2	5	32	4	2	2
			10	65	2	2	2	9	52	3	2	2	8	36	3	2	2	7	17	6	3	3
			12	45	3	3	3	11	35	3	3	3	10	23	4	3	3	9	10	8	4	4
50W PAR-30 NFL *	2,000	32°	6	49	3	3	3	5	45	4	3	3	4	39	5	3	3	3	24	9	3	3
			8	27	5	5	5	7	23	6	5	5	6	17	7	5	5	5	9	15	6	6
			10	18	6	6	6	9	14	7	6	6	8	10	10	6	6	7	4	21	8	8
75W PAR-30 NSP *	2,000	12°	12	73	3	3	3	11	56	3	3	3	10	37	4	3	3	9	16	8	4	4
			14	54	3	3	3	13	40	4	3	3	12	26	5	4	4	11	11	10	5	5
			16	41	3	3	3	15	30	4	4	4	14	19	6	4	4	13	8	11	5	5
75W PAR-30 NFL *	2,000	32°	6	83	3	3	3	5	78	4	3	3	4	66	5	3	3	3	42	9	3	3
			8	47	5	5	5	7	40	6	5	5	6	29	7	5	5	5	15	15	6	6
			10	30	6	6	6	9	24	7	6	6	8	17	10	6	6	7	8	21	8	8
150W PAR-38 NSP *	3,000	9°	18	116	3	3	3	17	84	4	3	3	16	52	5	4	4	15	21	10	5	5
			20	94	3	3	3	19	67	4	3	3	18	41	6	4	4	17	16	11	5	5
			22	77	3	3	3	21	55	4	4	4	20	33	6	4	4	19	13	12	6	6
150W PAR-38 SP *	3,000	10°	10	250	2	2	2	9	200	2	2	2	8	138	3	2	2	7	64	5	2	2
			12	174	2	2	2	11	134	3	2	2	10	88	4	2	2	9	39	6	3	3
			14	128	2	2	2	13	96	3	3	3	12	61	4	3	3	11	26	8	4	4
Q250W PAR-38 SP	6,000	12.8° × 12.8°	10	400	2	2	2	8	406	3	3	2	6	392	3	2	2	4	313	4	2	2
			15	178	3	3	3	12	180	4	4	3	9	174	4	3	3	6	139	6	3	3
			20	100	4	4	4	16	101	5	5	4	12	98	6	4	4	8	78	8	4	4
			25	64	6	6	5	20	65	6	7	6	15	63	7	5	5	10	50	10	5	4

Figure 12.31 Beam spread and illumination data for commonly used incandescent spot and flood lamps. Adapted with permission from *USI Lighting Catalogues*, © 1989, USI Lighting, 1251 Doolittle Drive, San Leandro, CA.

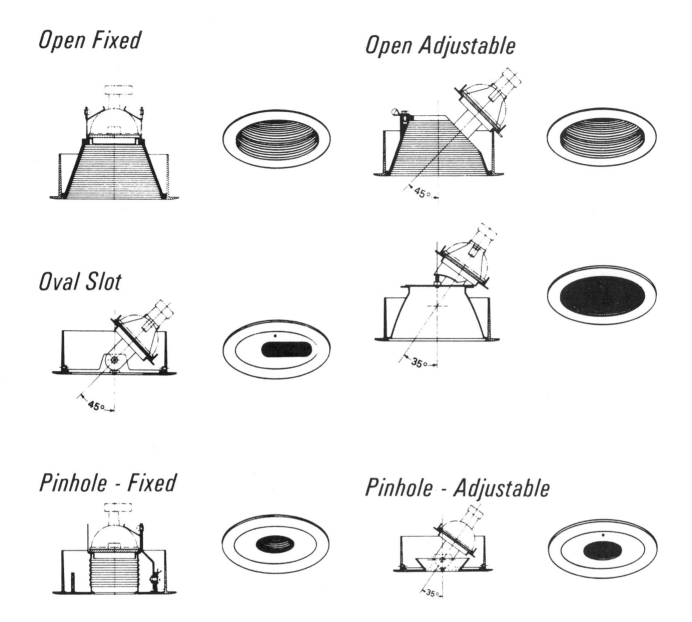

Figure 12.32 Low-voltage incandescent lamps can produce a very precise beam of light. This feature can be used to create downlights with minimum openings. The narrow, high-intensity beam of light can also be directed to a point of focus such as a piece of art or merchandise in a retail store. Adapted with permission from *USI Lighting Catalogues*, © 1989, USI Lighting, 1251 Doolittle Drive, San Leandro, CA.

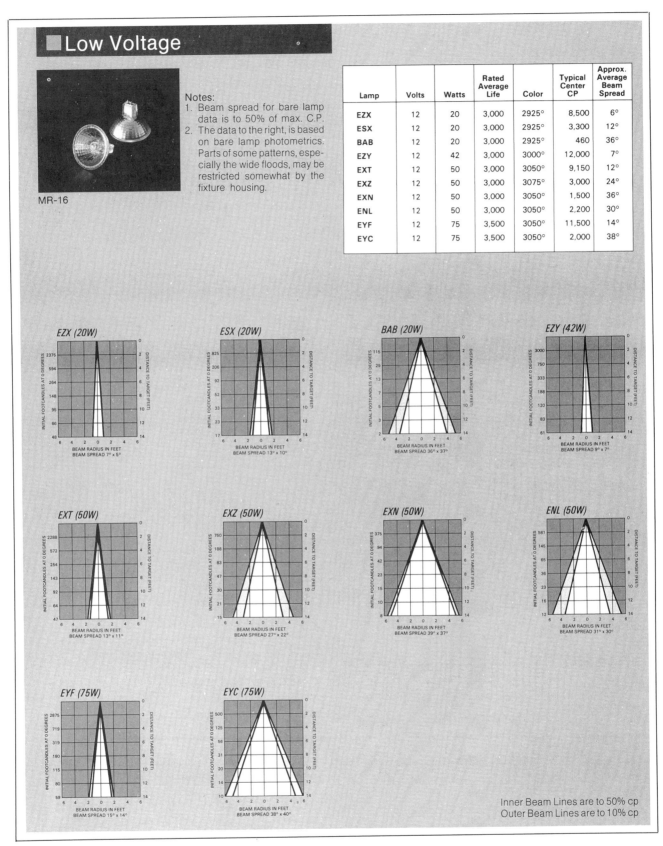

Low Voltage

MR-16

Notes:
1. Beam spread for bare lamp data is to 50% of max. C.P.
2. The data to the right, is based on bare lamp photometrics. Parts of some patterns, especially the wide floods, may be restricted somewhat by the fixture housing.

Lamp	Volts	Watts	Rated Average Life	Color	Typical Center CP	Approx. Average Beam Spread
EZX	12	20	3,000	2925°	8,500	6°
ESX	12	20	3,000	2925°	3,300	12°
BAB	12	20	3,000	2925°	460	36°
EZY	12	42	3,000	3000°	12,000	7°
EXT	12	50	3,000	3050°	9,150	12°
EXZ	12	50	3,000	3075°	3,000	24°
EXN	12	50	3,000	3050°	1,500	36°
ENL	12	50	3,000	3050°	2,200	30°
EYF	12	75	3,500	3050°	11,500	14°
EYC	12	75	3,500	3050°	2,000	38°

Inner Beam Lines are to 50% cp
Outer Beam Lines are to 10% cp

Figure 12.33 Beam spread and illumination data for low-voltage MR-16 lamps. Adapted with permission from *USI Lighting Catalogues*, © 1989, USI Lighting, 1251 Doolittle Drive, San Leandro, CA.

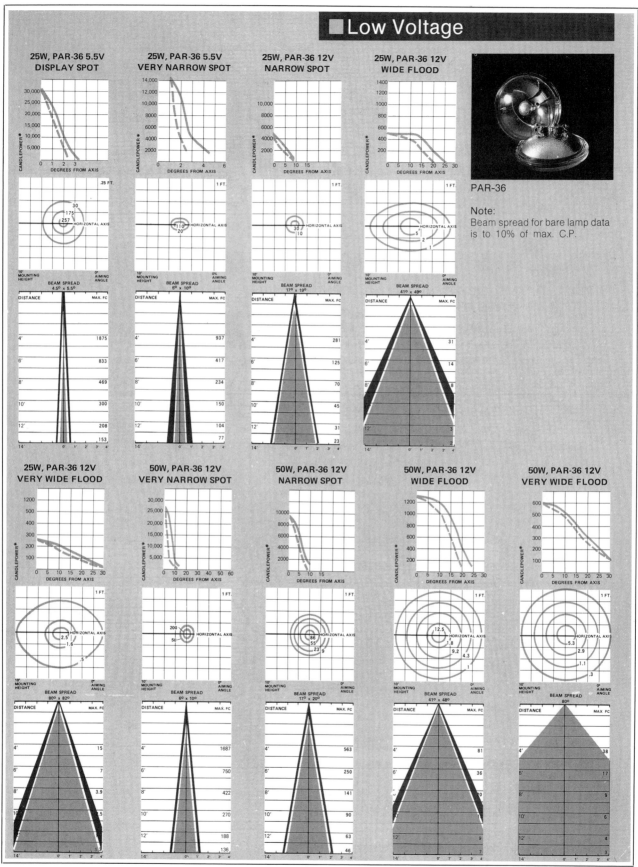

Figure 12.34 Beam spread and illumination data for low-voltage PAR-36 lamps. Adapted with permission from *USI Lighting Catalogues,* © 1989, USI Lighting, 1251 Doolittle Drive, San Leandro, CA.

The second is to use light fixtures that incorporate HVAC system supply and return diffusers into the design of the light fixture. With this option there is only the light fixture pattern on the ceiling. In fluorescent fixtures the diffuser is a slot diffuser on the sides of the fixture; in a recessed downlight the diffuser is a ring around the downlight reflector.

Surface reflectivity is an element that must be accounted for in the lighting design. The reflectivity of the walls, ceiling, and floor will affect the amount of light that reflects off their surfaces and thus their relative brightness. The walls are more important than the ceiling and floor because the users of the space naturally look directly at the walls but only obliquely at the ceiling and floor. It is the combination of illumination and reflectivity that will make a wall or other surface become a bright focal feature of an interior layout.

In the planning process, a modular grid is a useful means of coordinating the layout of lighting fixtures with other elements such as HVAC diffusers, sprinkler system heads, and acoustical treatments on the ceiling (See Figs. 12.36 and 12.37). All of these items need to be composed in a coherent pattern.

Lighting Calculations   Light fixture layout should be planned in an approximate manner during design formation. The overall strategy of the lighting plan should be the focus in the early design stage. Tables 12.1 and 12.2 provide a simplified and quick method of determining the number of fixtures needed for given illumination levels. Such simplified methods are appropriate for approximate lighting plan layout; when a design is formed, however, more detailed calculations should be performed to confirm that the proper illumination is being achieved.

Figure 12.38 outlines a zonal cavity lighting calculation. Figure 12.39 provides coefficients of utilization.

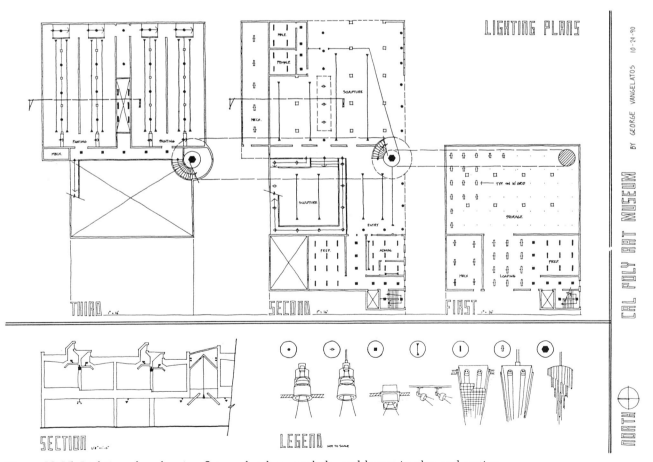

Figure 12.35 Lighting plan showing fixture sketches, symbols, and layout in plan and section.

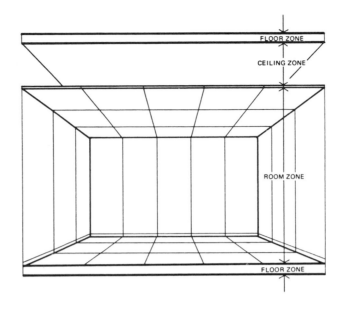

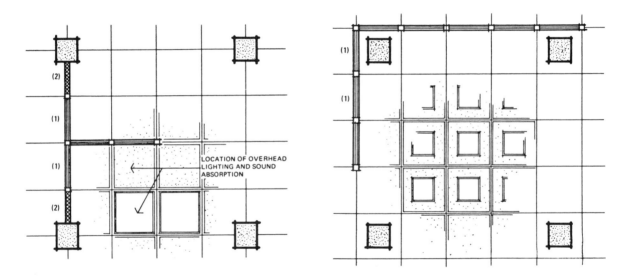

Figure 12.36 Example of a ceiling layout planning grid. Reproduced by permission from Flynn, Segil, and Steffy (1988).

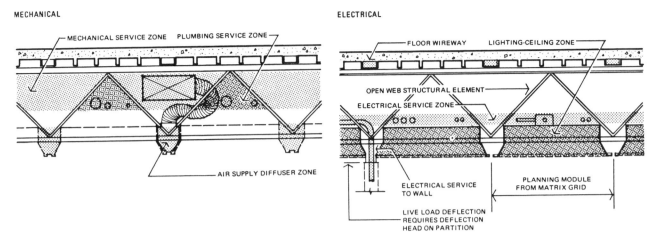

Figure 12.37 Service zones in the ceiling space. Reproduced by permission from Flynn, Segil, and Steffy (1988).

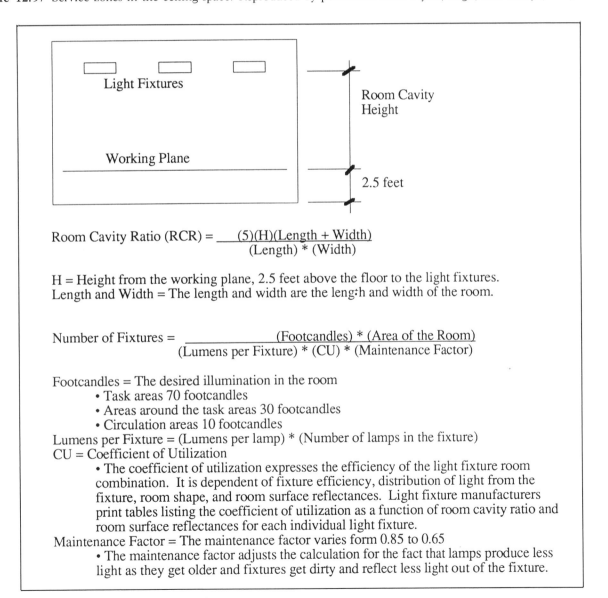

Room Cavity Ratio (RCR) = $\dfrac{(5)(H)(\text{Length} + \text{Width})}{(\text{Length}) * (\text{Width})}$

H = Height from the working plane, 2.5 feet above the floor to the light fixtures.
Length and Width = The length and width are the length and width of the room.

Number of Fixtures = $\dfrac{(\text{Footcandles}) * (\text{Area of the Room})}{(\text{Lumens per Fixture}) * (\text{CU}) * (\text{Maintenance Factor})}$

Footcandles = The desired illumination in the room
   • Task areas 70 footcandles
   • Areas around the task areas 30 footcandles
   • Circulation areas 10 footcandles
Lumens per Fixture = (Lumens per lamp) * (Number of lamps in the fixture)
CU = Coefficient of Utilization
   • The coefficient of utilization expresses the efficiency of the light fixture room
   combination. It is dependent of fixture efficiency, distribution of light from the
   fixture, room shape, and room surface reflectances. Light fixture manufacturers
   print tables listing the coefficient of utilization as a function of room cavity ratio and
   room surface reflectances for each individual light fixture.
Maintenance Factor = The maintenance factor varies form 0.85 to 0.65
   • The maintenance factor adjusts the calculation for the fact that lamps produce less
   light as they get older and fixtures get dirty and reflect less light out of the fixture.

Figure 12.38 Zonal cavity calculation method.

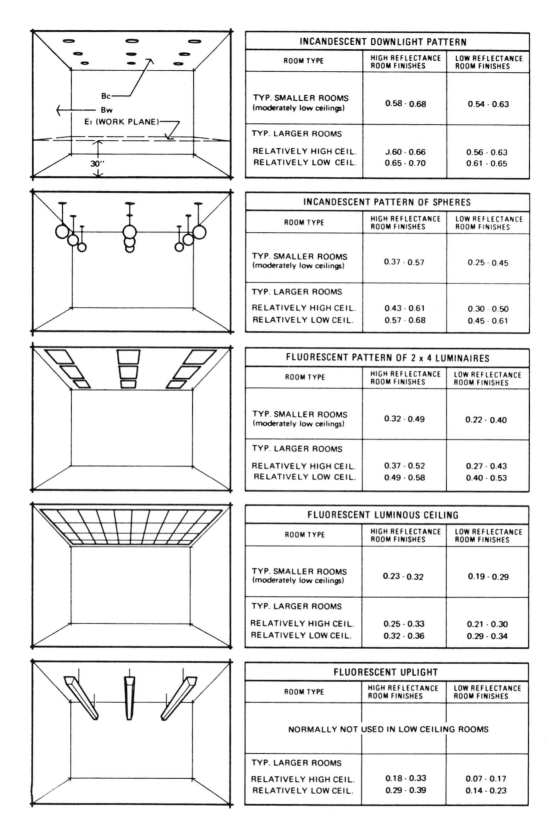

Figure 12.39 Typical coefficients of utilization. Reproduced by permission from Flynn, Segil, and Steffy (1988).

13

The Acoustic System

There is a negative and a positive function to consider in acoustic design. The positive function is to ensure that the reverberation characteristics of the spaces of a building are appropriate to their function. On the negative side, the task is to make certain that unwanted outside noises are kept out of quiet areas of the building. Reverberant and sound isolation characteristics of a building need to be carefully analyzed; problems are often not discovered until the building is in use, when correction may be costly and difficult.

ROOM ACOUSTICS

Sound is a pressure wave that moves through the air, alternating between relatively higher and lower pressure (Fig. 13.1). This pressure wave travels through the air in a fashion similar to a wave traveling across the surface of the ocean, except that the sound pressure wave is not confined to a surface—it is three dimensional. The sound pressure wave travels at the speed of sound (1100 feet per second), which is a slow enough speed that reflections of the original wave form can interfere with perception of the original, intended signal. Reverberation time is the measure of this problem.

Sound of any kind emitted in a room will be absorbed or reflected off the room surfaces. Soft materials absorb sound energy. Hard materials reflect sound energy back into the space. The reflected sound can reinforce the

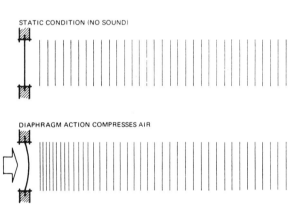

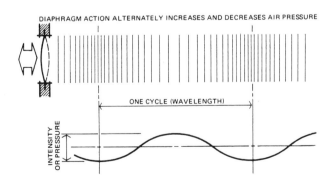

Figure 13.1 Sound is a three-dimensional pressure wave in air. Reproduced by permission from Flynn, Segil, and Steffy (1988).

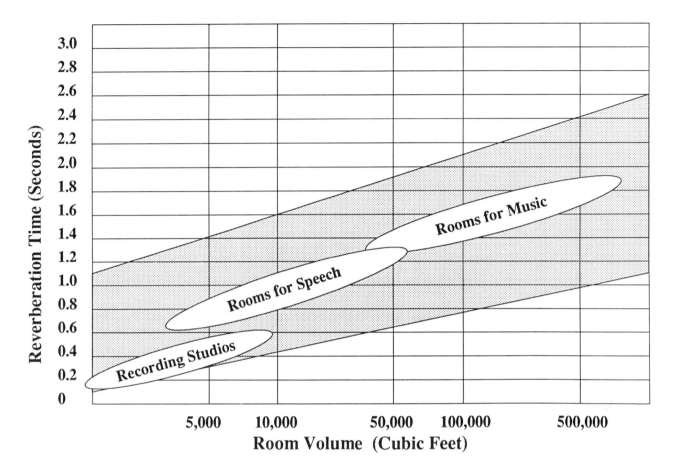

Figure 13.2 Reverberation time related to room size and occupancy.

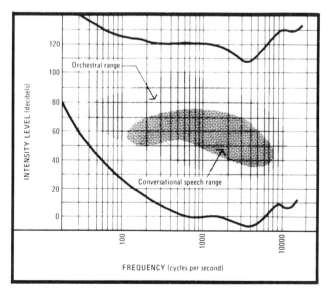

Figure 13.3 Sensitivity levels of the human ear to low- and high-frequency sound. Reproduced by permission from Flynn, Segil, and Steffy (1988).

direct sound and enhance communication if the room size and room surfaces are configured appropriately (Fig. 13.2 and 13.3). The room volume and surface characteristics will determine the reverberation time for the room. Reverberation time is the time in seconds that it takes for a sound to decay through 60 decibels. It is calculated as follows:

Reverberation time = (0.05)(room volume)/(sound absorption of the room)

where room volume is measured in cubic feet. The sound absorption of a surface is the product of the acoustic coefficient for the surface multiplied by the area of the surface. The sound absorption of the room is the sum of the sound absorptions for all the surfaces in the room. The following is a list of some common materials and their associated acoustic coefficients: concrete (0.1); gypsum board (0.1); carpet with a pad (0.6); acoustic tiles (0.8); cloth upholstered seats (0.8); an audience (0.8).

Auditoriums   In spaces where a large group of people can gather to hear a speech or musical performance, the sound energy should be distributed evenly over the room and be loud enough for everyone to hear the performance. The following guidelines can be used to aid in auditorium concept design.

· To achieve proper reverberation times, rooms must have an appropriate volume of space (Doelle 1972) (Table 13.1). Rooms for speech require 120 cubic feet per audience seat; rooms for music require 270 cubic feet.
· Rooms for speech should have a reverberation time of about 1 second.
· Rooms for music should have a longer reverberation time of about 1.5 seconds. (Churches traditionally have the longer reverberation times characteristic of rooms for music.)
· Proper reverberation times will be achieved by using the above room volumes, soft upholstered seats, carpeted aisles, and a soft back wall. The side walls and ceiling should be hard materials.
· The hard, sound-reflecting ceiling surface can be shaped to spread reflected sound evenly over the audience. Ray diagramming is a useful tool for achieving this purpose. Sound energy will reflect off of a hard surface at the same angle that it impinges onto the surface (Fig. 13.4). Lines can be drawn on a section through the auditorium concept (incident angle = reflected angle) to determine how sound will be reflected by various ceiling configurations (Fig. 13.5).
· Concave surfaces will focus sound energy (see Fig. 13.6) and thus should be avoided.
· Side walls should have faceted surfaces so that sound

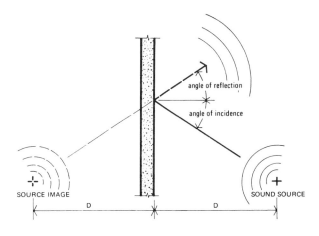

Figure 13.4 Ray diagramming to measure reflected sound. Reproduced by permission from Flynn, Segil, and Steffy (1988).

energy is bounced in all directions, diffused rather than reflected into the room. This is more important in large halls. The dimension of the faceting must be coordinated to the wavelength of the sound to be diffused. Low-frequency diffusion requires faceting on the order of 6 to 8 feet in dimension; while high-frequency diffusion requires faceting of 6 to 8 inches. An echo can form in a large hall when the first reflected path is approximately 70 feet longer than the direct sound path (see Fig. 13.7). This situation occurs because of sound reflection off the back wall or off a high ceiling just in front of the stage. The echo off the back wall is easily eliminated by covering the back wall with soft, sound-absorbing material. The echo off a high ceiling in front of the stage can be eliminated by lowering the ceiling or providing a throat on

TABLE 13.1.   Recommended volume-per-seat values for various types of auditoriums

Type of auditorium	Volume per seat (cubic feet)		
	Minimum	Optimum	Maximum
Rooms for speech	80	110	150
Concert halls	220	275	380
Opera houses	160	200	260
Roman Catholic churches	200	300	425
Protestant churches, synagogues	180	255	320
Multipurpose auditoriums	180	255	320
Motion-picture theaters	100	125	180

Source: Adapted with permission from Doelle 1972.

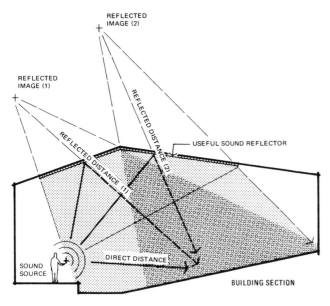

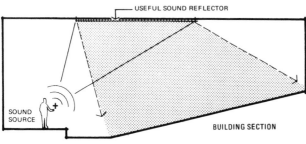

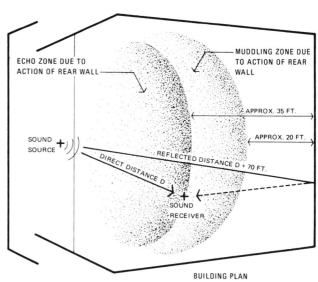

Figure 13.7 Echos can form in an auditorium if the back wall is not either soft or faceted. Reproduced by permission from Flynn, Segil, and Steffy (1988).

Figure 13.5 Planning ceiling shape in an auditorium to achieve the desired sound quality and quantity. Reproduced by permission from Flynn, Segil, and Steffy (1988).

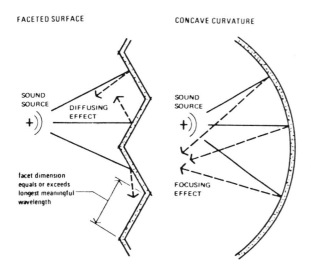

Figure 13.6 Illustration of how faceted surfaces diffuse sound and concave surfaces focus sound. Reproduced by permission from Flynn, Segil, and Steffy (1988).

the proscenium opening to reflect sound that would otherwise reach the high ceiling.

Unwanted exterior noises need to be excluded from the auditorium by not locating noisy functions near the auditorium and/or by providing high quality sound isolation walls. Thick massive walls are best. Circulation spaces surrounding an auditorium create a sound buffer.

Figures 13.8 and 13.9 illustrate various theater examples. Figure 13.10 is an example of a lecture hall. Figures 13.11 and 13.12 are examples of concert halls. Figure 13.13 is an example of a music practice facility.

Office and Commercial Space   Office and commercial space is an environment where speech communication between individuals at close range is important. Sound from other areas of the room becomes noise that should be muffled. Sound from one source does not need to fill an entire room as in an auditorium. This situation calls for a very short reverberation time on the order of 0.5 seconds. Typically this low reverberation time is achieved through the use of an acoustical ceiling and a carpeted floor. Additional speech privacy can be achieved through the use of partitions to intercept direct sound paths.

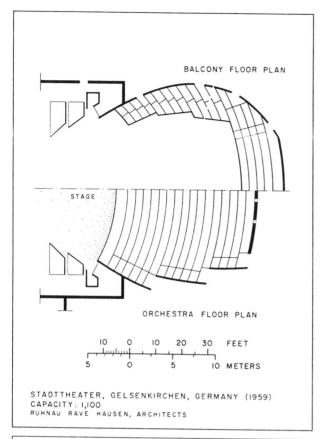

BALCONY FLOOR PLAN

STAGE

ORCHESTRA FLOOR PLAN

10   0   10   20   30   FEET
5   0   5   10   METERS

STADTTHEATER, GELSENKIRCHEN, GERMANY (1959)
CAPACITY: 1,100
RUHNAU RAVE HAUSEN, ARCHITECTS

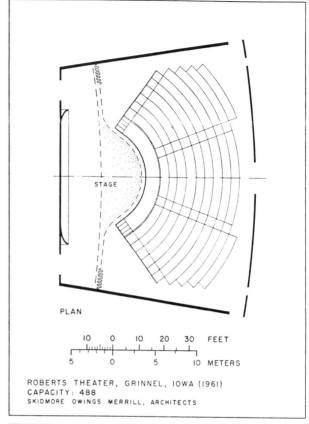

STAGE

PLAN

10   0   10   20   30   FEET
5   0   5   10   METERS

ROBERTS THEATER, GRINNEL, IOWA (1961)
CAPACITY: 488
SKIDMORE OWINGS MERRILL, ARCHITECTS

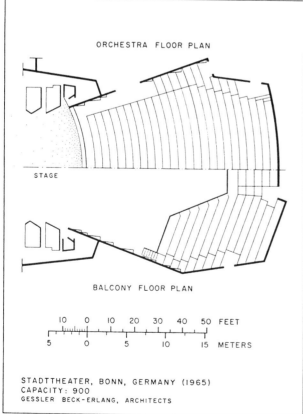

ORCHESTRA FLOOR PLAN

STAGE

BALCONY FLOOR PLAN

10   0   10   20   30   40   50   FEET
5   0   5   10   15   METERS

STADTTHEATER, BONN, GERMANY (1965)
CAPACITY: 900
GESSLER BECK-ERLANG, ARCHITECTS

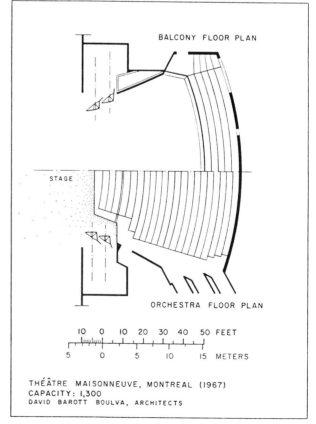

BALCONY FLOOR PLAN

STAGE

ORCHESTRA FLOOR PLAN

10   0   10   20   30   40   50   FEET
5   0   5   10   15   METERS

THÉÂTRE MAISONNEUVE, MONTREAL (1967)
CAPACITY: 1,300
DAVID BAROTT BOULVA, ARCHITECTS

Figure 13.8 Examples of theaters with proscenium stages. Reproduced by permission from Doelle (1972).

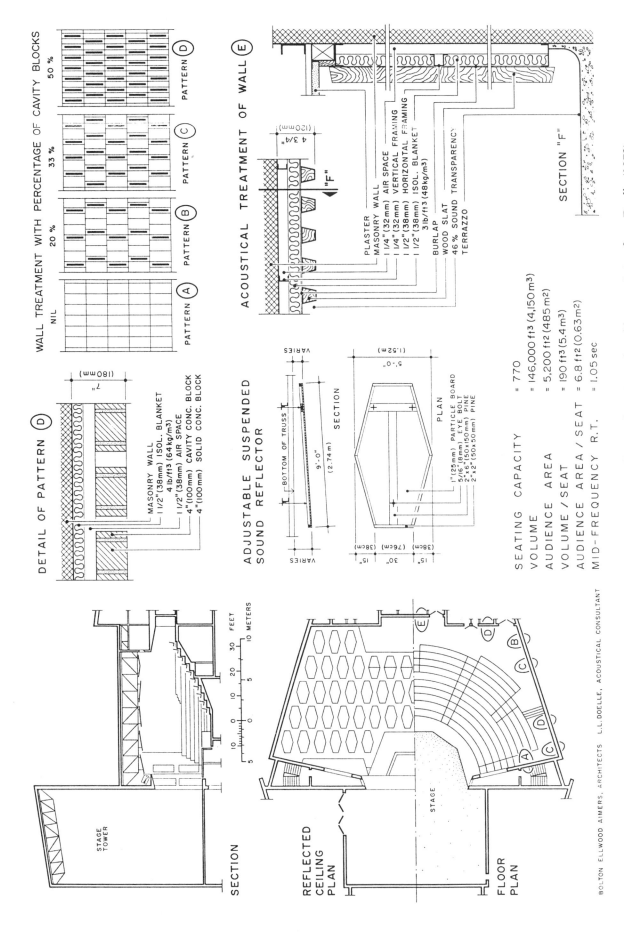

WALL TREATMENT WITH PERCENTAGE OF CAVITY BLOCKS

NIL   20 %   33 %   50 %

PATTERN (A)   PATTERN (B)   PATTERN (C)   PATTERN (D)

ACOUSTICAL TREATMENT OF WALL (E)

PLASTER
MASONRY WALL
1 1/4" (32mm) AIR SPACE
1 1/4" (32mm) VERTICAL FRAMING
1 1/2" (38mm) HORIZONTAL FRAMING
1 1/2" (38mm) ISOL. BLANKET
3 lb/ft3 (48kg/m3)
BURLAP
WOOD SLAT
46 % SOUND TRANSPARENCY
TERRAZZO

4 3/4" (120mm)

"F"

SECTION "F"

DETAIL OF PATTERN (D)

7" (180mm)

MASONRY WALL
1 1/2" (38mm) ISOL. BLANKET
4 lb/ft3 (64kg/m3)
1 1/2" (38mm) AIR SPACE
4" (100mm) CAVITY CONC. BLOCK
4" (100mm) SOLID CONC. BLOCK

ADJUSTABLE SUSPENDED SOUND REFLECTOR

BOTTOM OF TRUSS
VARIES

9'-0" (2.74 m)

SECTION

VARIES

5'-0" (1.52m)

15"   30"   15"
(38cm) (76cm) (38cm)

PLAN

1" (25mm) PARTICLE BOARD
5/16" (8mm) EYE BOLT
2"×6" (50×150mm) PINE
2"×2" (50×50mm) PINE

SEATING CAPACITY   = 770
VOLUME   = 146,000 ft3 (4,150 m3)
AUDIENCE AREA   = 5,200 ft2 (485 m2)
VOLUME / SEAT   = 190 ft3 (5.4 m3)
AUDIENCE AREA / SEAT   = 6.8 ft2 (0.63 m2)
MID-FREQUENCY R.T.   = 1.05 sec

BOLTON ELLWOOD AIMERS. ARCHITECTS   L.L. DOELLE, ACOUSTICAL CONSULTANT

SECTION

REFLECTED CEILING PLAN

FLOOR PLAN

STAGE TOWER

STAGE

FEET   0 10 20 30
METERS 0   5   10

Figure 13.9 Acoustic detailing of the theater at Bishop's University, Lennoxville, Quebec. Reproduced by permission from Doelle (1972).

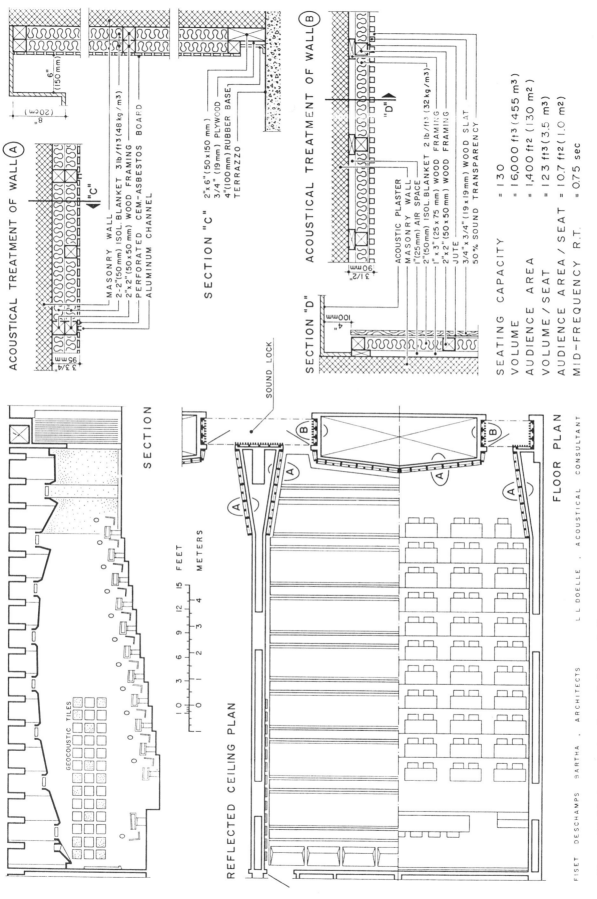

ACOUSTICAL TREATMENT OF WALL (A)

↓"C"

MASONRY WALL
2-2"(50 mm) ISOL. BLANKET 3 lb/ft3 (48 kg/m3)
2"x 2"(50 x 50 mm) WOOD FRAMING
PERFORATED CEM.-ASBESTOS BOARD
ALUMINUM CHANNEL

SECTION "C"
2"x 6"(50 x150 mm)
3/4"(19 mm) PLYWOOD
4"(100 mm) RUBBER BASE
TERRAZZO

ACOUSTICAL TREATMENT OF WALL (B)

↓"D"

ACOUSTIC PLASTER
MASONRY WALL
1"(25mm) AIR SPACE
2"(50mm) ISOL. BLANKET 2 lb/ft3 (32 kg/m3)
1"x 3"(25 x 75 mm) WOOD FRAMING
2"x 2"(50 x 50 mm) WOOD FRAMING
JUTE
3/4"x 3/4"(19 x19mm) WOOD SLAT
50% SOUND TRANSPARENCY

SECTION "D"

SEATING CAPACITY	= 130
VOLUME	= 16,000 ft3 (455 m3)
AUDIENCE AREA	= 1,400 ft2 (130 m2)
VOLUME / SEAT	= 123 ft3 (3.5 m3)
AUDIENCE AREA / SEAT	= 10.7 ft2 (1.0 m2)
MID-FREQUENCY R.T.	= 0.75 sec

SECTION

GEOCOUSTIC TILES

REFLECTED CEILING PLAN

SOUND LOCK

FEET
METERS

FLOOR PLAN

FISET DESCHAMPS BARTHA , ARCHITECTS   L L DOELLE , ACOUSTICAL CONSULTANT

Figure 13.10 Acoustic detailing of a lecture hall at University Laval, Quebec. Reproduced by permission from Doelle (1972).

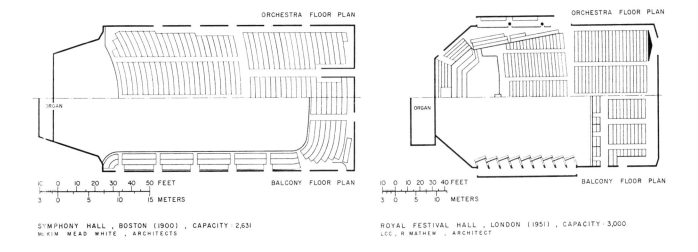

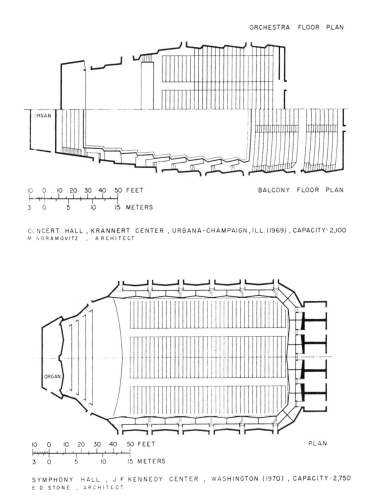

Figure 13.11 Music auditoriums with rectangular floor plans. Reproduced by permission from Doelle (1972).

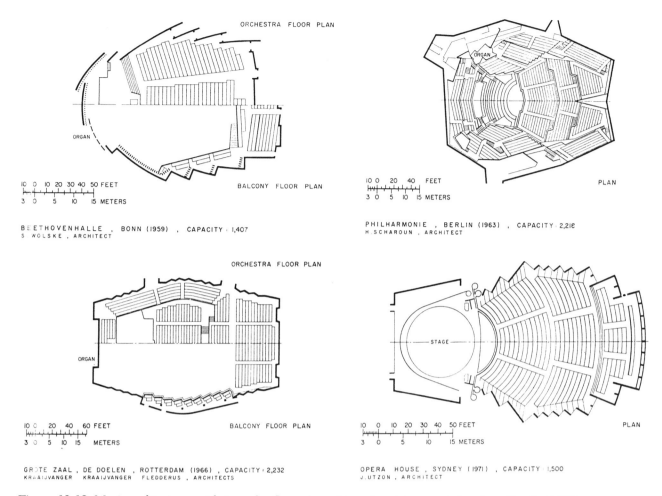

ORCHESTRA FLOOR PLAN

ORGAN

IO O IO 20 30 40 50 FEET

3 O 5 IO 15 METERS

BALCONY FLOOR PLAN

BEETHOVENHALLE , BONN (1959) , CAPACITY : 1,407
S WOLSKE , ARCHITECT

ORGAN

IO O 20 40 FEET

3 O 5 IO 15 METERS

PLAN

PHILHARMONIE , BERLIN (1963) , CAPACITY : 2,218
H.SCHAROUN , ARCHITECT

ORCHESTRA FLOOR PLAN

ORGAN

IO O 20 40 60 FEET

3 O 5 IO 15 METERS

BALCONY FLOOR PLAN

GROTE ZAAL , DE DOELEN , ROTTERDAM (1966) , CAPACITY : 2,232
KRAAIJVANGER KRAAIJVANGER FLEDDERUS , ARCHITECTS

STAGE

IO O IO 20 30 40 50 FEET

3 O 5 IO 15 METERS

PLAN

OPERA HOUSE , SYDNEY (1971) , CAPACITY : 1,500
J.UTZON , ARCHITECT

Figure 13.12 Music auditoriums with irregular floor plans. Reproduced by permission from Doelle (1972).

SOUND ISOLATION

Sound travels through walls and floors by causing building materials to vibrate and then broadcast the noise into the quiet space. There are two methods of setting up the vibration. Air-borne sound is a pressure vibration in the air. When it hits a wall, the wall materials are forced to vibrate. The vibration passes through the materials of the wall. The far side of the wall then passes the vibration back into the air. Structure-borne sound starts out differently. The vibration of the building materials is directly caused by a vibrating piece of equipment like an air handler, chiller, boiler, or pump. Another source of direct vibration is the impact caused by walking over a hard floor.

The following guidelines will be helpful in planning for noise reduction.

· The first line of defense against unwanted noise penetration into quiet areas is to avoid placing noisy areas near quiet areas.
· Areas with similar noise characteristics should be placed next to each other. Place bed rooms next to bed rooms and living rooms next to living rooms.
· Massive materials (concrete or masonry) are the best noise isolation materials.
· Background noise levels are specified with noise criteria curve levels (Fig. 13.14). These curves have a loudness-versus-frequency shape similar to the hu-

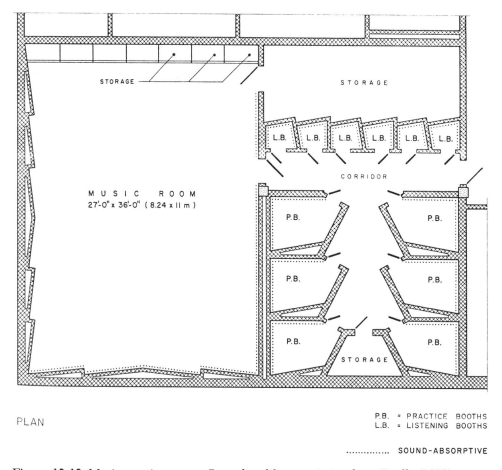

PLAN

P.B. = PRACTICE BOOTHS
L.B. = LISTENING BOOTHS

.... SOUND-ABSORPTIVE

Figure 13.13 Music practice rooms. Reproduced by permission from Doelle (1972).

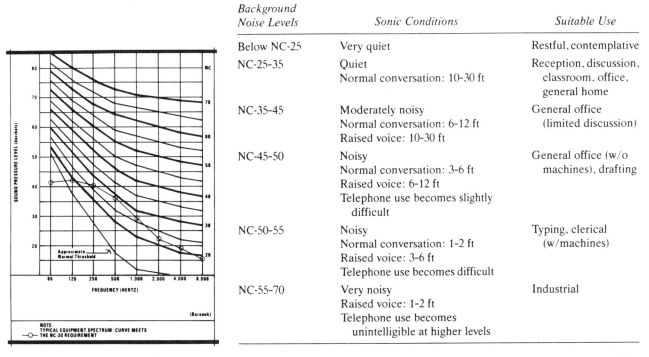

Background Noise Levels	Sonic Conditions	Suitable Use
Below NC-25	Very quiet	Restful, contemplative
NC-25-35	Quiet Normal conversation: 10-30 ft	Reception, discussion, classroom, office, general home
NC-35-45	Moderately noisy Normal conversation: 6-12 ft Raised voice: 10-30 ft	General office (limited discussion)
NC-45-50	Noisy Normal conversation: 3-6 ft Raised voice: 6-12 ft Telephone use becomes slightly difficult	General office (w/o machines), drafting
NC-50-55	Noisy Normal conversation: 1-2 ft Raised voice: 3-6 ft Telephone use becomes difficult	Typing, clerical (w/machines)
NC-55-70	Very noisy Raised voice: 1-2 ft Telephone use becomes unintelligible at higher levels	Industrial

Figure 13.14 Noise criteria curves and noise criteria levels related to typical situations and occupancies. Reproduced by permission from Flynn, Segil, and Steffy (1988).

man ear's sensitivity to loudness as a function of frequency.

• For an exterior noise to be unnoticeable, the separation wall must reduce it to a level that is less loud than the background noise level of the receiving room (Fig. 13.15).

• Walls and floors are classified by sound transmission class (STC), which is the amount of reduction in loudness of airborne sound that the wall will achieve (Figs. 13.16 and 13.17).

• Reducing structure-born sound from vibrating equipment is achieved by mounting the equipment on an inertial block that is supported on resilient mounts.

• Reducing structure-born sound from walking on floors is achieved by carpet on the floor surface to reduce the impact and/or resiliently mounting the floor (Fig. 13.18).

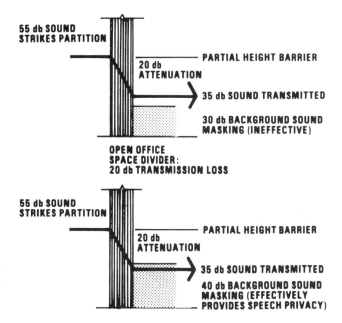

Figure 13.15 Planning sound barriers to reduce the sound level to below the ambient noise level in the receiving room. Reproduced by permission from Flynn, Segil, and Steffy (1988).

Noise Criteria Curve	Sonic Environment
NC-15-20	Concert halls, broadcast studios
NC-20-25	Assembly areas without amplification, theaters, auditoriums, courtrooms
NC-20-30	Sleeping spaces, such as hospital rooms, hotel and motel rooms, apartments
NC-25-35	Classrooms, music rooms
NC-30-35	Churches, library reading rooms, private offices, conference rooms
NC-35-40	Heavy occupancy areas where limited discussion occurs, such as stores, gymnasiums, cafeterias, large offices
NC-40-45	Heavy circulation areas, such as lobbies, corridors, large offices
NC-45-50	Machinery and equipment spaces, such as garages, laundries, equipment rooms
NC-50	Assembly areas with amplification

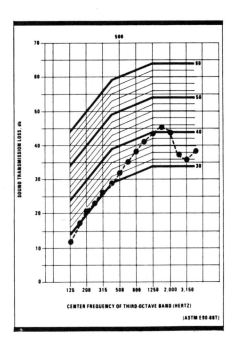

Typical partition sound transmission criteria and noise criteria combinations

(Partition Transmission Loss (STC))			Sonic Conditions in the Receiving Room	Typical Applications
NC 25[1]	NC 35[1]	NC 45[1]		
STC 35 (or less)	STC 30 (or less)	—	Normal speech can be easily and distinctly understood through the wall	Privacy not required; partition used only as a space divider
STC 35-40	STC 30-35	—	Loud speech (and loud radios) understood fairly well through the wall; normal speech can be heard, but not easily understood	Suitable for dividing noncritical areas; provides fair degree of freedom from distraction
STC 40-45	STC 35-40	STC 30-35	Loud speech can be heard through the wall, but is not easily intelligible; normal speech can be heard only faintly, if at all	Provides good degree of freedom from distraction; suitable for junior executives, engineers, apartment dwellers, and so on
STC 45-50	STC 40-45	STC 35-40	Loud speech can be heard faintly through the wall, but is not easily understood; normal speech is inaudible through the wall	Provides a confidential degree of conversational privacy; generally suitable for doctors, lawyers, senior executives, and apartment dwellers
STC 50	STC 45-50	STC 40-45	Loud sounds such as brass musical instruments and singing, or a radio at high volume can be heard only faintly through the wall	Suitable for dividing private or relaxing spaces from noisy adjacent spaces that house loud activities or equipment

1. NC values describe the background noise levels in the receiving room (space of interest).

Figure 13.16 Sound transmission class values related to the quality of the noise reduction job they are doing. Noise criteria background levels are included for reference. Reproduced by permission from Flynn, Segil, and Steffy (1988).

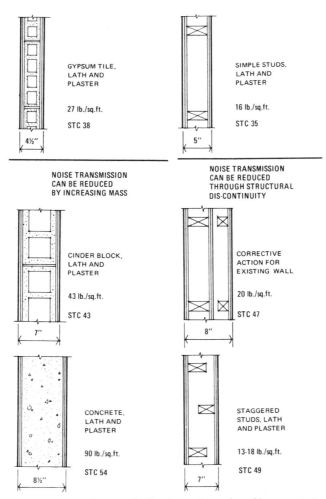

Figure 13.17 Walls with accompanying noise reduction STC values. Reproduced by permission from Flynn, Segil, and Steffy (1988).

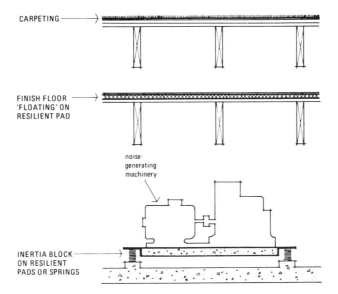

Figure 13.18 Reducing impact noise by cushioning the floor. Vibration noise is reduced by isolating the vibrating piece of equipment. Reproduced by permission from Flynn, Segil, and Steffy (1988).

14

The Vertical Transportation System

The vertical transportation system is an important feature of wayfinding through a building. Its clarity of location and use will enhance the public appreciation of the design.

ELEVATOR TYPES

Traction elevators hang on a counterweighted cable and are driven by a traction machine that pulls the cable up and down. Traction elevators can operate smoothly at fast speeds and have no height limits. (See Fig. 14.1, Table 14.1, and Table 14.2).

Hydraulic elevators are less expensive than traction elevators. They are moved up and down by a hydraulic piston (Fig. 14.2 and Table 14.3). Their operation is limited to buildings of about six stories in height, and they are slow and not as smooth as a traction elevator. This type of elevator is generally used in low-rise buildings (two to four stories) in which it is not necessary to move large numbers of people quickly.

COMMERCIAL ELEVATOR APPLICATIONS

Elevators are an important focus in the circulation system of a building. The vertical shaft that elevators are housed in can be used by the structural system as a tube form providing resistance to horizontal loads. As buildings get taller the elevator system becomes a more dominant design feature of the plan layout of the building and takes up a substantial amount of floor area. The following are guidelines for planning an elevator system.

- One passenger elevator is required for each 30,000 square feet of net floor area.
- One service elevator is required per each 300,000 square feet of net floor area.
- Enough space should be provided in the lobby to allow room (minimum 10 feet in width) for people to wait in front of the elevators.

- In high buildings the elevator system is broken down into zones serving groups of floors, typically zones of 10 to 15 floors. Elevators that serve the upper zones express from the lobby to the beginning of the upper zone. The elevator shafts that serve the lower zones terminate with a machine room above the highest floor served (Fig. 14.3).
- Very high buildings have sky lobbies served by express elevators. People arriving in the lobby take an express elevator to the appropriate sky lobby where they get off the express elevator and wait for the local elevator system.
- Elevators should be arranged to serve a zone together in a clear fashion so that the wayfinding problem of the building user is simplified. It should be possible to walk into an office building lobby and easily determine which bank of elevators to use.
- Banks of elevators should consist of four or fewer cars so that people can respond easily to the arrival of an elevator.

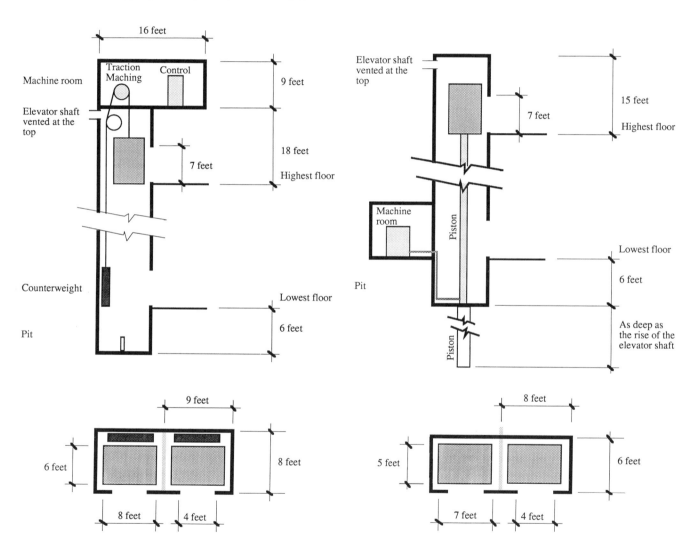

Figure 14.1 Approximate traction elevator layout information.

Figure 14.2 Approximate hydraulic elevator layout information.

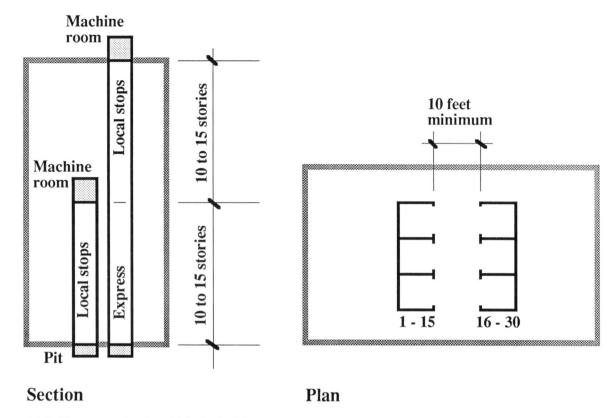

Section   **Plan**

Figure 14.3 Elevator zoning in a high-rise building.

ESCALATORS

When the building design requires moving large numbers of people up and down a few floors, escalators are a good choice. They are commonly used in department stores, commercial shopping centers, airports, and at the base of commercial high-rise buildings. The following provides general information for planning escalators (see also Fig. 14.4).

· All escalators rise at a 30 degree angle.
· Escalators come in two standard widths: 32 inches and 48 inches.
· There needs to be a minimum of 10 feet clear landing space at the top and bottom of the escalator for people to get on and off.
· The moving step assembly and support truss underneath the exposed part of the escalator take up approximately 4 feet of depth.
· The escalator will require structural support: a beam at the top and bottom for the escalator's internal truss structure to sit on.

· The escalator will require lighting that does not produce any distorting shadows that could cause safety problems.
· Escalators need to be laid out with a crowded flow of people in mind. Cross-over points where people will run into each other must be avoided.
· Current trends in the design of retail space use the escalators as a dramatic and dynamic focal feature of open atrium spaces.
· Because escalators create open holes through building floor assemblies, special smoke and fire protection provisions are necessary.

RESIDENTIAL ELEVATOR APPLICATIONS

Residential buildings are not as densely populated and do not require as rapid a service time as commercial buildings, thus fewer elevators are necessary. Residential buildings include apartment buildings, dormitories, and hotels. The following are rough guidelines for planning elevator service in residential buildings.

- The number of elevators is dependent on the number of apartments served and the height of the building (Macsai et al. 1976).
- In hotels and large apartment buildings, one elevator is required for every 70 to 100 units.
- In a 3- to 4-story building it is possible to walk up to the top floor if the elevator is broken. One elevator is acceptable. It will probably be a hydraulic elevator.
- In the 5- to 6-story range, two elevators are necessary so that there will always be an elevator available. Although elevators can be hydraulic in this height range, traction elevators will provide better service.
- In the 7- to 12-story range two traction elevators are needed. (This is above the range of hydraulic elevators.)

- Above 12 stories two to three traction elevators are necessary depending on elevator speed.
- Very tall buildings will require fast elevators and zoning of the elevator system as in commercial buildings.
- The configuration of the elevator lobby is a central feature in people's attitudes about the quality of a building.
- Apartments can be planned as 2-story units with internal stairs. This arrangement, called a skip stop system, allows the elevator to stop on every other floor.
- The elevator lobby on upper floors should be more than the space in the hallway in front of the elevator doors. The lobby should be a place distinguished from the hallway by extra width, access to natural light and a view out, and possibly some seating.

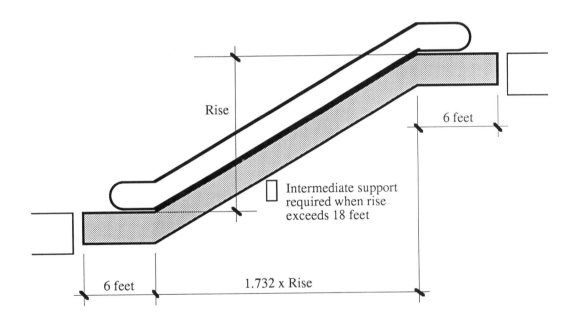

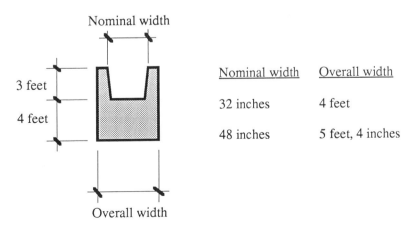

Nominal width	Overall width
32 inches	4 feet
48 inches	5 feet, 4 inches

Figure 14.4 Approximate escalator layout information.

TABLE 14.1.   Sizes and capacities of electric traction passenger elevators

A. Gearless—Speeds in Excess of 300 Fpm

Building	Rated capacity		Platform		Hoistway		Doors:[a]
	Lb	Passengers	Width w	Depth d	Clear width W	Clear depth D	Clear opening C
Office	2,500	16	7'-0"	5'-0"	8'-4"	6'-4"	3'-6"
Office or hotel	3,000	20	7'-0"	5'-6"	8'-4"	6'-10"	3'-6"
Large office	3,500	23	7'-0"	6'-2"	8'-4"	7'-6"	3'-6"
Store	3,500	23	8'-0"	5'-6"	9'-5"	6'-10"	4'-6"
Large office	4,000	27	8'-0"	6'-2"	9'-4"	7'-6"	4'-0"

B. Gearless Hospital—Speeds in Excess of 75 Fpm

Rated capacity	Passengers	Platform		Hoistway		Doors:[a]
		Width w	Depth d	Clear width W	Clear depth D	Clear opening C
4,000 Lb						
Front opening	26	5'-8"	8'-8"	7'-8"	9'-1"	4'-0"
Front & rear opening	26	5'-8"	9'-1½"	7'-8"	9'-6"	4'-0"
5,000 Lb[b]						
Front opening	33	6'-0"	9'-6"	8'-0"	9'-11"	4'-0"
Front & rear opening	33	6'-0"	10'-0"	8'-0"	10'-4½"	4'-0"

C. Geared—Speeds up to 350 Fpm

Building	Rated capacity		Platform		Hoistway		Doors[a]		
	Lb	Passengers	Width w	Depth d	Clear width W	Clear depth D	Type	Sill	Clear opening C
Apartment	1,200	8	5'-0"	4'-0"	6'-4"	5'-3"	Single swing[c]	None	2'-8"
							Two speed	5½"	3'-0"
Apartment and small factory	2,000	13	6'-4"	4'-5"	7'-8"	5'-8"	Single swing[c]	None	2'-8"
							Single slide	4"	3'-0"
	2,500	16	7'-0"	5'-0"	8'-4"	6'-3"	Center opening	4"	3'-6"
Small office and factory	3,000	20	7'-0"	5'-6"	8'-4"	6'-9"	Center opening	4"	3'-6"
Department store	3,500	23	8'-0"	5'-6"	9'-5"	6'-10"	Center opening	4"	4'-6"

Source: Merritt and Ambrose 1990.
[a]Standard door height 7 ft. Rough sills are usually 4 in. for single-slide or center-opening doors and 5½ in. for two-speed doors.
[b]5,000-lb hospital elevators have two-speed, center-opening doors.
[c]Recommended only for elevators with speeds of 100 fpm or less.

TABLE 14.2.   Sizes and capacities of electric traction freight elevators

A. Light Duty—25 Fpm					
	Platform		Hoistway		Doors:[a]
Capacity, lb	Width w	Depth d	Clear width W	Clear depth D	Clear opening C
1,500	5'-4"	6'-1"	6'-11"	6'-9"	4'-5"
2,000	6'-4"	7'-0"	7'-11"	7'-8"	5'-2"
2,500	6'-4"	8'-0"	7'-11"	8'-8"	5'-2"

B. General Purpose—Speeds 50-200 Fpm					
	Platform		Hoistway		Doors:[c]
Capacity, lb	Width w	Depth d	Clear width W	Clear depth D	Clear opening
3,000	5'-4"	7'-0"	7'-2"	7'-11"	5'-0"
2,500, 3,500, 4,000	6'-4"	8'-0"	8'-4"	8'-11"	6'-0"
4,000, 5,000, 6,000, 8,000	8'-4"	10'-0"	10'-4"	10'-11"	8'-0"
10,000	8'-4"	12'-0"	10'-6"	12'-11"	8'-0"

C. Heavy Duty—Speeds 50-200 Fpm					
	Platform		Hoistway		Doors:
Capacity, lb	Width w	Depth d	Clear width W[e]	Clear depth D[b]	Clear opening C
10,000	8'-4"	12'-4"	11'-4"	12'-11"	8'-0" × 8'-0"
12,000	10'-4"	14'-0"	13'-6"	14'-11"	10'-0" × 8'-0"
16,000	10'-4"	14'-0"	13'-10"	15'-3"	10'-0" × 10'-0"
18,000	10'-4"	16'-0"	13'-11"	17'-3"	10'-0" × 10'-0"
20,000	12'-0"	20'-0"	15'-9"	21'-3"	11'-8" × 10'-0"

Source: Merritt and Ambrose 1990.
[a]Standard door height is 7 ft.
[b]Hoistway, front to back, is large enough to allow for installation of a reverse or rear opening in the car.
[c]Standard door height is 8 ft.
[e]These dimensions inlude space for double column guide-rail supports.

TABLE 14.3. Sizes and capacities of hydraulic elevators

A. Passenger

Capacity, lb	Pas-sen-gers	Platform		Hoistway		Doors:[a] clear opening C	Pit	Over-head	Max. rise	Stops
		Width w	Depth d	Clear width W	Clear depth D					
1,500	10	5'-0"	4'-6"	6'-8"	4'-11"	2'-8"	4'-0"	10'-9"	29'-0"	3
2,000	13	6'-4"	4'-5"	7'-8"	4'-10"	3'-0"	4'-0"	11'-0"	41'-0"	5
2,500	16	7'-0"	5'-0"	8'-4"	5'-5"	3'-6"	4'-0"	11'-3"	42'-0"	5
3,000	20	7'-0"	5'-6"	8'-4"	5'-11"	3'-6"	4'-0"	11'-3"	42'-0"	5
3,500	23	7'-0"	6'-2"	8'-4"	6'-7"	3'-6"	4'-0"	11'-3"	42'-0"	5
4,000	26	8'-0"	6'-2"	9'-4"	6'-7"	4'-0"	4'-0"	11'-3"	42'-0"	5

B. Hospital

4,000	26	5'-8"	8'-8"	7'-3"	9'-1"	4'-0"	4'-0"	11'-3"	36'-0"	5

C. Freight

Capacity, lb	Platform		Hoistway		Doors: clear opening	Pit	Overhead
	Width w	Depth d	Clear width W	Clear depth D[b]			
2,500	5'-4"	7'-0"	6'-8"	7'-11"	4'-3" × 7'-6"	4'-3"	14'-0"
3,000	6'-4"	8'-0"	7'-8"	8'-11"	6'-0" × 7'-6"	4'-3"	14'-0"
3,500	6'-4"	8'-0"	7'-8"	8'-11"	6'-0" × 8'-0"	4'-6"	14'-3"
4,000	6'-4"	8'-0"	7'-8"	8'-11"	6'-0" × 8'-0"	4'-6"	14'-3"
5,000	8'-4"	10'-0"	9'-10"	10'-11"	8'-0" × 8'-0"	4'-6"	14'-3"
6,000	8'-4"	10'-0"	9'-10"	10'-11"	8'-0" × 8'-0"	4'-6"	14'-3"
8,000	8'-4"	12'-0"	9'-10"	12'-11"	8'-0" × 8'-0"	4'-6"	14'-3"
10,000	8'-4"	12'-0"	11'-4"[c]	12'-11"	8'-0" × 8'-0"	4'-10"	14'-3"
12,000	8'-4"	14'-0"	11'-6"[c]	14'-11"	8'-0" × 8'-0"	5'-0"	14'-3"
16,000	8'-4"	16'-0"	11'-8"[c]	17'-3"	8'-0" × 10'-0"	5'-6"	16'-3"
18,000	10'-4"	16'-0"	13'-8"[c]	17'-3"	10'-0" × 10'-0"	5'-6"	16'-3"
20,000	12'-0"	20'-0"	15'-4"[c]	21'-3"	11'-8" × 10'-0"	5'-6"	16'-3"

Source: Merritt and Ambrose 1990.
[a]Standard door height 7 ft.
[b]Hoistway, front to back, is large enough to allow for installation of a reverse or rear opening in the car.
[c]These dimensions include space for double column guide-rail supports.

15

The Plumbing System

The plumbing system is larger and bulkier than the electrical and telephone systems but not as bulky as the structural or HVAC systems. Thus the integration problem is less complicated. Restrooms need to be laid out and located, a hot water heater needs to be located, water supply and drainage systems need to be routed through the building and connected to the utility systems outside, and sprinkler systems and standpipes need to be positioned. In a tall building a water supply pumping system is required.

RESTROOMS

The men's and women's restrooms need to be laid out to determine their size, and they must be located in the developing building concept. Stacking bathrooms above each other minimizes the need to make horizontal pipe runs through the building. Handicapped access must be considered when laying out restroom fixtures, the clear space in the restroom, and the entrance door to the restroom. Basic restroom dimensions are given below.

- Water closet stalls are 3 by 5 feet. The door opens into the stall except for the handicapped stalls, where the door opens out.
- Urinals are approximately 12 inches deep by 18 inches wide.
- Lavatories are about 20 inches by 20 inches, and are often set in a 24-inch wide counter.
- A clear space five feet in diameter must be provided inside the restroom for a wheelchair to turn around in (Fig. 15.1).
- To provide a good vertical plumbing chase between bathrooms, 12 to 18 inches is needed.

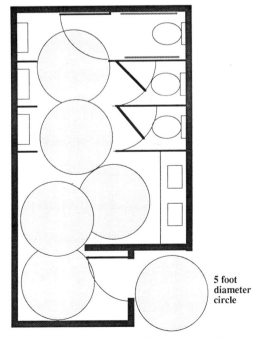

5 foot diameter circle

Figure 15.1 Bathroom layout allowing space for a wheelchair to turn around.

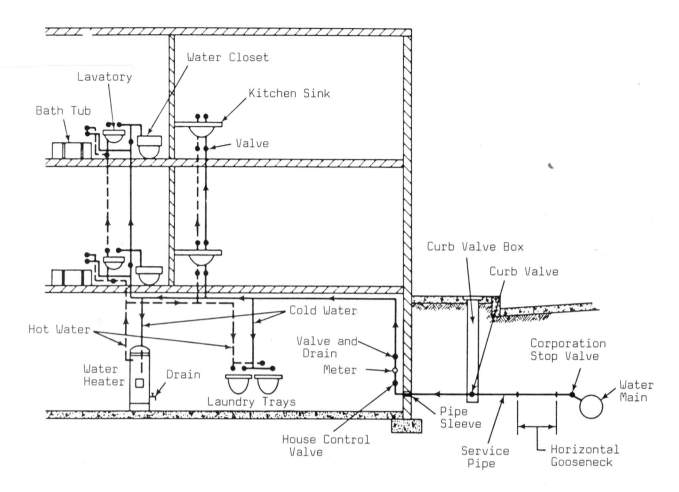

Figure 15.2 Water supply system for a low-rise building. Reproduced by permission from Merritt and Ambrose (1990).

OTHER FIXTURE REQUIREMENTS

Locate any special plumbing requirements in other areas of the building. Keep in mind that horizontal runs of drainage piping are difficult to achieve inside the building. The best arrangement is to bring the plumbing straight down—often along a column—and make connections horizontally under the building.

WATER SUPPLY

After the water supply enters the building, it divides into a hot and a cold water distribution system. This division occurs at the hot water heater, which can often be located in the HVAC mechanical room. Where bathrooms are spread far apart horizontally, consideration should be given to multiple hot water heaters.

Water supply pipes range from ½ inch to about 2 inches in diameter. Hot and cold pipes are usually laid out parallel to each other.

Water Supply Pumps The city water pressure will push water up through two or three stories. (Figure 15.2 shows a typical water supply system operating from city water pressure.) Buildings taller than this will need a surge tank and water pressure pumps. This equipment takes up approximately 100 to 200 square feet of space. Figure 15.3 shows a typical high-rise water supply system.

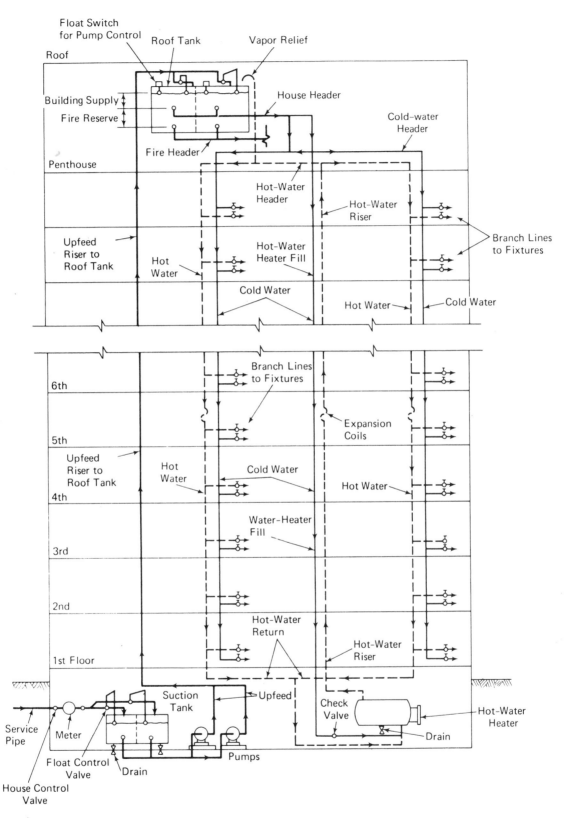

Figure 15.3 Water supply system for a high-rise building. Reproduced by permission from Merritt and Ambrose (1990).

SANITARY DRAINAGE

Waste water will be generated at the bathrooms and other plumbing fixtures in the building. The sanitary drainage system collects this wastewater, which flows by gravity down through the building and out into the city sanitary sewer system (Fig. 15.4). The gravity flow requirement makes it more difficult to lay out than the water supply system.

Because of the slope requirement, long horizontal runs of drainage pipe will run out of ceiling space to fit in. Ideally sanitary drainage pipes should run vertically down through the building collecting short branch lines from stacked bathrooms. This drainage line is called a plumbing stack.

A 4-inch plumbing stack can serve approximately 50 water closets and their accompanying lavatories. (A stack is never less than 4 inches.) A 6-inch plumbing stack can serve approximately 150 watercloset and accompanying lavatories.

The building drain runs horizontally under the building collecting wastewater from multiple vertical stacks. A 4- to 6-inch pipe requires a minimum slope of ⅛ inch per foot. A pipe 8 inches or larger requires a minimum slope of ¹⁄₁₆ inch per foot.

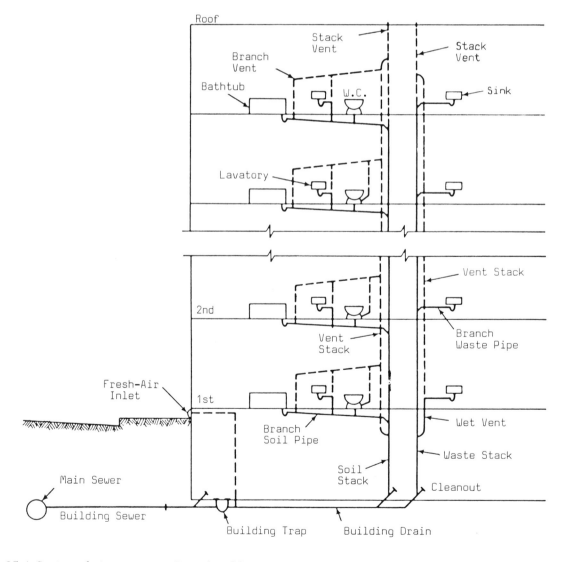

Figure 15.4 Sanitary drainage system. Reproduced by permission from Merritt and Ambrose (1990).

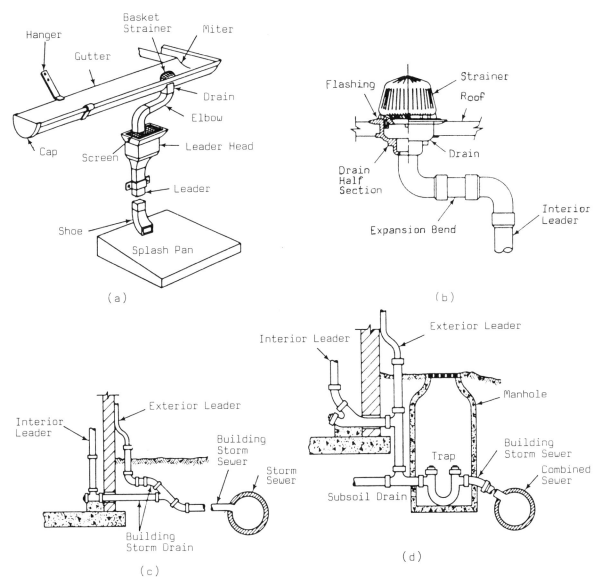

Figure 15.5 Storm drainage system components. (a) Roof gutter, exterior leader, and splash pan; (b) roof drain and top portion of interior leader; (c) piping to a storm sewer; (d) piping to a combined sewer. Reproduced by permission from Merritt and Ambrose (1990).

STORM DRAINAGE

The rainwater that falls on the roof and the grounds of a building needs to be collected and channeled into the city storm drainage system. The roof slope must be arranged to channel water to drain points, where drainage pipes can carry the water down through the building and out into the storm drainage system. The storm drainage water is kept separate from the sanitary drainage water so that the sewage treatment system will not become overloaded in a rainstorm. Storm drainage system components are shown in Figure 15.5.

The following guidelines can be used in planning a storm drainage system.
· Flat roofs need a minimum slope to drain points of ¼ inch per foot.
· Except for small roof areas, there should be more than one drain point on a roof area.
· Back-up drains or scuppers should be provided in case the main drains become clogged. These should be located about 4 inches up slope from the main drains. In a low-rise building they should discharge directly to the outside so that any drainage problem on the roof can be easily identified.

- Horizontal storm drainage pipes have a minimum slope of $\frac{1}{8}$ inch per foot. As in the sanitary drainage system, the best strategy is therefore to route them vertically down through the building with a minimum of horizontal collection lines. The multiple vertical lines can be fed into a main drainage line in the basement or below the building.
- For a maximum rainfall of 2 inches per hour, the required vertical, roof drain pipe sizes are as follows:
  - A 4-inch pipe for 9000 square feet of roof
  - A 5-inch pipe for 17,000 square feet of roof
  - A 6-inch pipe for 27,000 square feet of roof
- For a maximum rainfall of 3 inches per hour, pipe sizes are
  - A 4-inch pipe for 6000 square feet of roof
  - A 5-inch pipe for 11,000 square feet of roof
  - A 6-inch pipe for 18,000 square feet of roof

THE SPRINKLER SYSTEM

A sprinkler system is the most effective way to provide for fire safety in a building. A correctly operating sprinkler system will extinguish a fire before it can spread out of control. The pumps and valves for the sprinkler system take up a about 100 to 500 square feet depending on building size.

16

The Electrical and Signal Systems

Because they are not big and bulky like the structural and HVAC systems, or visually dominant like the lighting system, electrical and signal systems do not pose a major integration problem. They do require equipment rooms and access chases through the building, however.

THE ELECTRICAL SYSTEM

Electrical systems vary widely in complexity by building size and building type. The basic system includes a transformer, main switchboard, motor control panels, distribution panel boards, and a local circuit distribution system of some sort. The architect will have to provide room for a transformer, space for the main switchboard, space for motor control panel boards, chases through the building for electrical wiring, and closets for branch circuit panel boards spaced throughout the building.

The Transformer The utility company distributes electrical power at high voltage. The aim is efficiency: to push a large amount of power through fairly small wires with a minimum voltage drop. Transformers are necessary at the point of use to step the voltage down to safer levels.

In the case of small or residential scale buildings, the utility company owns the transformers and sells low-voltage power to the user at 120/240-volt single phase. The transformers are often pole mounted, oil cooled, about 18 inches in diameter, and three feet high. Where power is run underground, the transformer is a dry type mounted on a concrete pad outside. The components of residential scale electrical service are shown in Figure 16.1.

A commercial building has a much larger electrical load and consequently needs a more complex electrical system (see Fig. 16.2). The electrical load—for lighting, outlets, the HVAC system, elevators, and so on—is approximately 10 watts per square foot of floor area. The large motors driving HVAC equipment, elevators, and escalators run more efficiently on three-phase power because it produces a rotating magnetic field inside a motor that smoothly drives the rotation of the motor.

Medium-sized commercial buildings can purchase their power at cheaper higher voltage rates and operate their own transformer. The transformer, which can be located outside on a concrete pad or inside as part of a unit substation, is usually a dry type supplying 120/208-volt three-phase power. The size of the transformer can be approximated from the square feet of floor area to be served:

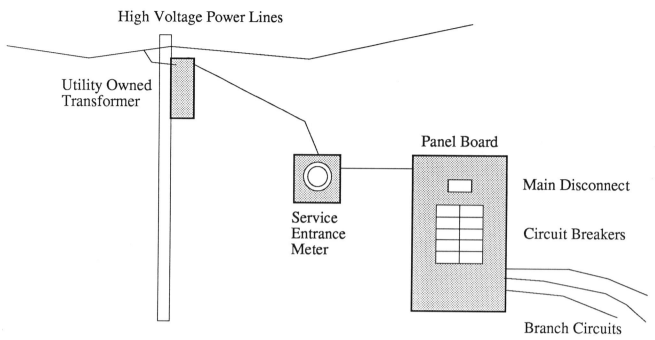

Figure 16.1 Residential scale electrical service.

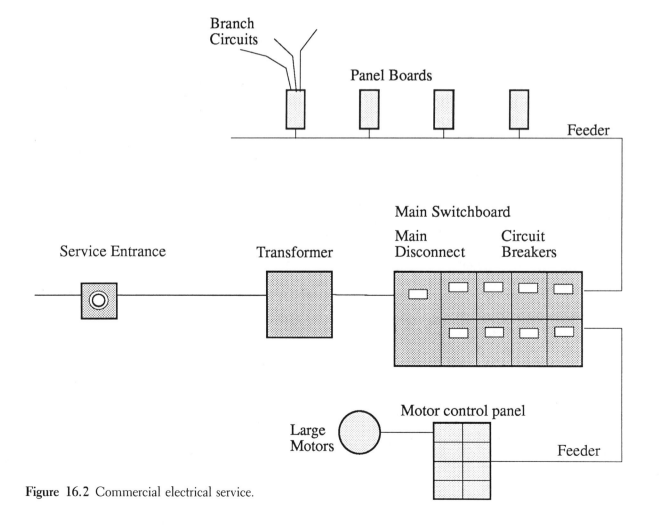

Figure 16.2 Commercial electrical service.

· A unit 12 inches by 8 inches by 18 inches high can serve up to 10,000 square feet.
· A unit 4 feet by 2 feet by 3.5 feet high can serve 100,000 square feet.
· A unit 6 feet by 3 feet by 6 feet high can serve 500,000 square feet.

To minimize electrical feeder conductor size and voltage drop, large buildings will purchase high-voltage power and step it down to a still relatively high 277/480 volts in a large transformer enclosed in a transformer vault for fire safety. The vault can be located inside the building or underground outside. In either location provision for ventilation must be made. Smaller dry transformers located throughout the building will then step the 480 volts down to 120 volts for electrical outlets.

The Main Switchboard   The main switchboard is generally located near the place where the electrical power enters the building. It groups a main disconnect switch and circuit breakers that divide the electrical power into feeder circuits that serve separate systems or areas of the building.

In residential scale buildings the main switchboard is an electrical panel board with a main disconnect switch and a collection of circuit breakers dividing up the load. The panel board is normally 20 inches wide by 5 inches deep by 30 inches high. Branch circuits should not extend more than 100 feet from a panel board because of wire size and the potential for voltage drop.

In a small commercial building using 5 watts per square foot for lighting and electrical outlets, a panel board with 120-volt 20-amp circuit breakers (a 20-amp breaker is loaded to 16 amps) could serve the following areas:

$$(400 \text{ sq. ft./breaker}) \times (30 \text{ breakers}) = 12,000 \text{ sq. ft.}$$
$$(400 \text{ sq. ft./breaker}) \times (42 \text{ breakers}) = 16,800 \text{ sq. ft.}$$

In medium-sized commercial or apartment buildings, the main switchboard is a more elaborate piece of equipment because the electrical power used is much greater. The switchboard contains a main disconnect and the main circuit breakers that divide the electrical load into major components. The major components of the electrical load are large motors for the HVAC equipment, large motors for the elevators and escalators, and lighting and receptacle panel boards throughout the building.

For maintenance, 4 to 6 feet of access space in front of the switchboard are necessary. Switchboard equipment is available in front access only for modest loads, and front and back access for more substantial loads. A low-voltage metal enclosed front-access switchboard is approximately 6 feet long by 2 feet deep by 7 feet high. (The transformer will be located elsewhere, usually outside on a concrete pad.) This type of switchboard is limited to 2000 amps, which, depending on the load mix, can serve about 70,000 square feet of commercial space.

The main step-down transformer can be included along with the switchboard. This combination, called a unit substation, is approximately 10 to 15 feet long by 5 feet deep by 7 feet high (Fig. 16.3). The length varies according to the number of circuit breakers included. Four to 6 feet of access is required all around.

In large and tall buildings the main switchboard functions in the same way as in a medium-sized building, but the voltages distributed are higher (277/480). The distribution system is therefore more complex (Fig. 16.4). Dry transformers are located at power distribu-

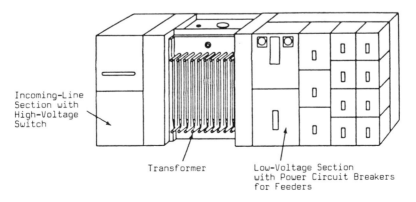

Incoming-Line Section with High-Voltage Switch

Transformer

Low-Voltage Section with Power Circuit Breakers for Feeders

Figure 16.3 A commercial unit substation. Reproduced by permission from Merritt and Ambrose (1990).

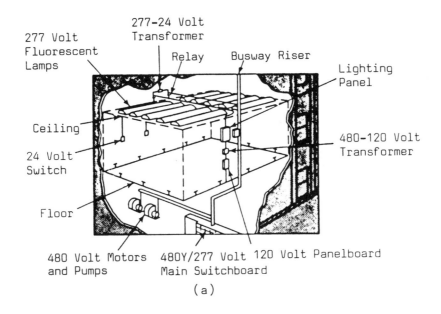

277-24 Volt Transformer

277 Volt Fluorescent Lamps

Relay

Busway Riser

Lighting Panel

Ceiling

480-120 Volt Transformer

24 Volt Switch

Floor

480 Volt Motors and Pumps

480Y/277 Volt Main Switchboard

120 Volt Panelboard

(a)

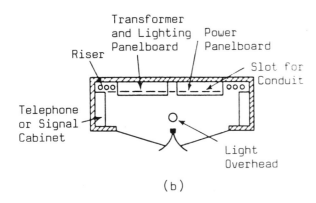

Transformer and Lighting Panelboard

Power Panelboard

Riser

Slot for Conduit

Telephone or Signal Cabinet

Light Overhead

(b)

Figure 16.4 A typical electrical distribution system for tall and large buildings. (a) Busway riser supplies power to panelboard in each story; (b) plan of electrical closet on each building floor. Reproduced by permission from Merritt and Ambrose (1990).

tion panel boards inside the building to supply the lighting and receptacle panel boards with 120 volts.

A large building main switchboard is approximately 10 to 15 feet long by 5 feet deep by 7 feet high. The length will vary with the number of circuit breakers. For maintenance, 4 to 6 feet of access is necessary all around the switchboard.

Figure 16.5 is a diagram of a large metal-enclosed switchboard.

Motor Controller Panel Boards The large motors driving the HVAC equipment, the elevators, and other large motors that are in the building require separate motor control panels. These units are a combination starter and circuit breaker. In a large mechanical room with many large motors, the motor control equipment is grouped together into a motor control panel board. Motor control panel boards can be mounted against the wall.

A motor control center for large motors varies in length according to the number of motor controllers involved. A basic panel module is approximately 1 foot wide by 1.5 feet deep by 7 feet high. A module 1 foot wide can accommodate two to four motor control units stacked on top of one another. Smaller motors in isolated locations require individual motor control units approximately 12 inches wide by 6 inches deep by 18 inches high.

Lighting and Branch Circuit Panel Boards Lighting and receptacle branch circuits originate at panel boards spaced around the building for convenient access (Fig. 16.6). There is at least one panel board on each floor of a building. The panel boards are generally related to the functional groupings of the building. For example, the panel containing the circuits serving a small auditorium would be located in the projection booth at the back of the room.

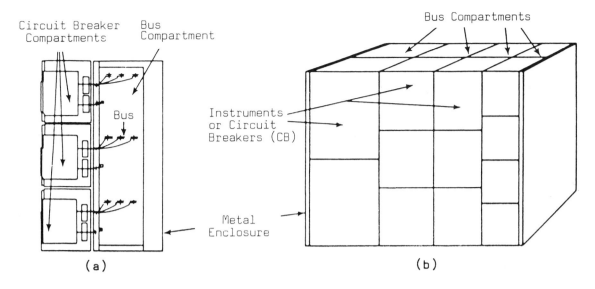

Figure 16.5 Commercial switchgear. (a) Transverse section through low-voltage switchgear; (b) arrangements of stacked compartments. Reproduced by permission from Merritt and Ambrose (1990).

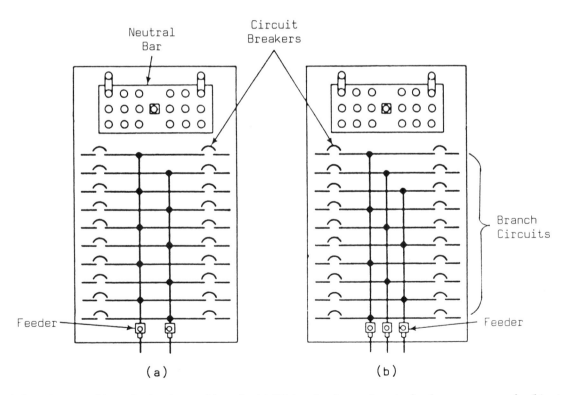

Figure 16.6 Lighting and branch circuit panel boards. (a) Wiring for three-wire, single-phase power supply; (b) wiring for four-wire, three-phase power supply. Reproduced by permission from Merritt and Ambrose (1990).

Branch circuit length is limited to 80 to 100 feet of extension from the panel board. Beyond 100 feet the voltage drop restrictions on wire size create too large a wire for convenient use. In a commercial building using 5 watts per square foot for lighting and electrical outlets, a panel board with 120-volt 20-amp circuit breakers (a 20-amp breaker is loaded to 16 amps) could serve the following areas:

$$(400 \text{ sq. ft./breaker}) \times (30 \text{ breakers}) = 12,000 \text{ sq. ft.}$$
$$(400 \text{ sq. ft./breaker}) \times (42 \text{ breakers}) = 16,800 \text{ sq. ft.}$$

Panel boards are approximately 20 inches wide by 5 inches deep by 30 to 60 inches high, depending on the number of circuit breakers. The maximum number of breakers in a panel board is 42. Panel boards are often mounted in a closet with the telephone distribution equipment. The area needed is approximately 0.005 times the building area served.

Branch Circuit Distribution System Commercial buildings, especially commercial office buildings, often require the capability of locating electrical power and telephone service anywhere on the floor surface. This flexibility can be provided in a variety of different ways:

· "Poke through" is the simplest distribution system (Fig. 16.7). The power is run in conduits under the floor; where someone wants power, a hole is drilled to bring the power up. The hole must be properly sealed to maintain fire safety.
· In steel construction, raceways incorporated into the metal deck can be used for power and telephone wiring.
· In concrete construction, under-floor metal ducts can be cast into the floor system to provide wire raceways.
· Raceways and under-floor ducts are spaced at about 5 feet on center under an office floor.
· Where there are a lot of wires and flexibility is important, as in a computer installation, a raised floor can be constructed. This arrangement provides ample and easy access for rewiring everywhere in the space.

THE TELEPHONE SYSTEM

The telephone and other signal systems in buildings will vary in complexity over a wide range. This section outlines parameters for a generic telephone system (Fig. 16.8). Exact determination of signal system space requirements cannot be accurate without detailed knowledge of the complexity of the system being planned for.

Telephone service entrance space requirements will vary with the size and complexity of the building. A large building will have a 400-square-foot telephone terminal room with telephone closets located at secondary distribution points throughout the building. A small building can be served by a 4- to 6-foot telephone closet.

Large buildings need apparatus closets to house the telephone switching equipment for each area or each floor of the building. Often the telephone and electrical distribution equipment is located together. This space takes the form of a closet that has an area approximately 0.005 times the building floor area served.

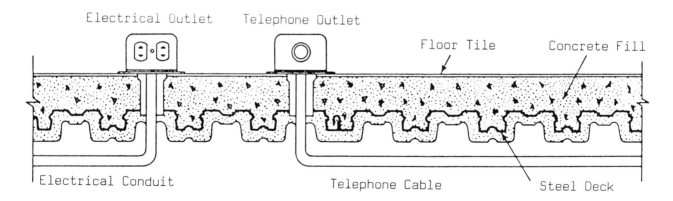

Figure 16.7 "Poke through" electrical and telephone distribution system. Reproduced by permission from Merritt and Ambrose (1990).

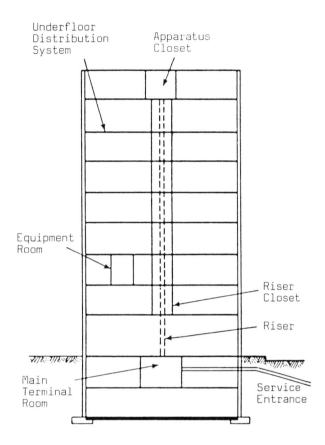

Figure 16.8 Typical telephone distribution system. Reproduced by permission from Merritt and Ambrose (1990).

17

The Technical Integration Game

The integration of the many components that are required to design a constructible building is a complex problem that has no direct algorithmic solution. The problem is beyond logic. A tool that can take the designer beyond logic is play. Technical integration can be conceived as a cooperative game played between the technical systems, interlinked with a cooperative game played between the designer's logical and intuitive minds (Minai 1989). It is the combination of rule systems explored with logic, and chance provided by the intuitive leaps of a well-prepared mind that is responsible for the creation of harmonious form.

TWO SIDES OF EXISTENCE

The world of phenomena presents itself in two forms (Rucker 1987). One aspect is digital, like the number of trees in a row, the number of pebbles I am holding in my hand, or the amount of money I should be paid to do a certain job. The other aspect is continuous, like the area of the lawn in front of a house, the volume of water in a glass, or how happy I am with the way my life is going. Our minds have a structure to deal with this situation. The mind has a digital logical side and a continuous intuitive side. The digital logical side has become very powerful in recent history. Scientific method has allowed the digital logical side of the brain to achieve important tasks on demand. It is the continuous intuitive side of the mind, always monitoring the continuity of life, from which new creative ideas come, however. We need both sides of the mind to function.

COOPERATIVE GAMES

In *The Laws of the Game*, Eigen and Winkler (1981) explore the ways in which the combination of game rules and the element of chance create form. The authors introduce the reader to games and play in the following manner:

Chance and rules are the elements that underlie games and play. Play began among the elementary particles, atoms, and molecules, and now our brain cells carry it on. Human beings did not invent play, but it is play and only play that makes man complete.

All our capabilities arise from play. First there is the play of limbs and muscles. The aimless grasping and kicking of an infant develop into carefully coordinated movements. Then there is the play of our senses. Playful curiosity sends us in search of profound knowledge. From play with colors, shapes, and sounds emerge immortal works of art. The first expressions of love take the form of play: the secret exchange of glances, dancing, the interplay of thoughts and emotions, the yielding of partners to each other. In Sanskrit, the union of lovers is called *kridaratnam*, the jewel of games.

Games do not have to be a competition, with one player trying to beat another. In cooperative games, the players coordinate strategies to achieve some larger goal. An example of a cooperative game is warming up for a volleyball game with a group of players in a circle. The object of the game is to keep the ball in the air. All the players win as long as the ball stays in the air. All the players lose if the ball falls on the sand.

PLAYING THE TECHNICAL INTEGRATION GAME

Technical integration is a cooperative game played on two levels. The architectural, building code, structural, HVAC, lighting, acoustic, vertical transportation, plumbing, and electrical systems are playing together to create a harmonious composition. Overlaid on top of this game the designer's digital logical mind is playing a cooperative game with his continuous intuitive mind.

The rules of the game are the architectural program, the site constraints, and the technical system sizing and composition constraints. This book provides easy access to the technical system rule structures.

The chance element comes from the continuous intuitive side of the designer's brain. Where constraints conflict, intuition often leaps in to reconfigure the situation. These creative leaps are unpredictable in timing and in where they lead. Creative leaps do not come out of nowhere, however; they emerge from a well-prepared mind.

The game structure outlined below is an attempt to coordinate the logical rule structure of technical system constraints with the chance event of the creative leap from a prepared intuition.

1. Begin the game with the architectural concept and organization of spaces to meet that concept (see Chapter 10). Developing the basic concept of the architecture is a game in itself that must be played before but also during the technical integration game.
2. Over the concept layout of spaces, sketch a solution to each of the technical systems. Keep the drawings small enough to draw quickly and change easily but large enough to present the needed information. Annotate the drawings to store information. Do not worry about conflict between systems on this first pass.
3. After all the technical systems have been initially laid out, identify and explore the conflict points between systems. Creative inspiration lives on conflict. Learn to follow intuition as well as logic.
4. Do not be afraid of intuitive leaps that restructure things. Chance is as important as rules in the creation of form.
5. The technical system integration should aid the design concept of the building. The following visual design scales (Dondis 1974) can help produce intuitive leap ideas: Balance/Instability; Symmetry/Asymmetry; Regularity/Irregularity; Unity/Fragmentation; Economy/Intricacy; Understatement/Exaggeration; Predictability/Spontaneity; Activeness/Stasis; Subtlety/Boldness; Neutrality/Accent; Transparency/Opacity; Consistency/Variation; Accuracy/Distortion; Flatness/Depth; Singularity/Juxtaposition; Sequentiality/Randomness; Sharpness/Diffusion; Repetition/Episodicity.
6. The heart of a cooperative game is the development of coordinated strategies between the players. Develop strategies of relative importance. In a cooperative game any player or group of players might become dominant.
7. Play the game. Do not settle on the first solution or force system interactions that do not feel right. An old piece of design advice applies here. When the design concept is right the pieces start falling easily into place.
8. Remember that this is a multiplayer game. The designer cannot ignore any of the players. He can let some dominate others but he cannot ignore any. All the players have to play.
9. Remember that play is fun.

APPENDIX A

Student Drawings

The following drawings were produced by Greg Blaylock in the structural and mechanical integration design studio in the School of Architecture at the University of Tennessee. The drawings were produced by photocopying pencil drawings of the floor plans and sections. The technical systems were then drawn on the photocopies with a bold felt tipped pen. This procedure minimizes redrawing.

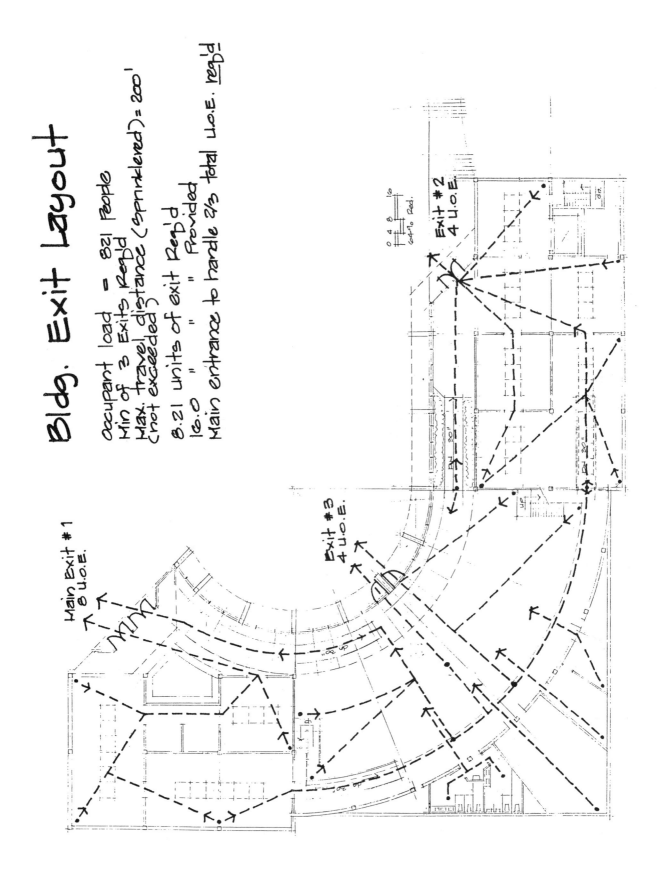

Bldg. Exit Layout

Occupant load = 821 People
Min. of 3 Exits Req'd
Max. travel distance (Sprinkled) = 200'
(not exceeded)

8.21 units of exit Req'd
16.0 " = " Provided
Main entrance to handle 2/3 total u.o.E. req'd

Main Exit #1
7 8 u.o.E.

Exit #3
4 u.o.E.

Exit #2
4 u.o.E.

0 4 8   16
64% Red.

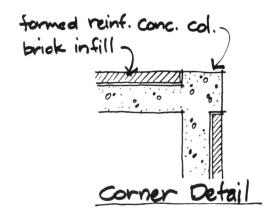

formed reinf. conc. col.
brick infill

Corner Detail

Structural Concepts

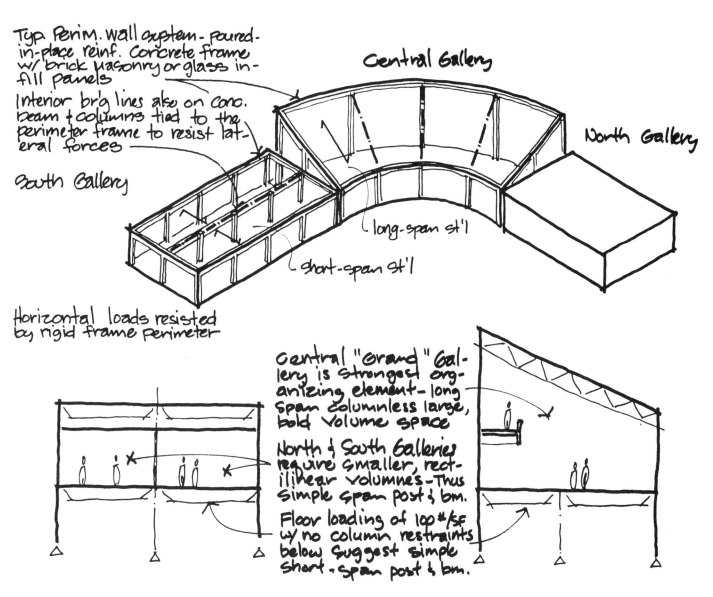

Typ. Perim. wall system - poured-in-place reinf. Concrete frame w/ brick masonry or glass in-fill panels

Interior br'g lines also on conc. beam & columns tied to the perimeter frame to resist lat-eral forces

South Gallery

Central Gallery

North Gallery

long-span st'l

short-span st'l

Horizontal loads resisted by rigid frame perimeter

Central "Grand" Gal-lery is strongest org-anizing element - long span columnless large, bold volume space

North & South Galleries require smaller, rect-ilinear volumes - Thus simple span post & bm.

Floor loading of 100#/sf w/ no column restraints below Suggest simple short-span post & bm.

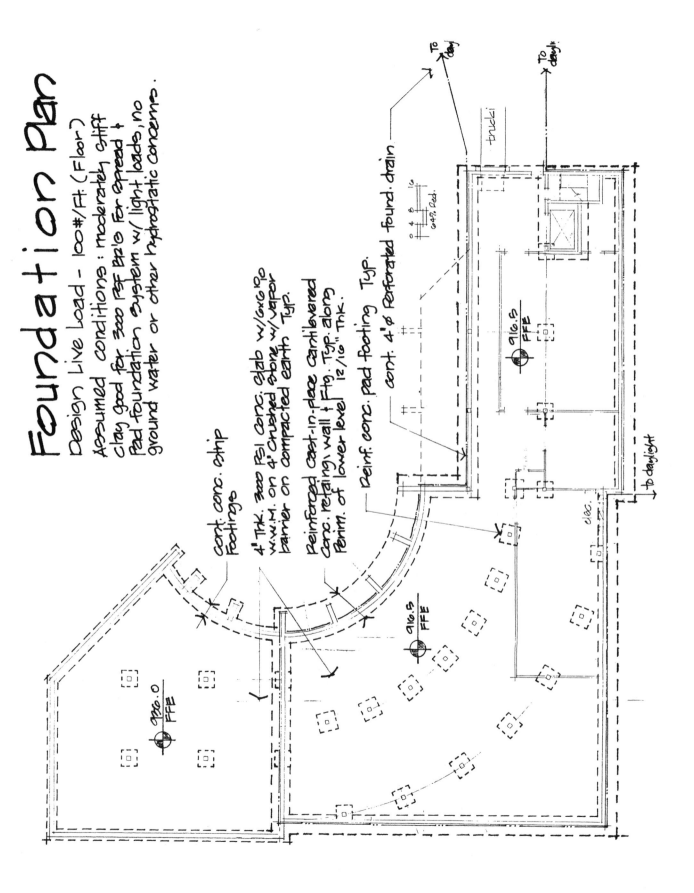

Foundation Plan

Design Live Load – 100#/ft.² (floor)
Assumed conditions: moderately stiff
clay good for 3000 psf BRG for spread +
Pad foundation system w/ light loads, no
ground water or other hydrostatic concerns.

cont. conc. strip
footings

4" thk. 3000 PSI conc. slab w/ 6x6 10
w.w.m. on 4" crushed stone w/ vapor
barrier on compacted earth. Typ.

Reinforced cast-in-place cantilevered
conc. retaining wall + ftg. Typ. along
Perim. of lower level 12/16" thk.

Reinf. conc. pad footing Typ.

cont. 4" Ø Perforated found. drain

916.5
FFE

916.0
FFE

916.5
FFE

To daylight

To daylight

to daylight

trench

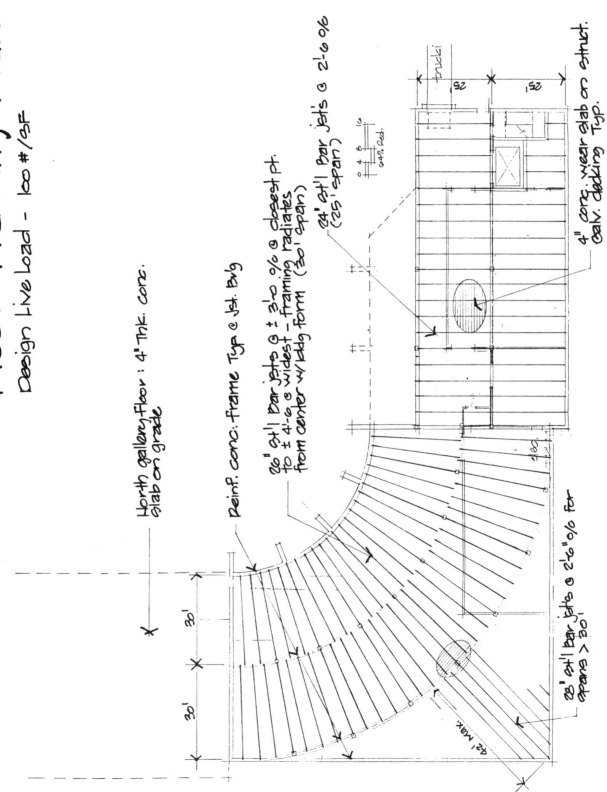

Floor Framing Plan

Design Live Load - 100 #/SF

North gallery floor : 4" Thk. conc. slab on grade

Reinf. conc. frame Typ @ Jst. Brg

26" @ 4" Bar Jsts @ ± 3'-0 % @ closest pt. to ± 4'-6 @ widest - framing radiates from center w/ bldg form (30' span)

24" @ 4" Bar Jst's @ 2'-6 % (25' span)

4" conc. wear slab on struct. galv. decking Typ.

28' @ 4" Bar Jsts @ 2'-6 % @ grade < 30' for

42' Max.

truck

25'

25'

Roof Framing Plan

Design Live Load - 20 lb/sf

North Gallery Fram'g
Same as South

Sloped Glazing System - structural alum. tube
frame supports w/ insul. tempered glass

24" O.H. bar jsts w/ sloped big seats @ ± 4'-0 o/c
@ lower brg - spacing increases to ± 6'-6 o/c @ top

40" Deep O.H. Girder Truss (60' span)
w/ panel point in 15' from brg. @ truss.
Designed interactive w/ truss (Typ.) for 3
spans

Reinf. conc.
frame Typ.

18" O.H. bar jsts
@ 5'-0 o/c Typ.
25' span

1½" Type 'B' Mtl. Deck Typ.

when jst span is
< 12' use 8" Mtl channels
w/ 4's as req'd

Truss

Slope
12'

Truss

Truss

segment 1½" Mtl deck
from jst to jst to con-
form to roof shape

20" O.H. Bar jsts @
5'-0 o/c > 28' span
18" jsts @ 5'-0 o/c
< 28' span

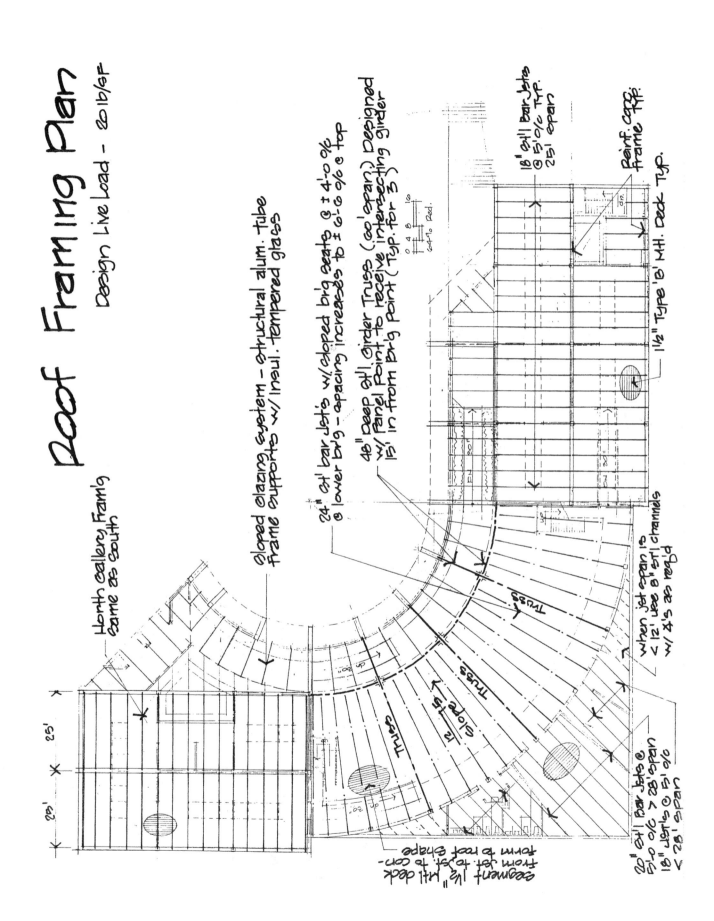

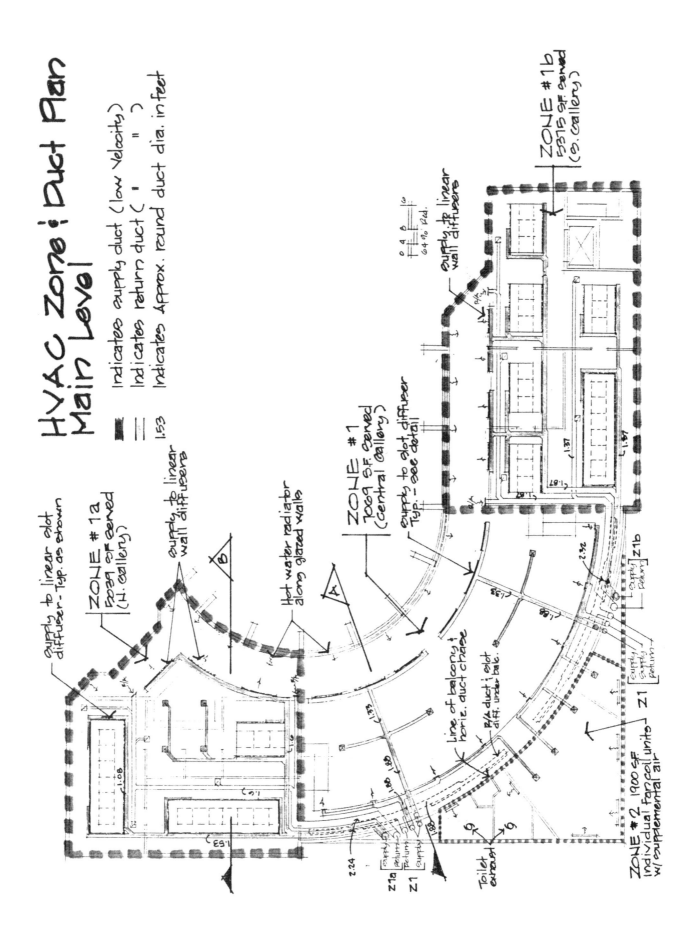

HVAC Zone & Duct Plan
Main Level

▆▆ — Indicates supply duct (low velocity)
═══ — Indicates return duct (| " =)
1.53 — Indicates approx. round duct dia. in feet

supply to linear slot
diffuser - Typ. as shown

ZONE #1a
1024 S.F. served
(N. Gallery)

supply to linear
wall diffusers

Hot water radiator
along glazed walls

ZONE #1
7069 S.F. served
(Central Gallery)

supply to slot diffuser
Typ. - see detail

Line of balcony &
horiz. duct chase

R/A duct & slot
diff. under bac.

Toilet exhaust

ZONE #2 1900 SF
individual farcoil units
w/ supplemental air

ZONE #1b
5375 sf served
(S. Gallery)

supply to linear
wall diffusers

HVAC Zone & Duct Plan Lower Level

HVAC Custom Equipment & Zone

Exhibition Spaces - Zone 1, 1a & 1b single duct, constant volume system w/supplemental hot water radiation along glazed walls. Served by A.H.U. #1 18,000 CFM

Office/Toilet Zone #2 - 4 Pipe Fan Coils w/ some supplemental air "spilled" in from Zone #1 sys. Individual units sized to suit.

Lower Level Zone #3 - Game as Zone 2 but w/o radiators. Served by A.H.U. #2 12,000 CFM

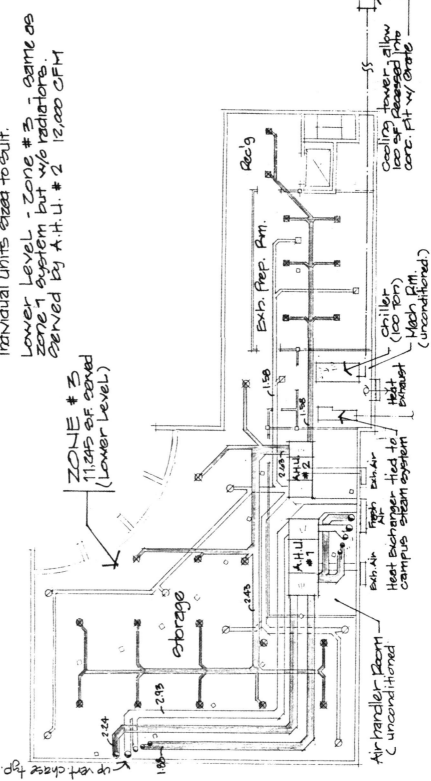

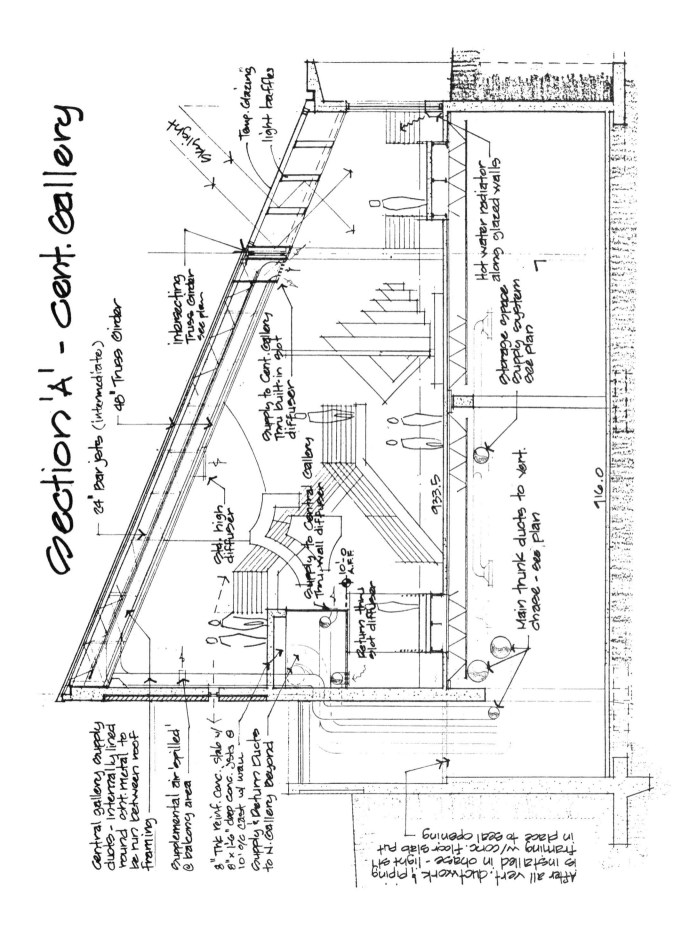

Section 'A' - Cent. Gallery

24" Bar jets (intermediate)
48" Truss Girder

intersecting
Truss Girder
see plan

Temp. drawing
light baffles

Skylight

Supply to Cent. Gallery
thru built-in slot
diffuser

Std. high
diffuser

Supply to Central Gallery
thru wall diffuser

10'-0"
A.F.F.

Hot water radiator
along glazed walls

Storage space
supply system
see plan

Return thru
slot diffuser

Main trunk ducts to vert.
chase - see plan

933.5

716.0

Central gallery supply
ducts - internally lined
round sht. metal to
be run between roof
framing

Supplemental air spilled
@ balcony area

8" Thk. reinf. conc. slab w/
8" x 16" deep conc. jobs @
10' o/c cast w/ wall

Supply & Return Ducts
to N. Gallery beyond

After all vert. ductwork & piping
is installed in chase - light sht
framing w/ conc. floor slab put
in place to seal opening

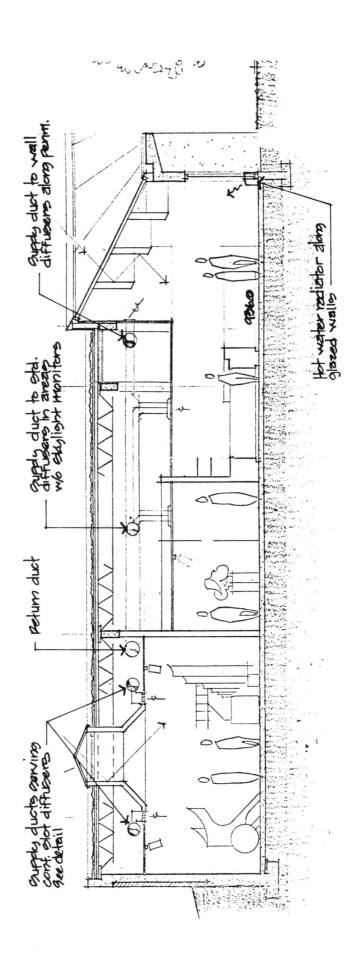

Section 'B' - N. Gallery

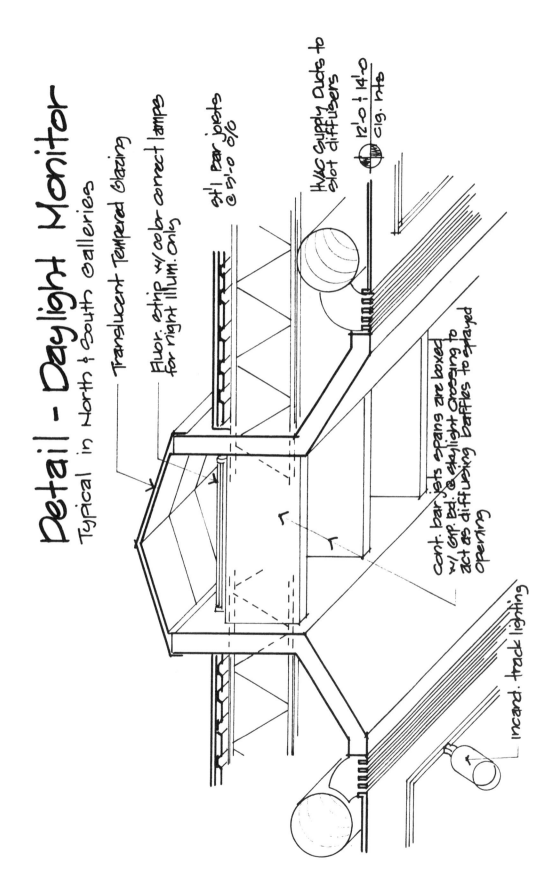

Detail - Daylight Monitor
Typical in North & South Galleries

Translucent Tempered Glazing

Fluor. strip w/ color correct lamps for night illum. only

3⅟₁ bar joists @ 5'-0 o/c

HVAC supply ducts to slot diffusers

12'-0 to 14'-0 clg. htd

painted steel baffle prevents direct glare @ skylights. gap in baffle @ skylight step

curved cont. bar joist

incand. track lighting

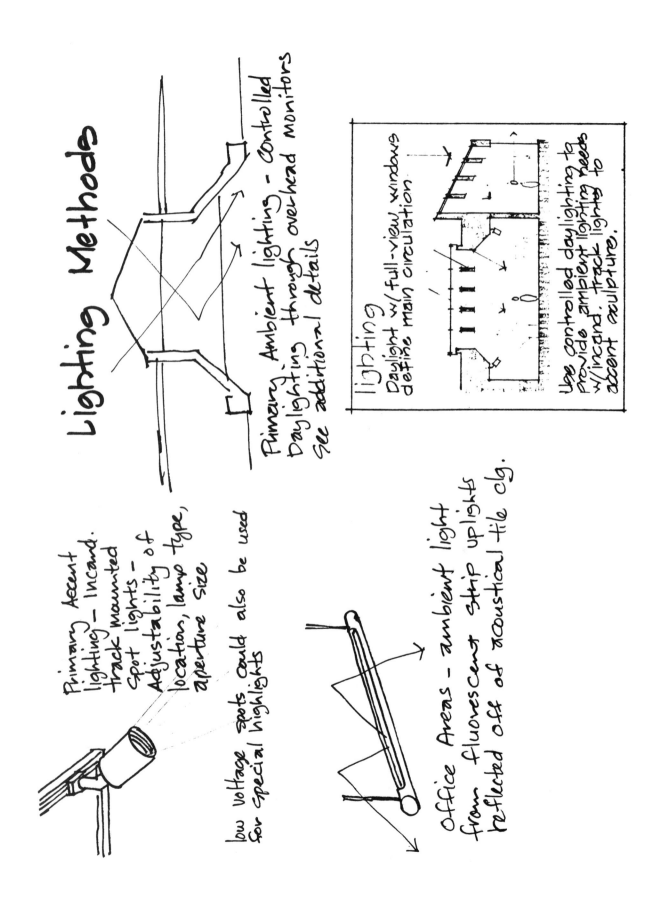

Lighting Methods

Primary Ambient lighting - Controlled
Daylighting through overhead monitors
See additional details

lighting

Daylight w/ full-view windows
define main circulation

Use controlled daylighting to
provide ambient lighting needs
Supplement w/ artificial incand. spots to
achieve focal illuminance

Primary Accent
lighting - incand.
track mounted
spot lights -
Adjustability of
location, lamp type,
aperture size

low voltage spots could also be used
for special highlights

Office Areas - ambient light
from fluorescent strip uplights
reflected off of acoustical tile clg.

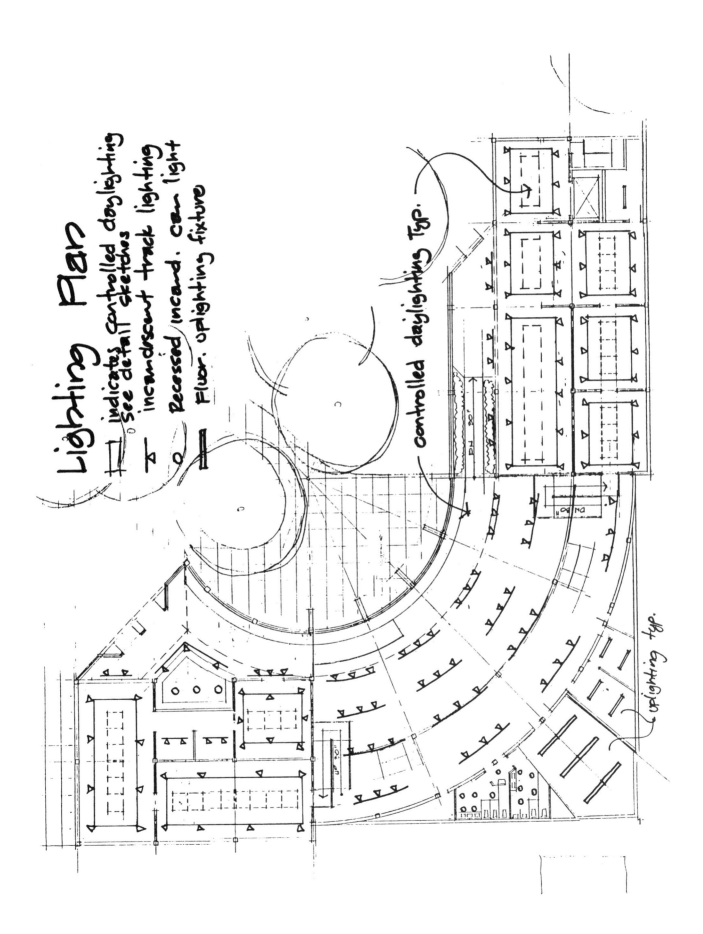

Lighting Plan

☐☐ Indicates controlled daylighting
○ See detail sketches
↑ Incandescent track lighting
○ Recessed incand. can light
○ Fluor. uplighting fixture

Controlled daylighting Typ.

Controlled daylighting Typ.

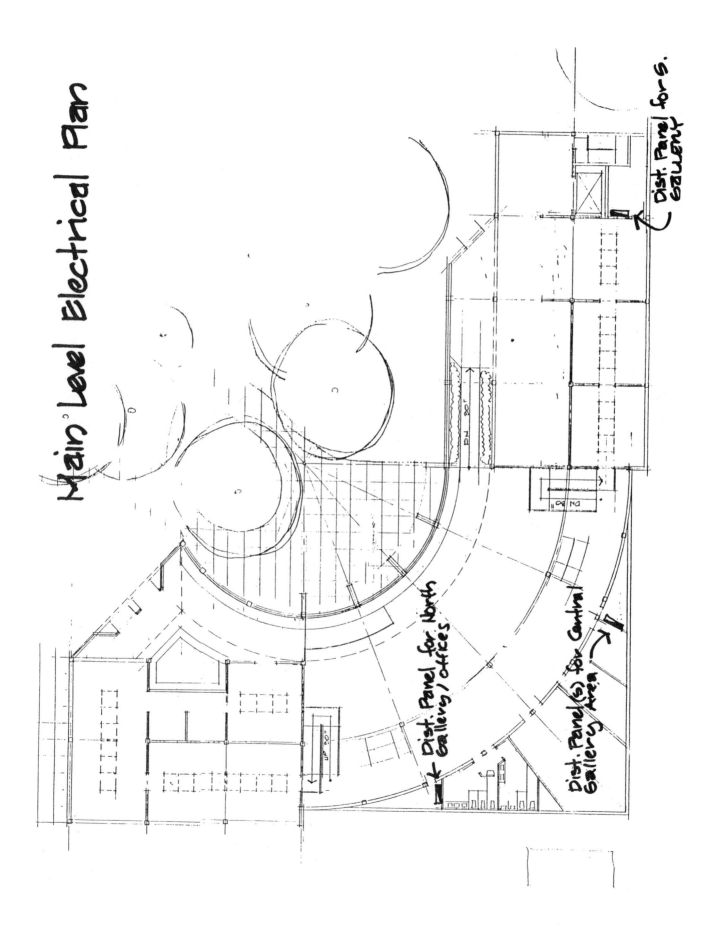

Main Level Electrical Plan

Dist. Panel for S. Gallery

Dist. Panel for North Gallery/offices

Dist. Panel(s) for Central Gallery Area

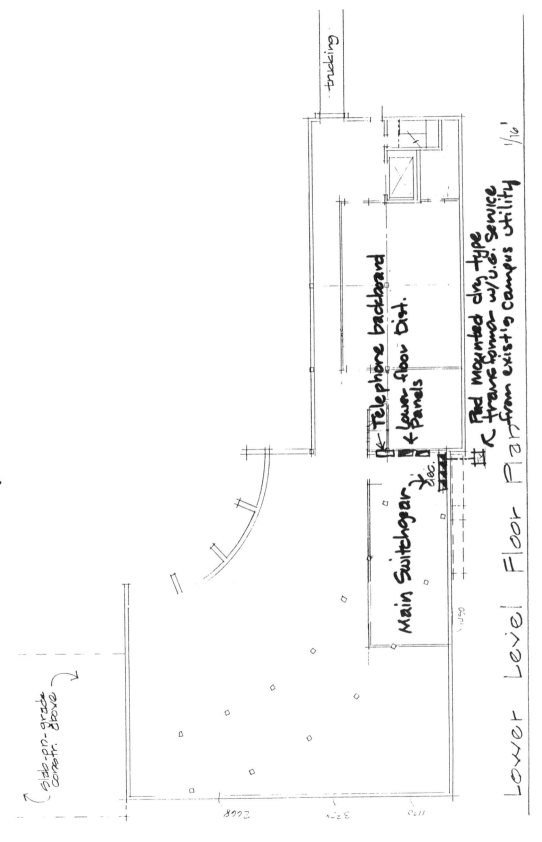

Lower Level Electrical Plan

trucking

Telephone backboard

lower floor Dist.
Panels

Main Switchgear

Elec.

Pad mounted dry type
transformer w/U.G. service
from existing campus utility

Lower Level Floor Plan   1/16'

slab-on-grade
constr. above

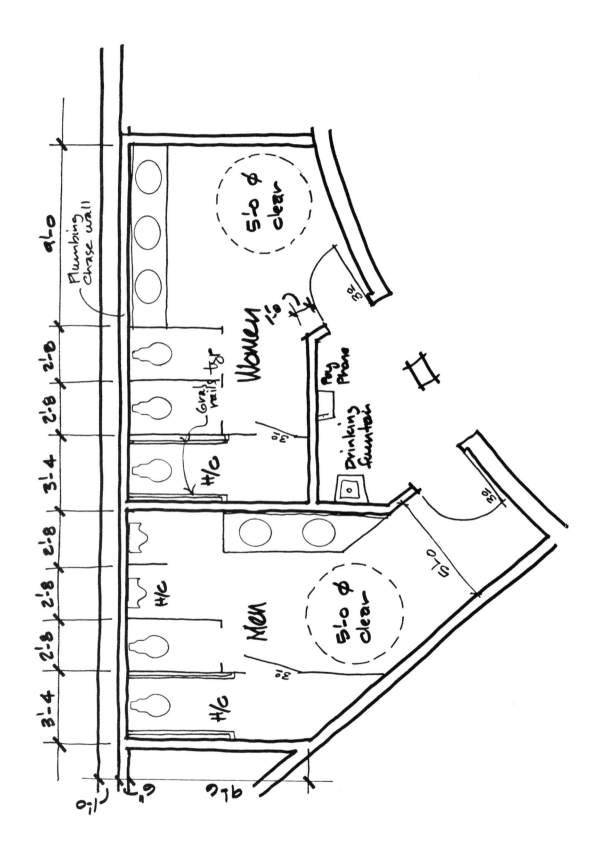

Enlarged Toilet Plan

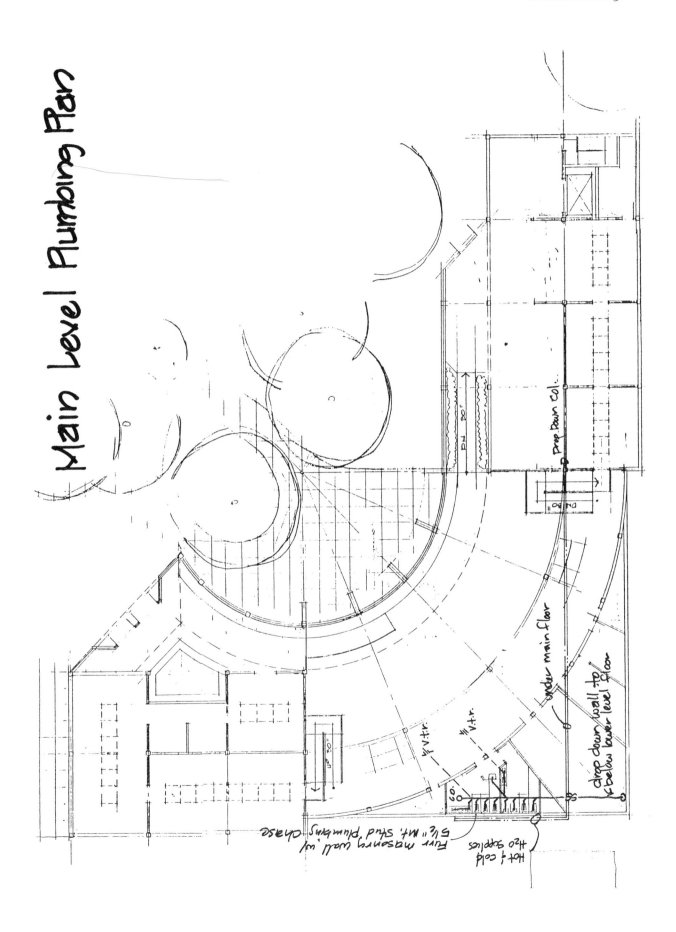

Main Level Plumbing Plan

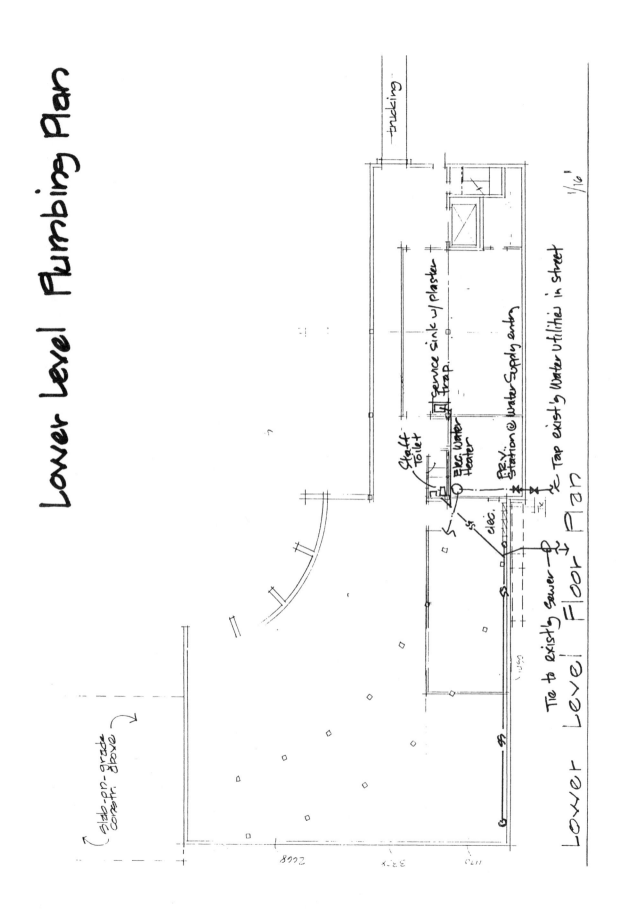

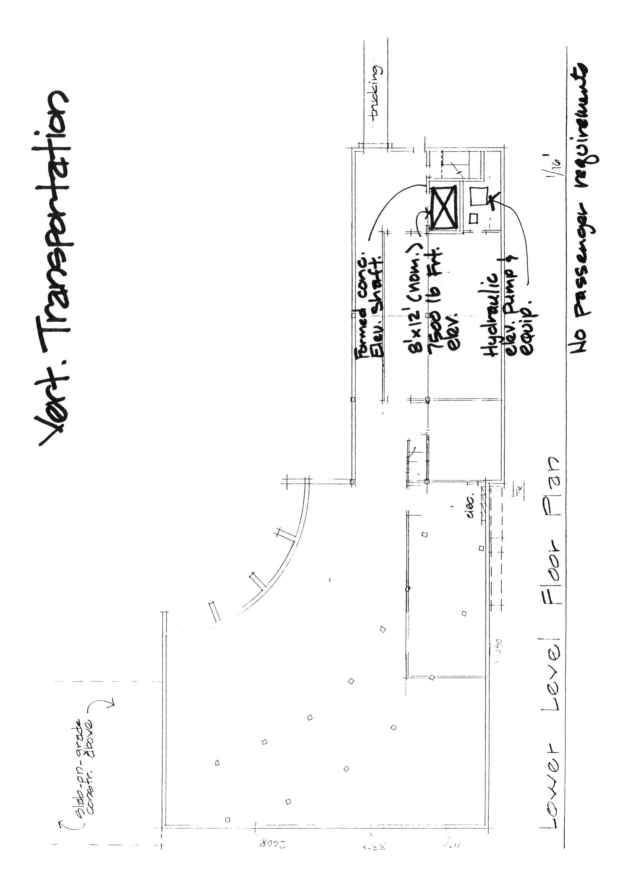

Vert. Transportation

Formed conc. Elev. shaft.

8'x12' (nom.) 7500 lb Fht. elev.

Hydraulic elev. Pump & equip.

trucking

elec.

(slab-on-grade constr. above)

Lower Level Floor Plan

1/16'

No Passenger requirements

Roof Drainage Plan

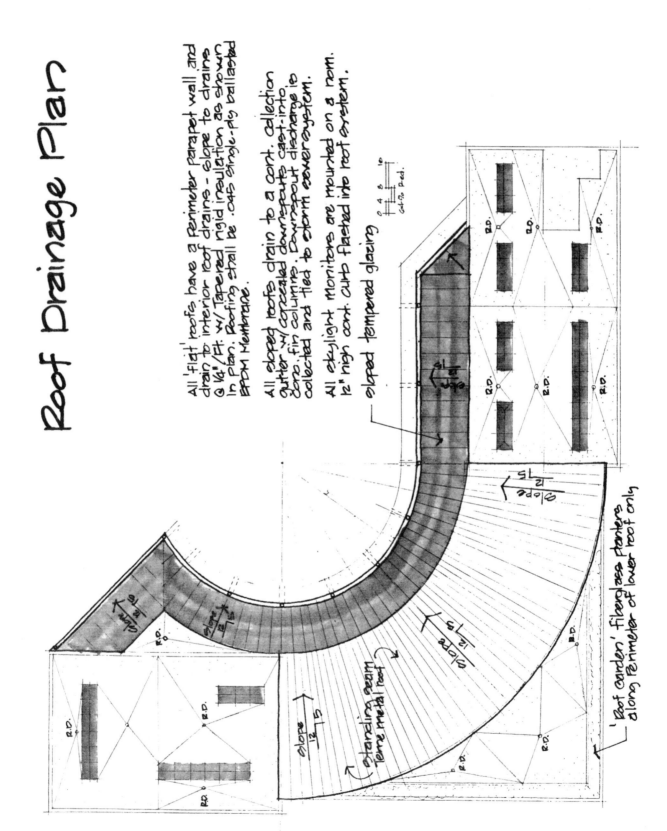

All 'flat' roofs have a perimeter parapet wall and drain to interior roof drains - slope to drains @ 1/4"/ft. w/ Tapered rigid insulation as shown in plan. Roofing shall be .045 single-ply ballasted EPDM Membrane.

All sloped roofs drain to a cont. collection gutter w/ concealed downspouts cast into conc. fin columns. Downspout discharge is collected and tied to storm sewer system.

All skylight monitors are mounted on a nom. 12" high conc. curb flashed into roof system.

sloped tempered glazing

slope 12/15

slope 12/15

slope 12/10

slope 12/5

'standing seam' terne metal roof

slope 12/15

slope 12/10

'Roof garden' fiberglass planters along perimeter of lower roof only

0 4 8 16
cut-a-way ped.

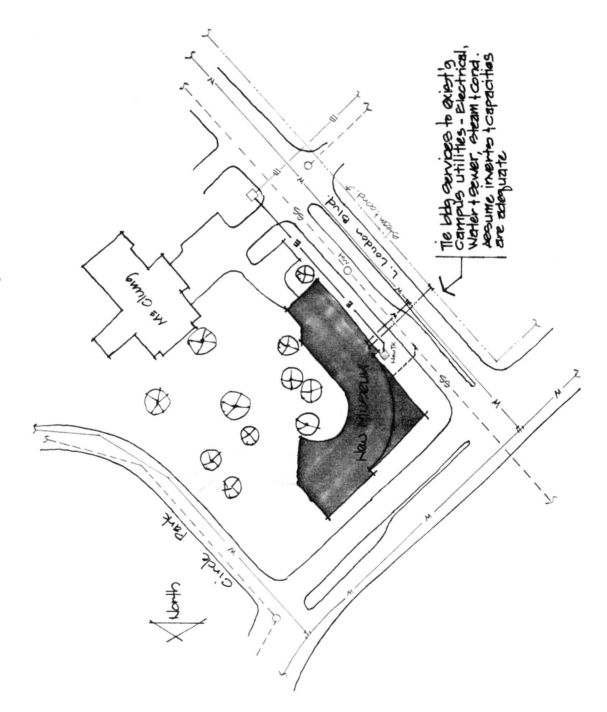

Utility Site Plan

APPENDIX B

Sun Path Diagrams

Sun path diagrams for 24, 28, 32, 36, 40, 44, 48, and 52 degrees north latitude are reprinted here by permission from Moore (1985).

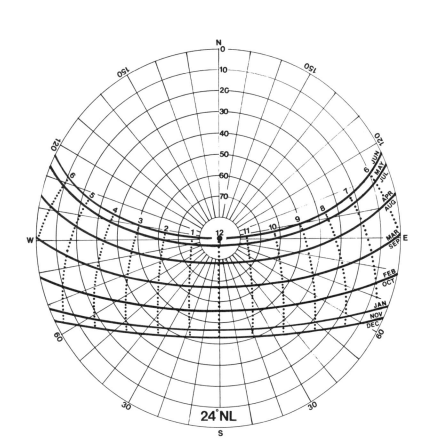

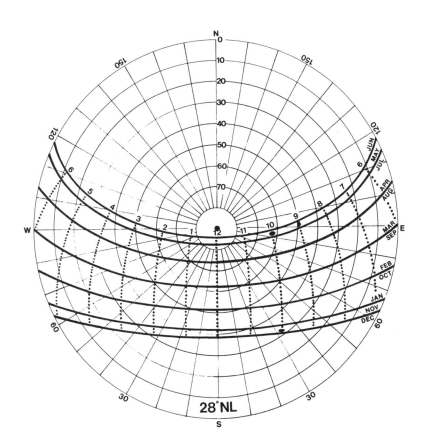

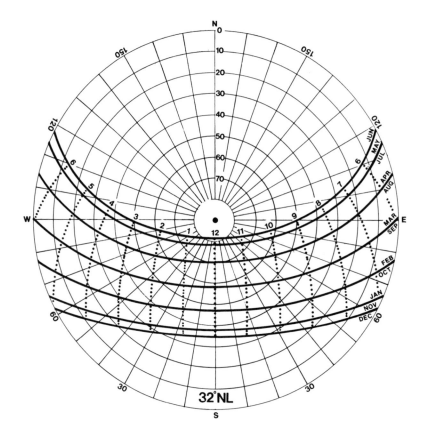

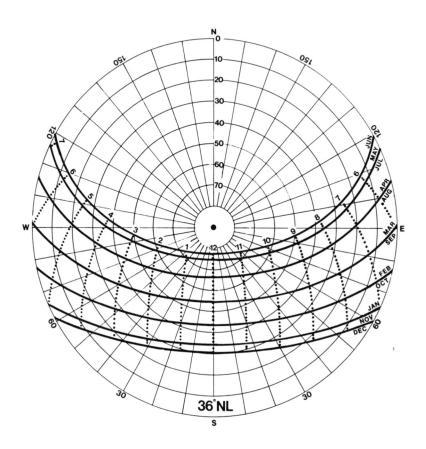

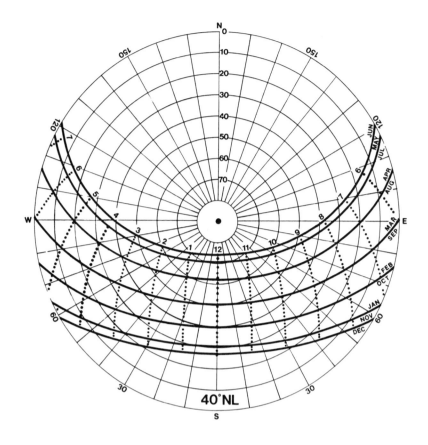

40°NL

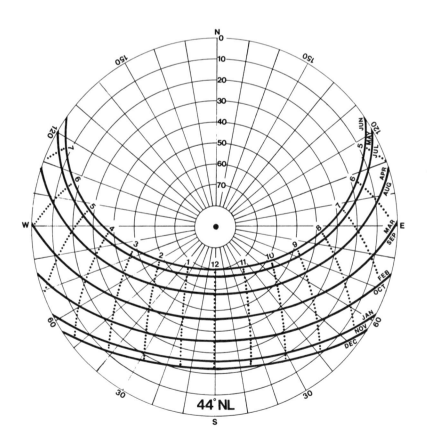

44°NL

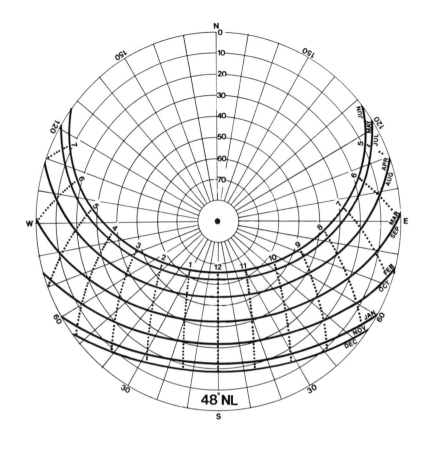

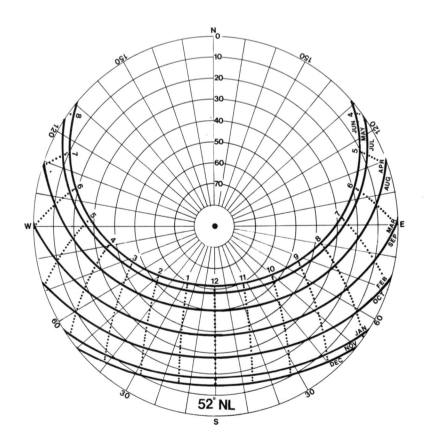

APPENDIX C

Sundials

Sundials for 28, 32, 36, 40, 44, 48, 52, and 56 degrees north latitude are reprinted here by permission from Moore (1985).

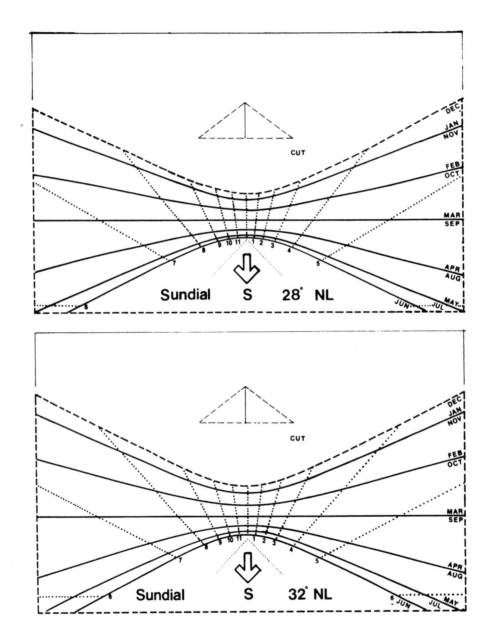

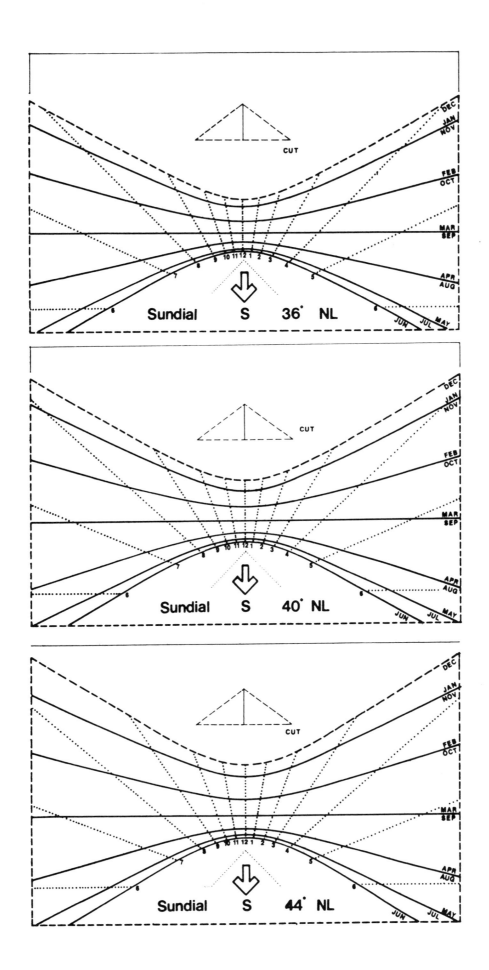

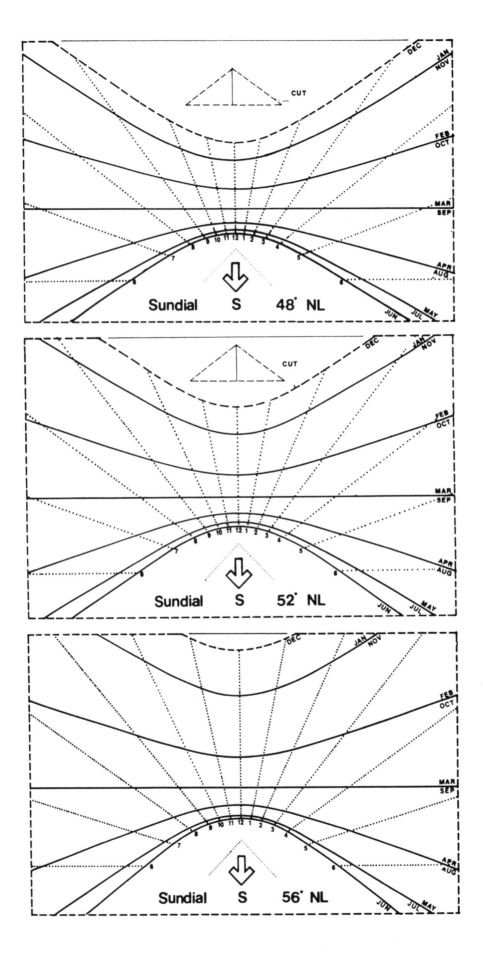

References

Archea, John. 1987. Puzzle Making: What Architects Do When No One Is Looking. In *Computability of Design*, Yehuda Kalay, (ed.) pp. 37–52. New York: Wiley.

Baglivo, Jenny, and Jack Graver. 1983. *Incidence and Symmetry in Design and Architecture*. London: Cambridge Univ. Press.

Corkill, P. A., H. Puderbaugh, and H. K. Sawers. 1974. *Structure and Architectural Design, 2nd Ed*. Davenport, Iowa: Lindsay Industries (Market Publishing).

Doelle, Leslie. 1972. *Environmental Acoustics*. New York: McGraw Hill.

Dondis, Donis. 1974. *A Primer of Visual Literacy*. Cambridge, Mass.: MIT Press.

Eigen, Manfred, and Ruthild Winkler. 1981. *Laws of the Game: How the Principles of Nature Govern Chance*. New York: Knopf.

Evans, Benjamin. 1981. *Daylight in Architecture*. New York: Architectural Record Books, McGraw Hill.

Flynn, John, and Samuel Mills. 1962. *Architectural Lighting Graphics*. New York: Van Nostrand Reinhold.

Flynn, John, Arthur Segil, and Gary Steffy. 1988. *Architectural Interior Systems*. New York: Van Nostrand Reinhold.

Hughes, David. 1988. *Electrical Systems in Buildings*. Boston: PWS-Kent.

International Association of Plumbing and Mechanical Officials. *Uniform Plumbing Code*. 1988. Walnut, Calif.

International Conference of Building Officials. 1988. *Uniform Building Code*. Whittier, Calif.: International Conference of Building Officials.

Jones, A. F.. 1980. *Game Theory, Mathematical Models of Conflict*. New York: Wiley.

Jones, Robert. 1984. *Noise and Vibration Control in Buildings*. New York: McGraw Hill.

Lin, T. Y., and Sidney Stotesbury. 1988. *Structural Concepts and Systems for Architects and Engineers*. New York: Van Nostrand Reinhold.

Macsai, John, Eugene Holland, Harry Nachman, and Julius Yacker. 1976. *Housing*. New York: Wiley.

McPartland, J. F. 1984. *Handbook of Practical Electrical Design*. New York: McGraw Hill.

Means Assemblies Cost Data. 1989. Kingston, Mass.: R. S. Means Co.

Mequiston, Faye, and Jerald Parker. 1977. *Heating, Ventilating, and Air Conditioning Analysis and Design*. New York: Wiley.

Merritt, Frederick, and James Ambrose. 1990. *Building Engineering and Systems Design*. New York: Van Nostrand Reinhold.

Minai, Asghar. 1989. *Design as Aesthetic Communication: Structuring Random Order; Deconstruction of Formal Rationality*. New York: Peter Lang.

Moore, Fuller. 1985. *Concepts and Practice of Architectural Daylighting*. New York: Van Nostrand Reinhold.

National Fire Protection Association. 1988. *Life Safety Code Handbook*. Quincy, Mass.: National Fire Protection Association.

Nielsen, Louis. 1982. *Standard Plumbing Engineering Design*. New York: McGraw Hill.

Passini, Romedi. 1984. *Wayfinding in Architecture*. New York: Van Nostrand Reinhold.

Rucker, Rudy. 1987. *Mind Tools: The Five Levels of Mathematical Reality*. Boston: Houghton Mifflin.

Schneider, Raymond. 1981. *HVAC Control Systems*. New York: Wiley.

Smith, Fran, and Fred Bertolone. 1986. *Bringing Interiors to Light*. New York: Whitney Library of Design, an Imprint of Watson-Guptill Publications.

Sorcar, Prafulla. 1979. *Rapid Lighting Design and Cost Estimating*. New York: McGraw Hill.

Starr, Williams. 1983. *Electrical Wiring and Design: A Practical Approach*. New York: Wiley.

Summers, Wilford. 1981. *American Electricians Handbook*. New York: McGraw Hill.

Index